Grimm Fairy Tales
presents

Wonderland

Volume Three

zenescope

Wonderland
Volume Three

Grimm Fairy Tales

WONDERLAND CREATED BY
RAVEN GREGORY
JOE BRUSHA
RALPH TEDESCO

WRITERS
PAT SHAND
RAVEN GREGORY

ART DIRECTOR
ANTHONY SPAY

TRADE DESIGN
CHRISTOPHER COTE

EDITOR
RALPH TEDESCO

THIS VOLUME REPRINTS THE
COMIC SERIES GRIMM FAIRY TALES
PRESENTS WONDERLAND ISSUES
#11-15 PUBLISHED BY ZENESCOPE
ENTERTAINMENT.

WWW.ZENESCOPE.COM

FIRST EDITION, DECEMBER 2013
ISBN: 978-1-939683-30-4

WWW.ZENESCOPE.COM
FACEBOOK.COM/ZENESCOPE

ZENESCOPE ENTERTAINMENT, INC.
Joe Brusha • President & Chief Creative Officer
Ralph Tedesco • Editor-in-Chief
Jennifer Bermel • Director of Licensing & Business Development
Raven Gregory • Executive Editor
Anthony Spay • Art Director
Christopher Cote • Senior Designer & Production Manager
Dave Franchini • Direct Market Sales & Customer Service
Stephen Haberman • Marketing Manager

Grimm Fairy Tales presents
Wonderland

Volume Three

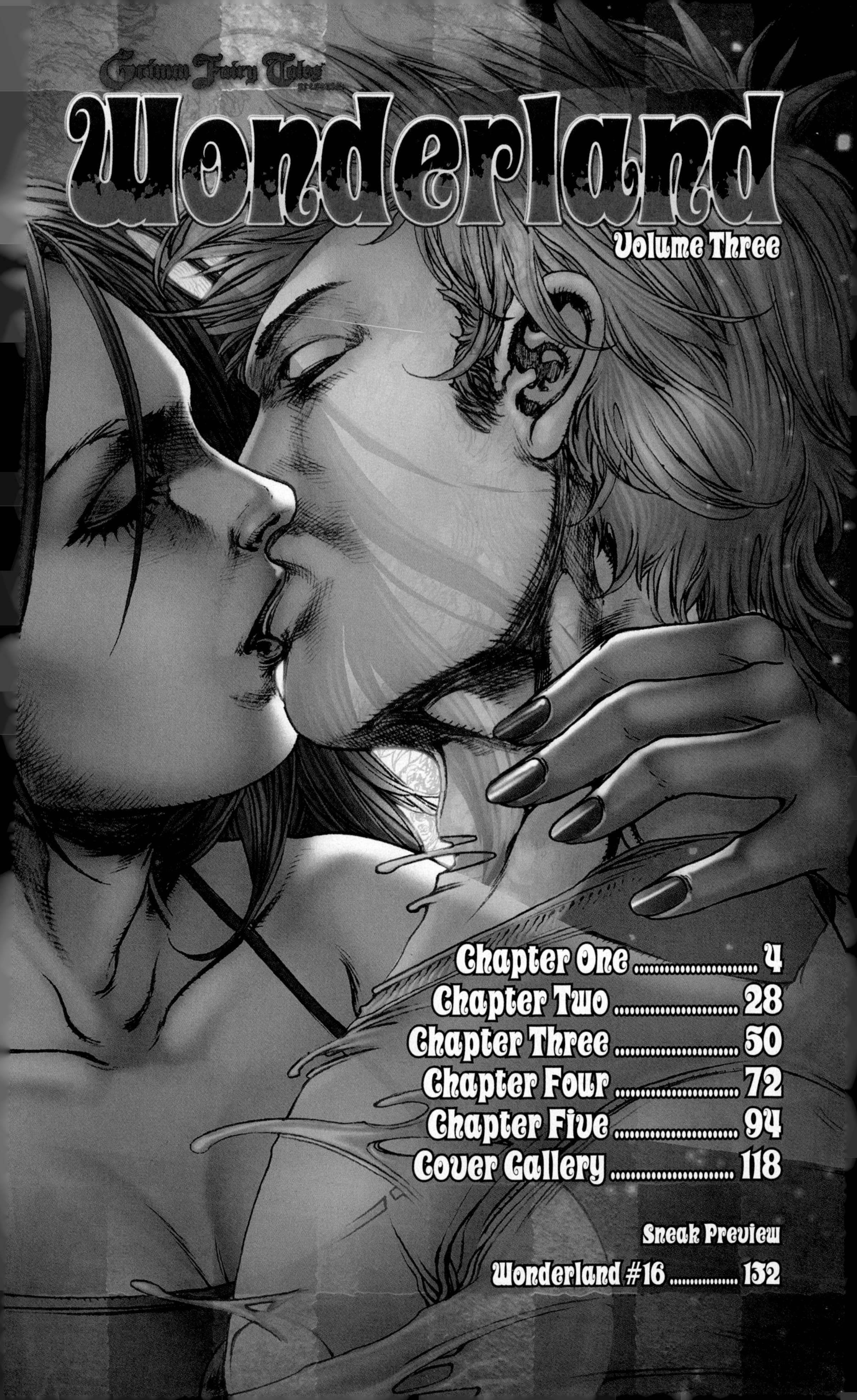

Chapter One 4

Chapter Two 28

Chapter Three 50

Chapter Four 72

Chapter Five 94

Cover Gallery 118

Sneak Preview

Wonderland #16 132

Chapter One

STORY RAVEN GREGORY
WRITER PAT SHAND
PENCILS SHELDON GOH
COLORS GROSTIETA
LETTERS JIM CAMPBELL

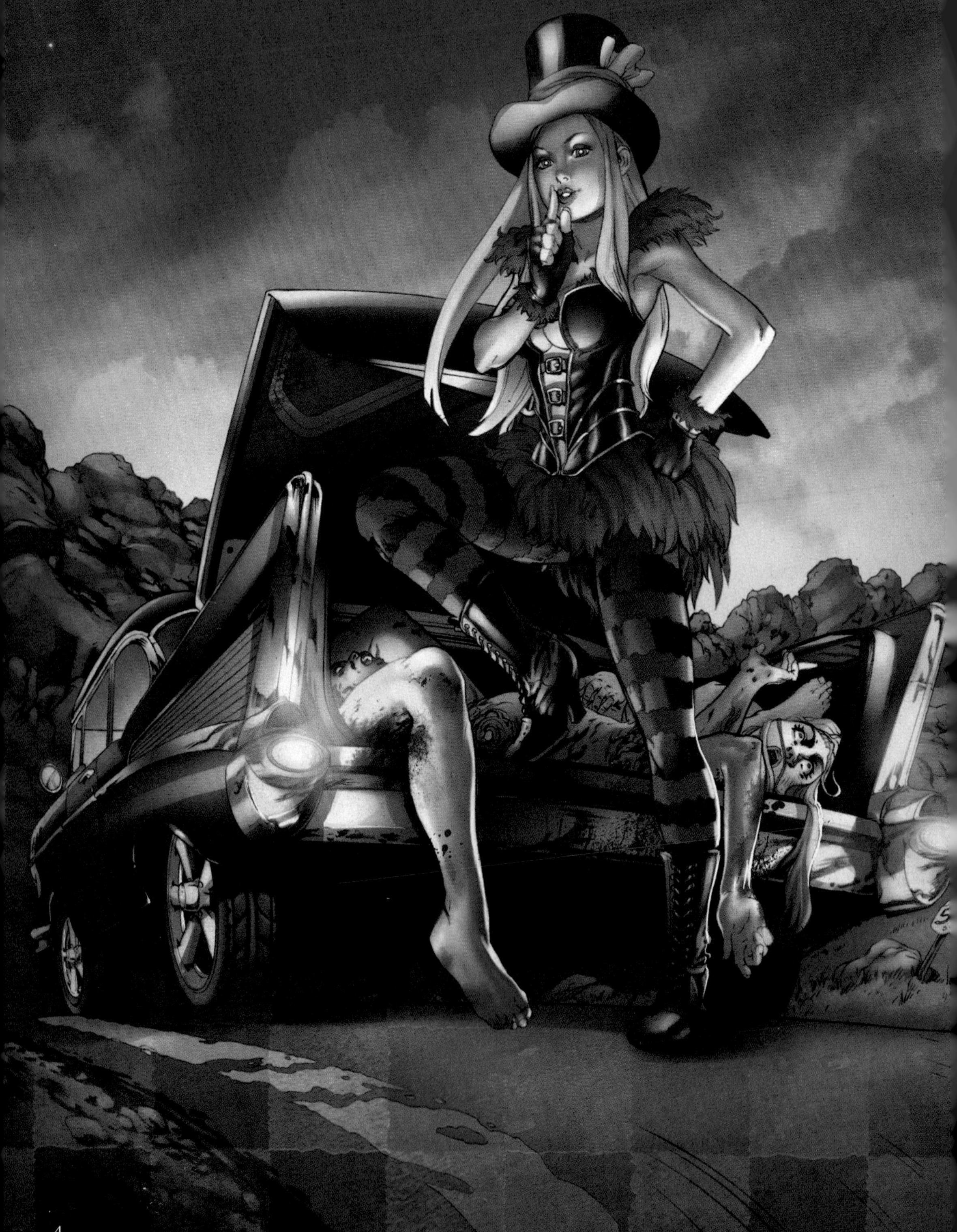

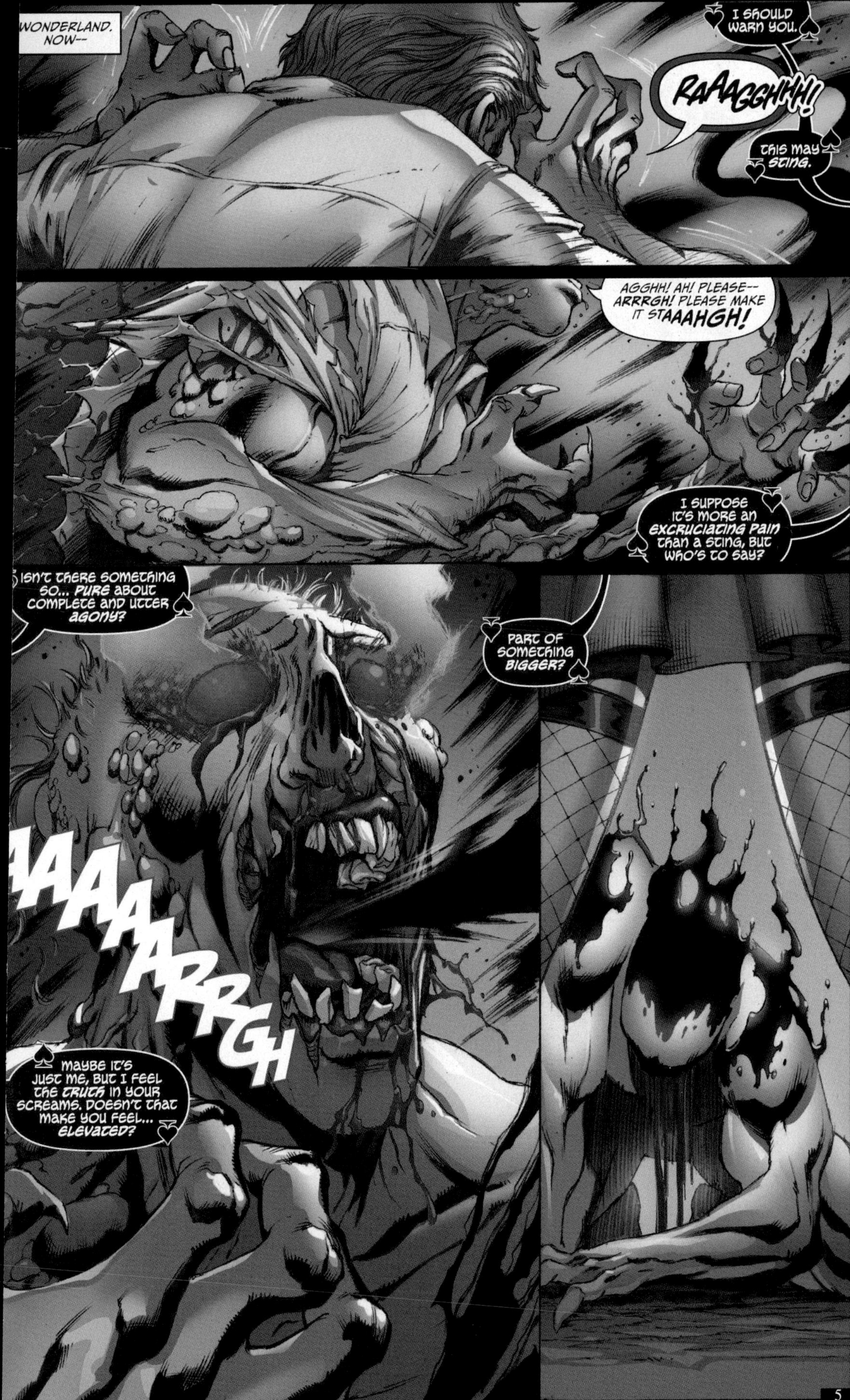
WONDERLAND. NOW--
I SHOULD WARN YOU.
RAAAGGHHH!
THIS MAY STING.
AGGHH! AH! PLEASE-- ARRRGH! PLEASE MAKE IT STAAAHGH!
I SUPPOSE IT'S MORE AN EXCRUCIATING PAIN THAN A STING, BUT WHO'S TO SAY?
ISN'T THERE SOMETHING SO... PURE ABOUT COMPLETE AND UTTER AGONY?
PART OF SOMETHING BIGGER?
AAAAAARRRGH
MAYBE IT'S JUST ME, BUT I FEEL THE TRUTH IN YOUR SCREAMS. DOESN'T THAT MAKE YOU FEEL... ELEVATED?

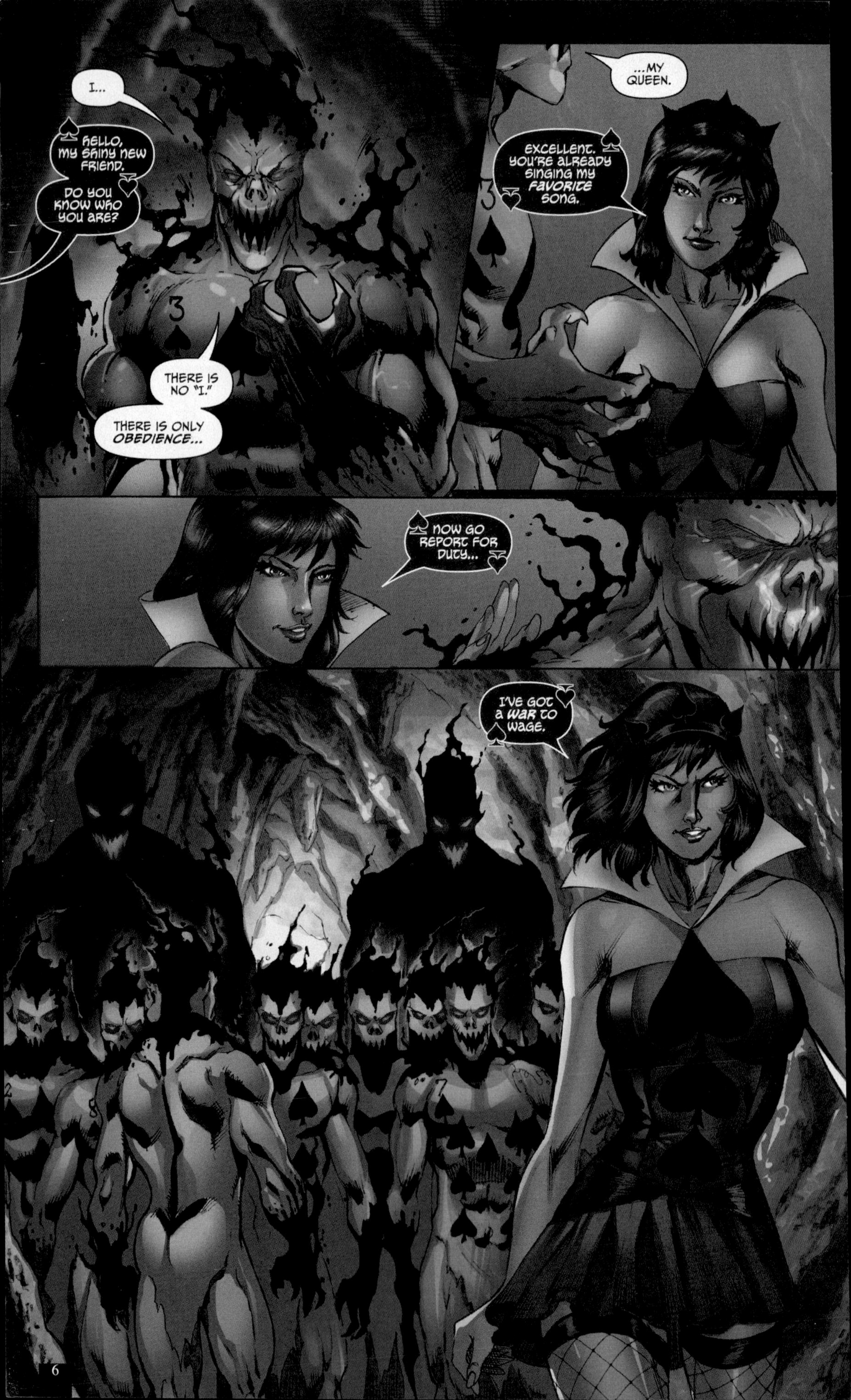

I...
HELLO, MY SHINY NEW FRIEND.
DO YOU KNOW WHO YOU ARE?
THERE IS NO "I."
THERE IS ONLY OBEDIENCE...
...MY QUEEN.
EXCELLENT. YOU'RE ALREADY SINGING MY FAVORITE SONG.
NOW GO REPORT FOR DUTY...
I'VE GOT A WAR TO WAGE.

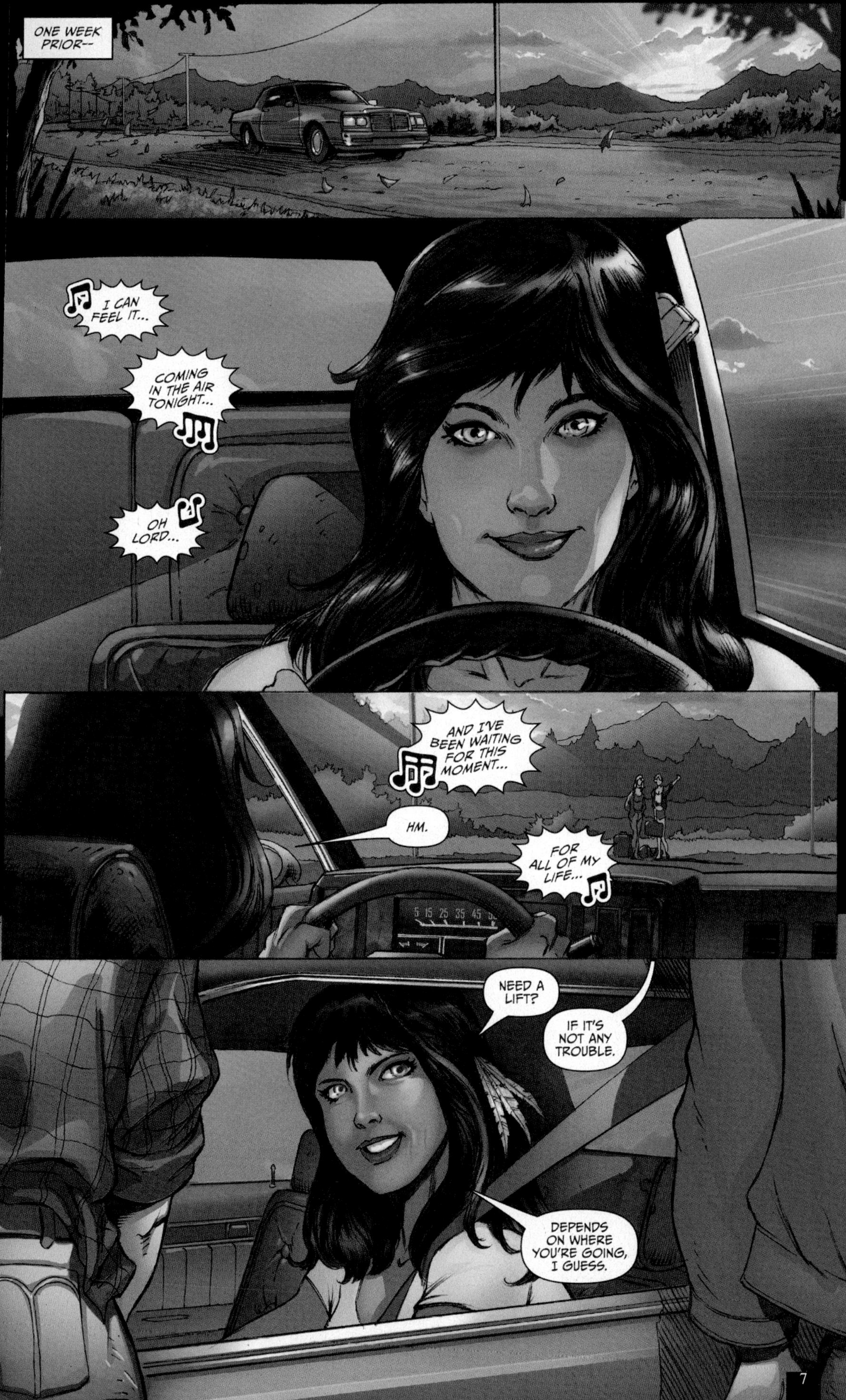
ONE WEEK PRIOR--
I CAN FEEL IT...
COMING IN THE AIR TONIGHT...
OH LORD...
AND I'VE BEEN WAITING FOR THIS MOMENT...
HM.
FOR ALL OF MY LIFE...
NEED A LIFT?
IF IT'S NOT ANY TROUBLE.
DEPENDS ON WHERE YOU'RE GOING, I GUESS.

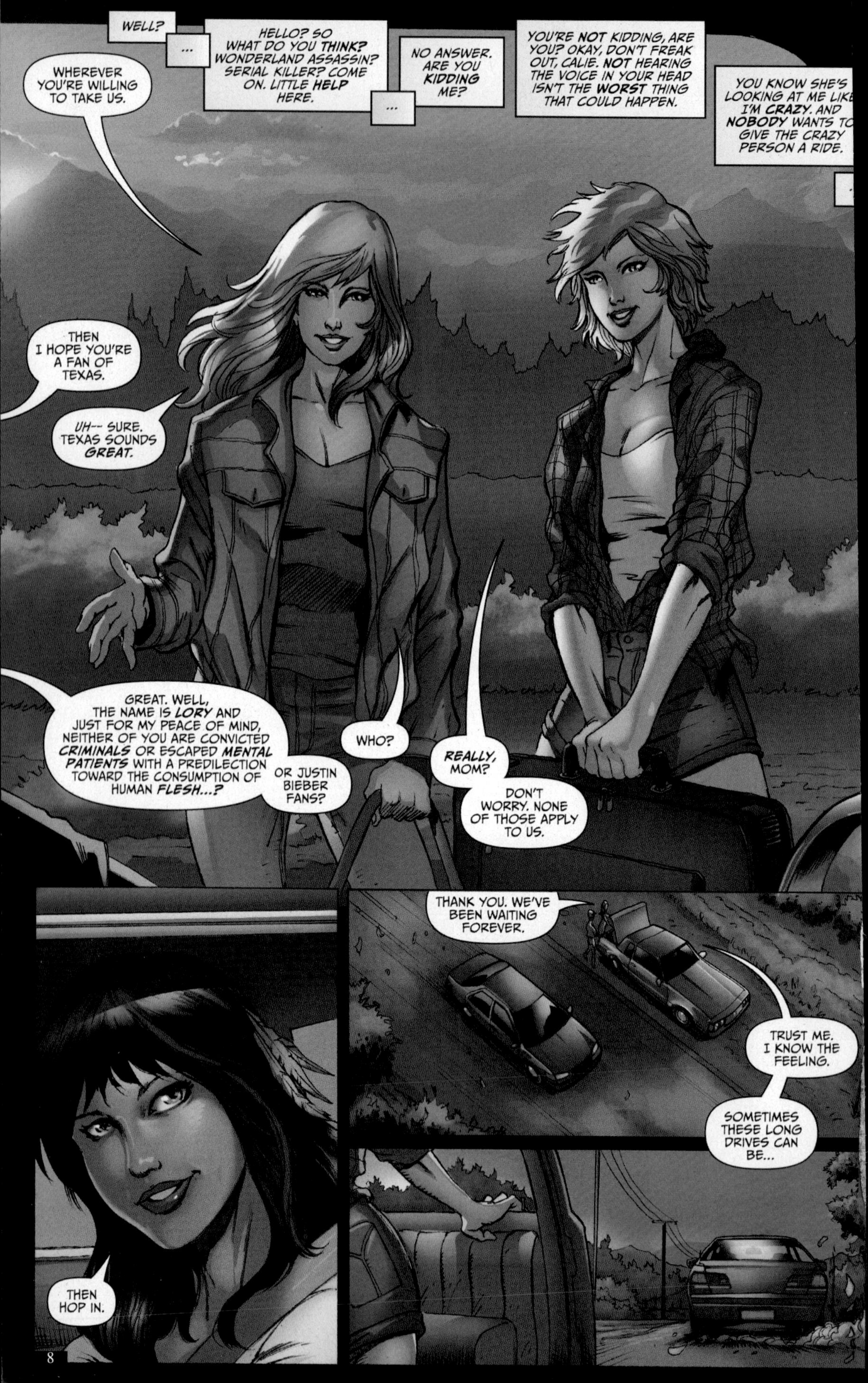
WELL?
...
HELLO? SO WHAT DO YOU THINK? WONDERLAND ASSASSIN? SERIAL KILLER? COME ON. LITTLE HELP HERE.
...
NO ANSWER. ARE YOU KIDDING ME?
YOU'RE NOT KIDDING, ARE YOU? OKAY, DON'T FREAK OUT, CALIE. NOT HEARING THE VOICE IN YOUR HEAD ISN'T THE WORST THING THAT COULD HAPPEN.
YOU KNOW SHE'S LOOKING AT ME LIK I'M CRAZY. AND NOBODY WANTS TO GIVE THE CRAZY PERSON A RIDE.
WHEREVER YOU'RE WILLING TO TAKE US.
THEN I HOPE YOU'RE A FAN OF TEXAS.
UH-- SURE. TEXAS SOUNDS GREAT.
GREAT. WELL, THE NAME IS LORY AND JUST FOR MY PEACE OF MIND, NEITHER OF YOU ARE CONVICTED CRIMINALS OR ESCAPED MENTAL PATIENTS WITH A PREDILECTION TOWARD THE CONSUMPTION OF HUMAN FLESH...?
OR JUSTIN BIEBER FANS?
WHO?
REALLY, MOM?
DON'T WORRY. NONE OF THOSE APPLY TO US.
THEN HOP IN.
THANK YOU. WE'VE BEEN WAITING FOREVER.
TRUST ME. I KNOW THE FEELING.
SOMETIMES THESE LONG DRIVES CAN BE...

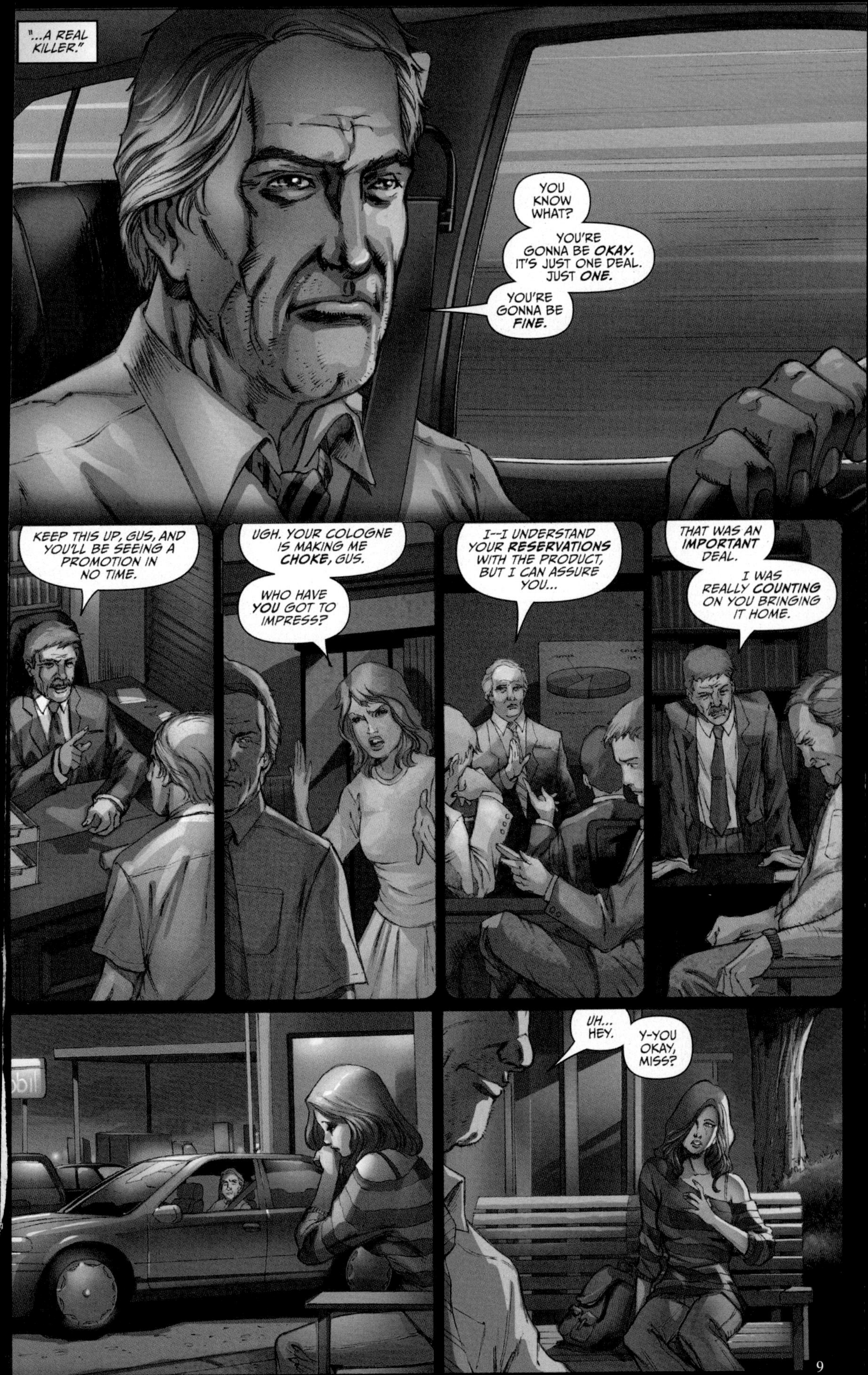
"...A REAL KILLER."
YOU KNOW WHAT?
YOU'RE GONNA BE OKAY. IT'S JUST ONE DEAL. JUST ONE.
YOU'RE GONNA BE FINE.
KEEP THIS UP, GUS, AND YOU'LL BE SEEING A PROMOTION IN NO TIME.
UGH. YOUR COLOGNE IS MAKING ME CHOKE, GUS.
WHO HAVE YOU GOT TO IMPRESS?
I--I UNDERSTAND YOUR RESERVATIONS WITH THE PRODUCT, BUT I CAN ASSURE YOU...
THAT WAS AN IMPORTANT DEAL.
I WAS REALLY COUNTING ON YOU BRINGING IT HOME.
UH... HEY.
Y-YOU OKAY, MISS?

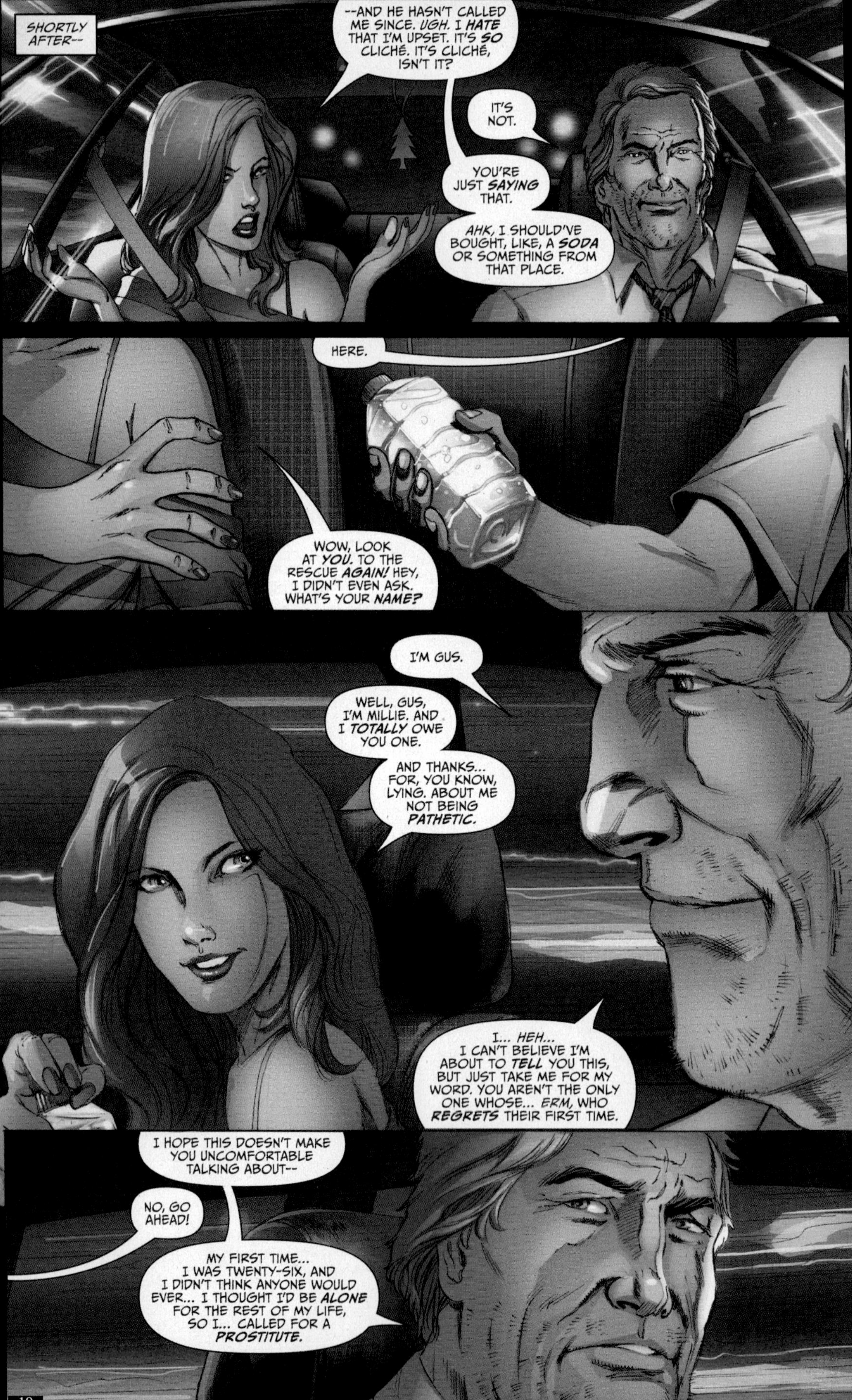
SHORTLY AFTER--
--AND HE HASN'T CALLED ME SINCE. UGH. I HATE THAT I'M UPSET. IT'S SO CLICHÉ. IT'S CLICHÉ, ISN'T IT?
IT'S NOT.
YOU'RE JUST SAYING THAT.
AHK, I SHOULD'VE BOUGHT, LIKE, A SODA OR SOMETHING FROM THAT PLACE.
HERE.
WOW, LOOK AT YOU. TO THE RESCUE AGAIN! HEY, I DIDN'T EVEN ASK. WHAT'S YOUR NAME?
I'M GUS.
WELL, GUS, I'M MILLIE. AND I TOTALLY OWE YOU ONE.
AND THANKS... FOR, YOU KNOW, LYING. ABOUT ME NOT BEING PATHETIC.
I... HEH... I CAN'T BELIEVE I'M ABOUT TO TELL YOU THIS, BUT JUST TAKE ME FOR MY WORD. YOU AREN'T THE ONLY ONE WHOSE... ERM, WHO REGRETS THEIR FIRST TIME.
I HOPE THIS DOESN'T MAKE YOU UNCOMFORTABLE TALKING ABOUT--
NO, GO AHEAD!
MY FIRST TIME... I WAS TWENTY-SIX, AND I DIDN'T THINK ANYONE WOULD EVER... I THOUGHT I'D BE ALONE FOR THE REST OF MY LIFE, SO I... CALLED FOR A PROSTITUTE.

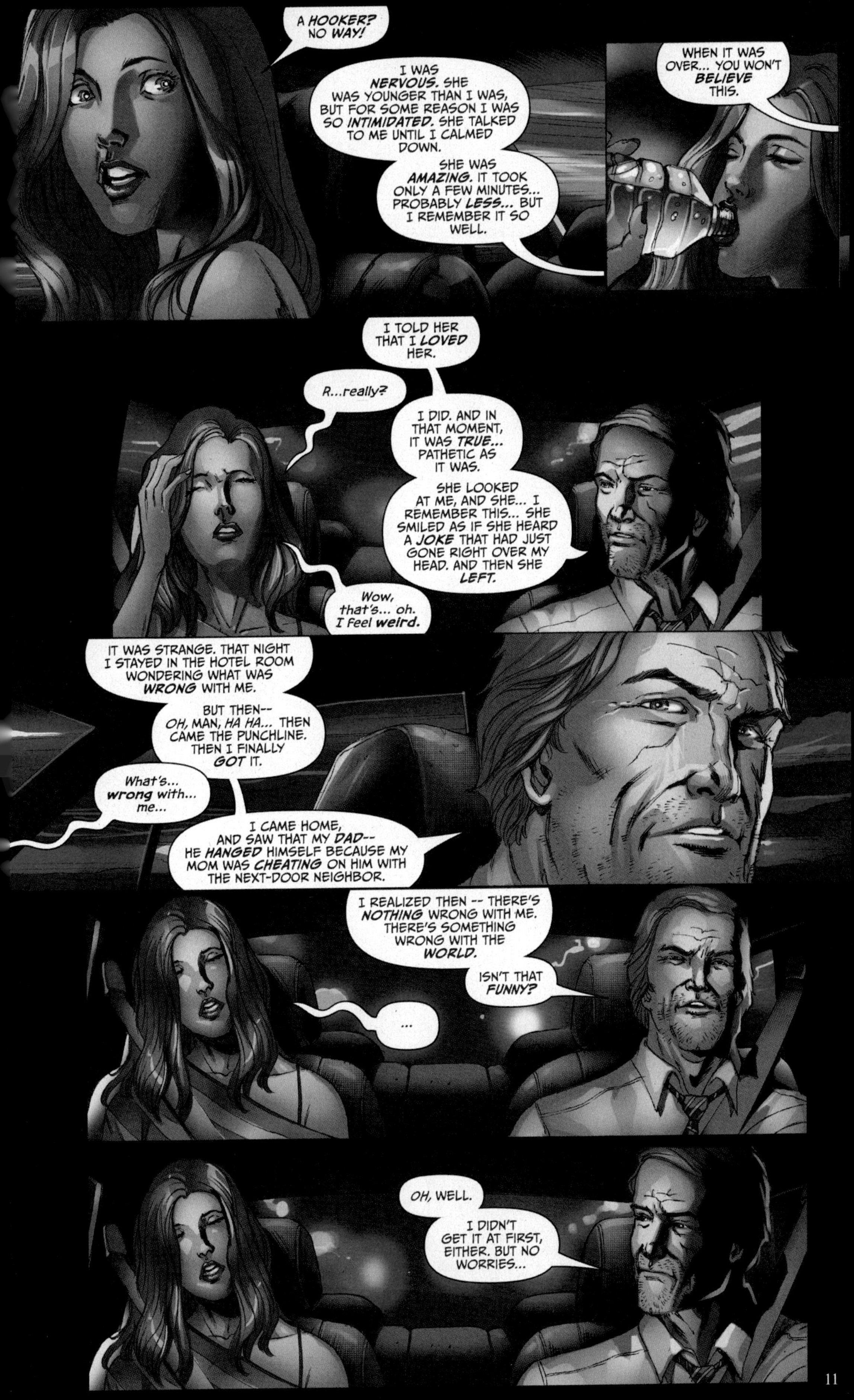

A HOOKER? NO WAY!
I WAS NERVOUS. SHE WAS YOUNGER THAN I WAS, BUT FOR SOME REASON I WAS SO INTIMIDATED. SHE TALKED TO ME UNTIL I CALMED DOWN.
SHE WAS AMAZING. IT TOOK ONLY A FEW MINUTES... PROBABLY LESS... BUT I REMEMBER IT SO WELL.
WHEN IT WAS OVER... YOU WON'T BELIEVE THIS.
I TOLD HER THAT I LOVED HER.
R...really?
I DID. AND IN THAT MOMENT, IT WAS TRUE... PATHETIC AS IT WAS.
SHE LOOKED AT ME, AND SHE... I REMEMBER THIS... SHE SMILED AS IF SHE HEARD A JOKE THAT HAD JUST GONE RIGHT OVER MY HEAD. AND THEN SHE LEFT.
Wow, that's... oh. I feel weird.
IT WAS STRANGE. THAT NIGHT I STAYED IN THE HOTEL ROOM WONDERING WHAT WAS WRONG WITH ME.
BUT THEN-- OH, MAN, HA HA... THEN CAME THE PUNCHLINE. THEN I FINALLY GOT IT.
What's... wrong with... me...
I CAME HOME, AND SAW THAT MY DAD-- HE HANGED HIMSELF BECAUSE MY MOM WAS CHEATING ON HIM WITH THE NEXT-DOOR NEIGHBOR.
I REALIZED THEN -- THERE'S NOTHING WRONG WITH ME. THERE'S SOMETHING WRONG WITH THE WORLD.
ISN'T THAT FUNNY?
...
OH, WELL.
I DIDN'T GET IT AT FIRST, EITHER. BUT NO WORRIES...

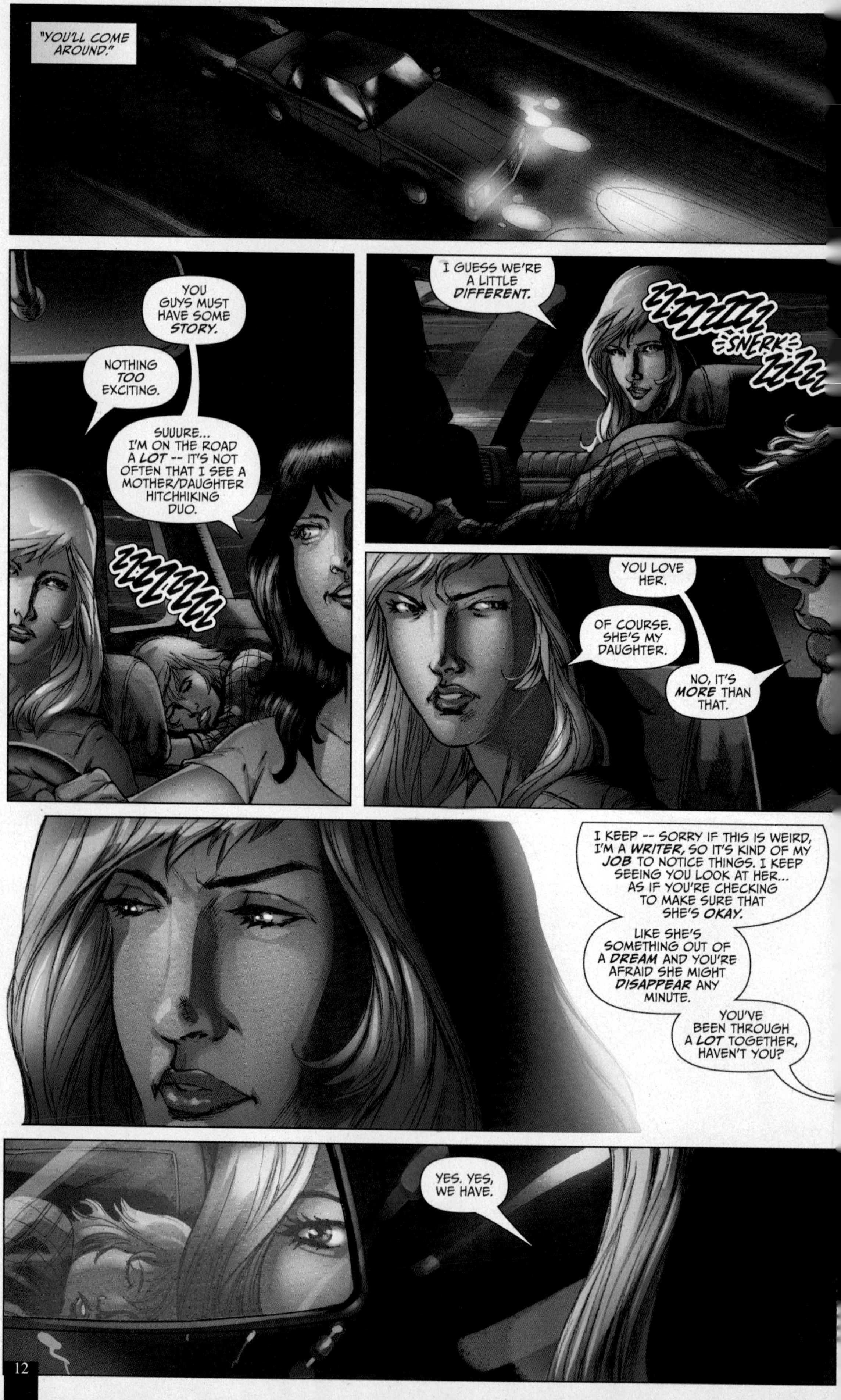
"YOU'LL COME AROUND."
YOU GUYS MUST HAVE SOME STORY.
NOTHING TOO EXCITING.
SUUURE... I'M ON THE ROAD A LOT -- IT'S NOT OFTEN THAT I SEE A MOTHER/DAUGHTER HITCHHIKING DUO.
ZZZZZZZ
I GUESS WE'RE A LITTLE DIFFERENT.
ZZZZZZZ
SNERK
ZZZZZ
YOU LOVE HER.
OF COURSE. SHE'S MY DAUGHTER.
NO, IT'S MORE THAN THAT.
I KEEP -- SORRY IF THIS IS WEIRD, I'M A WRITER, SO IT'S KIND OF MY JOB TO NOTICE THINGS. I KEEP SEEING YOU LOOK AT HER... AS IF YOU'RE CHECKING TO MAKE SURE THAT SHE'S OKAY.
LIKE SHE'S SOMETHING OUT OF A DREAM AND YOU'RE AFRAID SHE MIGHT DISAPPEAR ANY MINUTE.
YOU'VE BEEN THROUGH A LOT TOGETHER, HAVEN'T YOU?
YES. YES, WE HAVE.

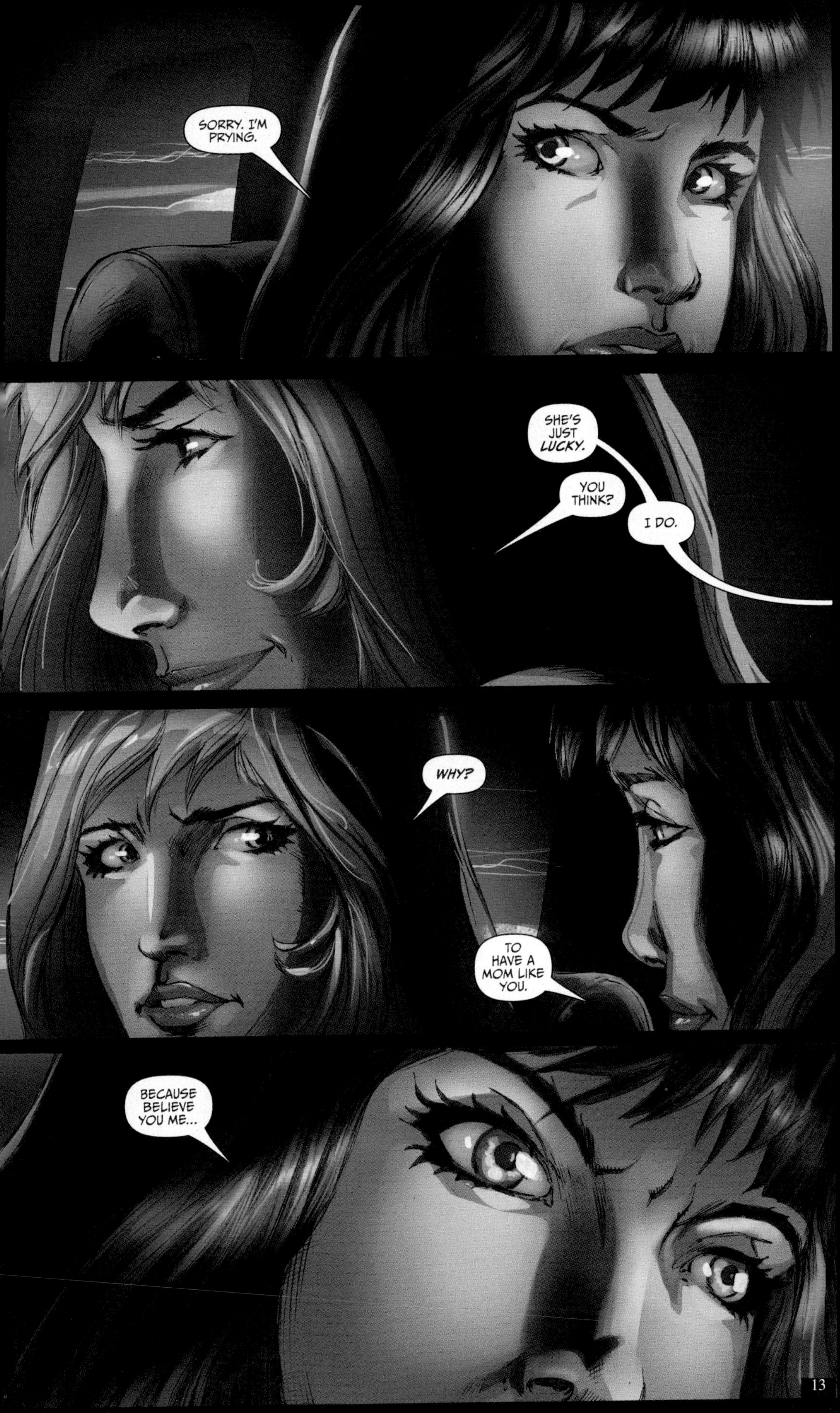
SORRY. I'M PRYING.
SHE'S JUST LUCKY.
YOU THINK?
I DO.
WHY?
TO HAVE A MOM LIKE YOU.
BECAUSE BELIEVE YOU ME...

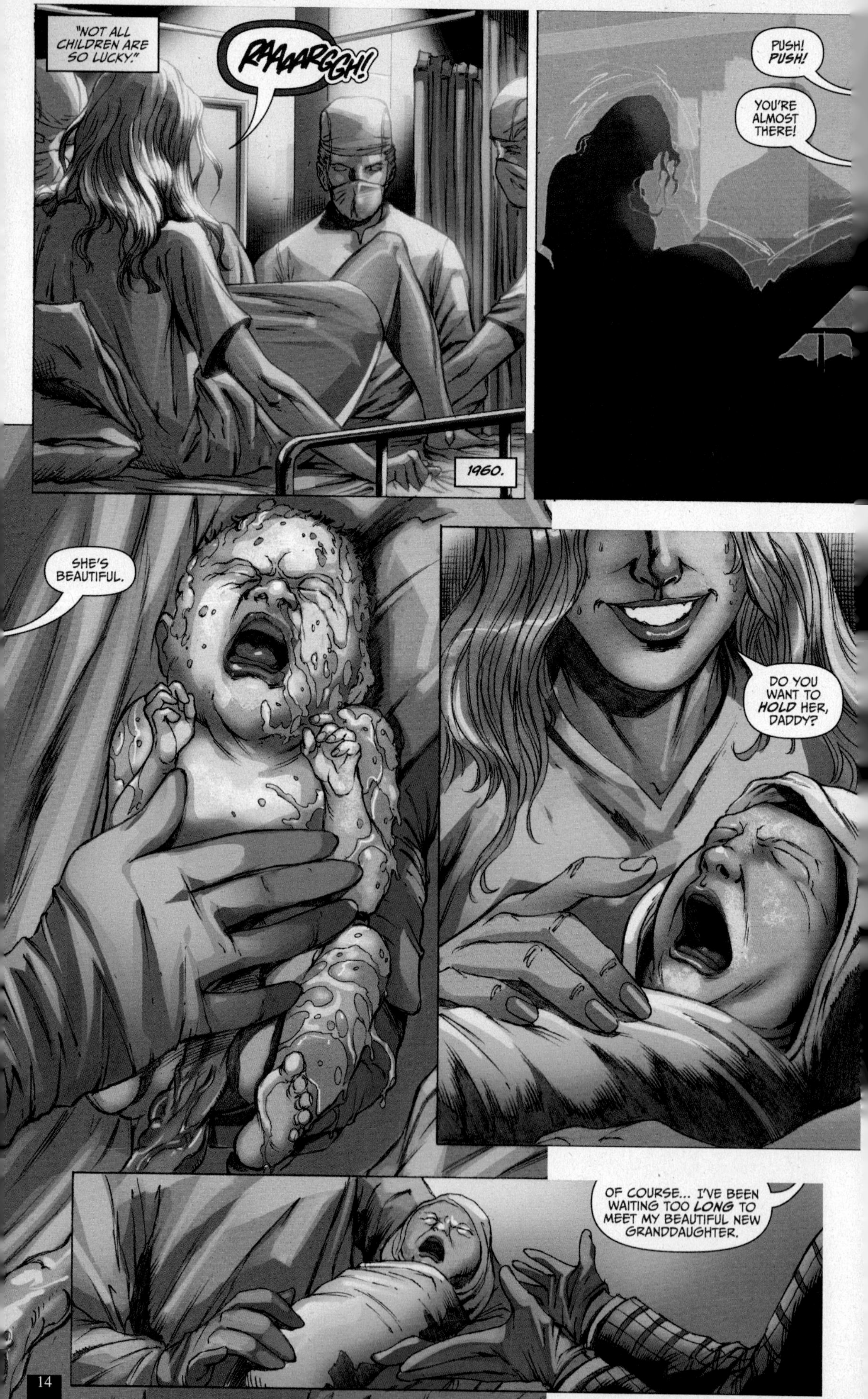
"NOT ALL CHILDREN ARE SO LUCKY."
RAAAARGGH!
1960.
PUSH! PUSH!
YOU'RE ALMOST THERE!
SHE'S BEAUTIFUL.
DO YOU WANT TO HOLD HER, DADDY?
OF COURSE... I'VE BEEN WAITING TOO LONG TO MEET MY BEAUTIFUL NEW GRANDDAUGHTER.

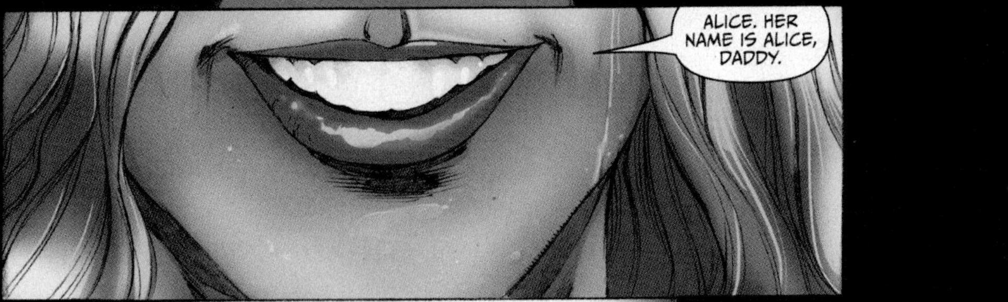
ALICE. HER NAME IS ALICE, DADDY.

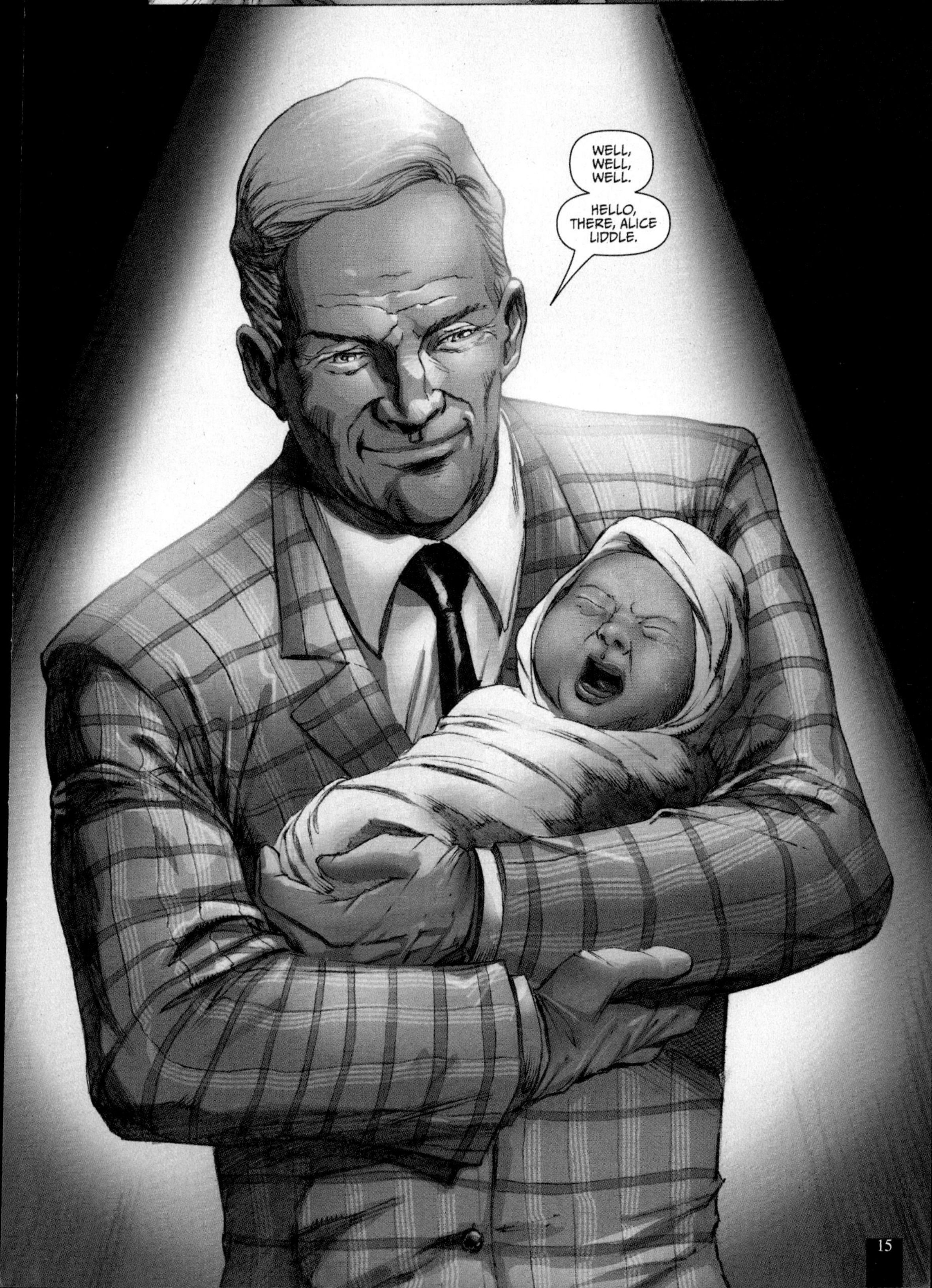
WELL, WELL, WELL.
HELLO, THERE, ALICE LIDDLE.

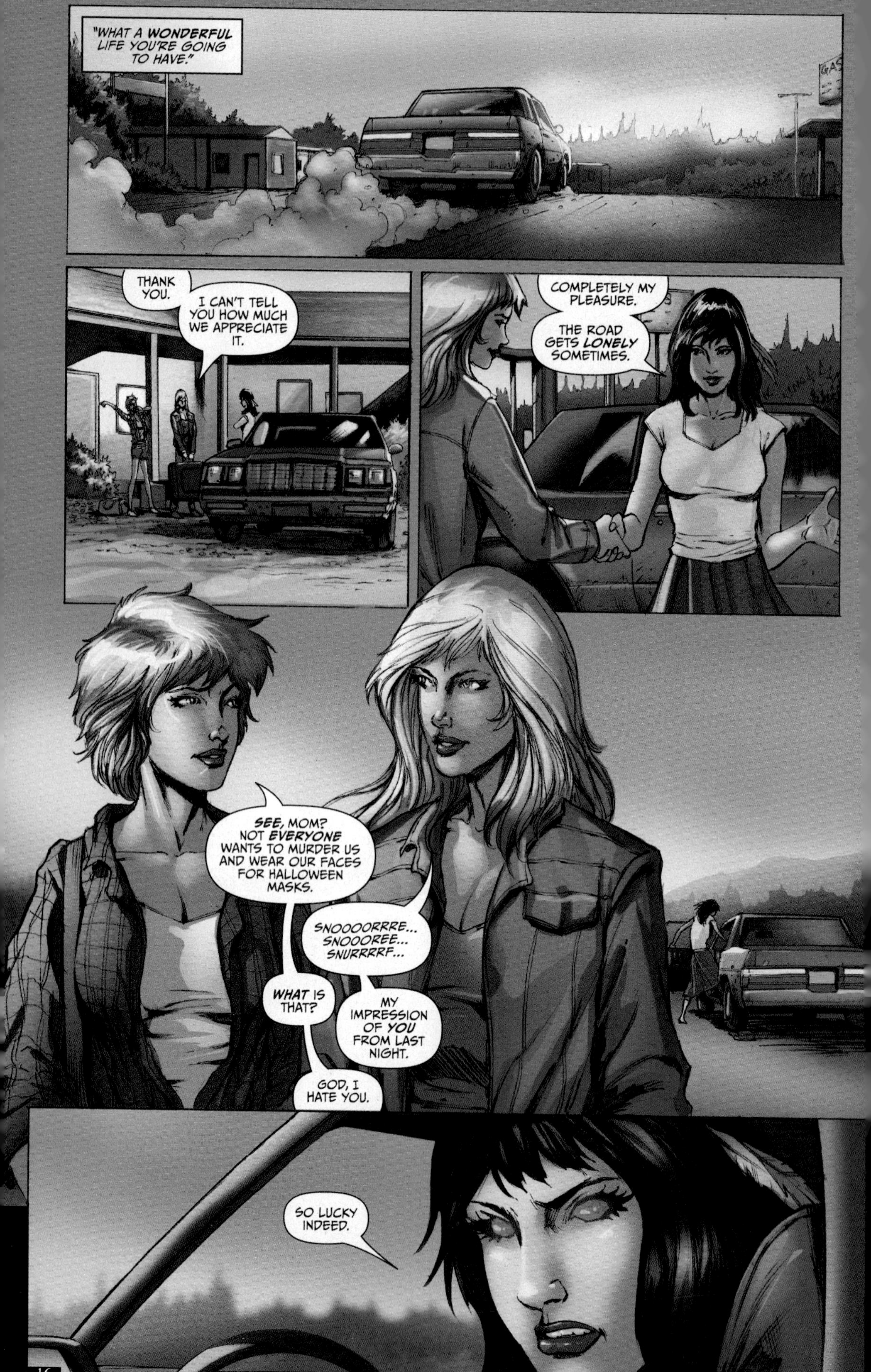
"WHAT A WONDERFUL LIFE YOU'RE GOING TO HAVE."
THANK YOU.
I CAN'T TELL YOU HOW MUCH WE APPRECIATE IT.
COMPLETELY MY PLEASURE.
THE ROAD GETS LONELY SOMETIMES.
SEE, MOM? NOT EVERYONE WANTS TO MURDER US AND WEAR OUR FACES FOR HALLOWEEN MASKS.
SNOOOORRRE... SNOOOREE... SNURRRRF...
WHAT IS THAT?
MY IMPRESSION OF YOU FROM LAST NIGHT.
GOD, I HATE YOU.
SO LUCKY INDEED.

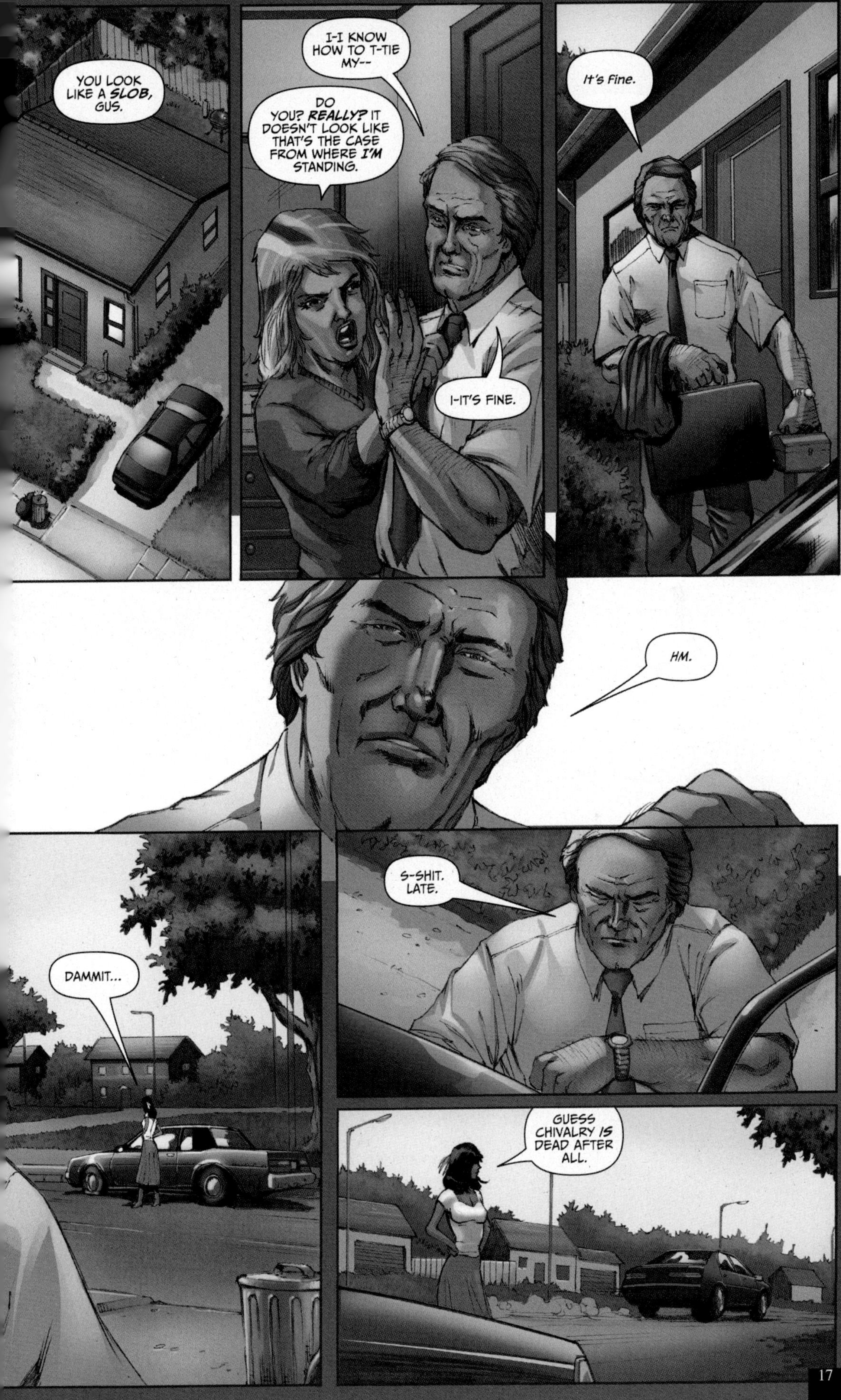

YOU LOOK LIKE A **SLOB,** GUS.
I-I KNOW HOW TO T-TIE MY--
DO YOU? **REALLY?** IT DOESN'T LOOK LIKE THAT'S THE CASE FROM WHERE ***I'M*** STANDING.
I-IT'S FINE.
It's fine.
HM.
DAMMIT...
S-SHIT. LATE.
GUESS CHIVALRY ***IS*** DEAD AFTER ALL.

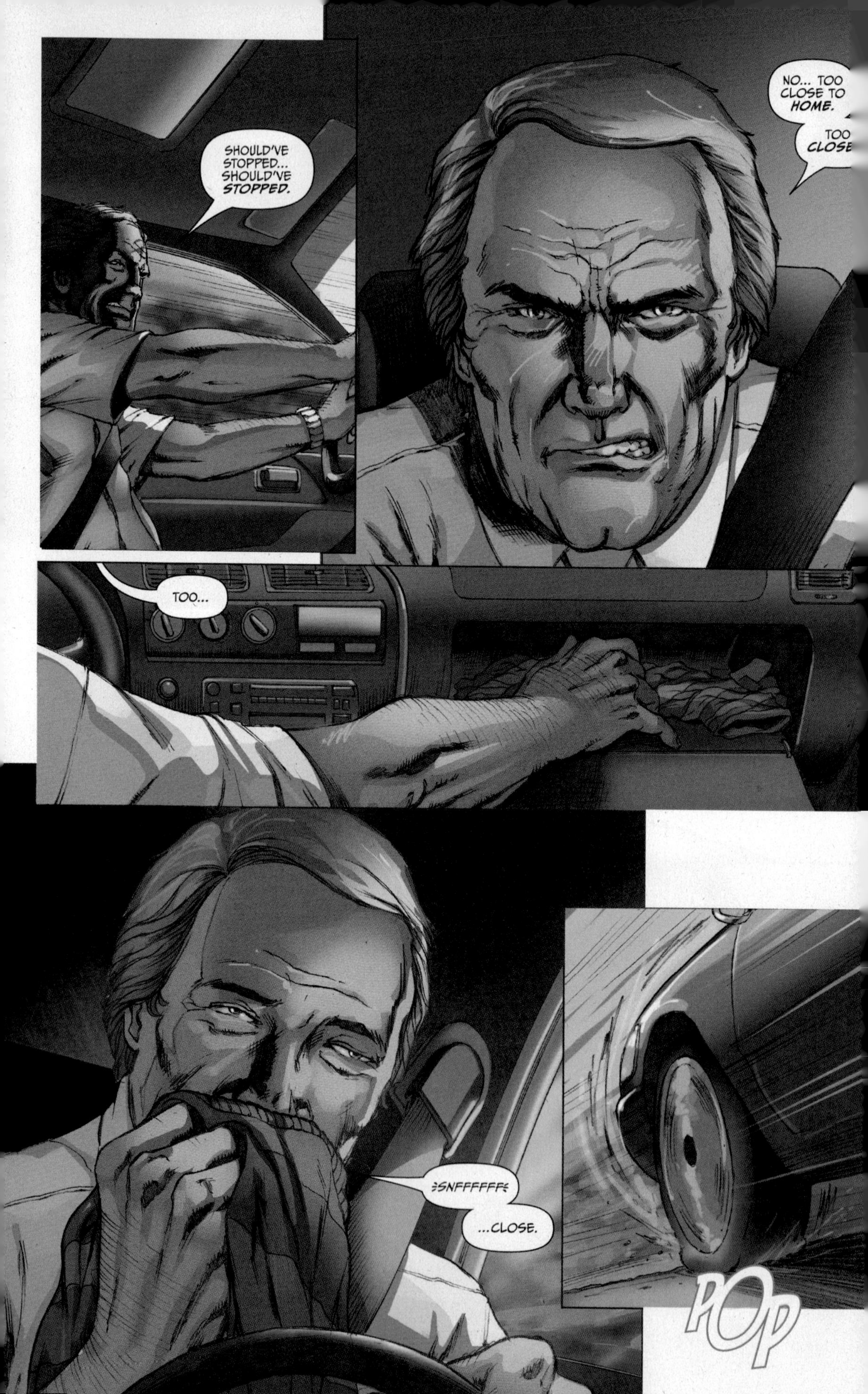
SHOULD'VE STOPPED... SHOULD'VE STOPPED.
NO... TOO CLOSE TO HOME.
TOO CLOSE
TOO...
SNFFFFFF
...CLOSE.
POP

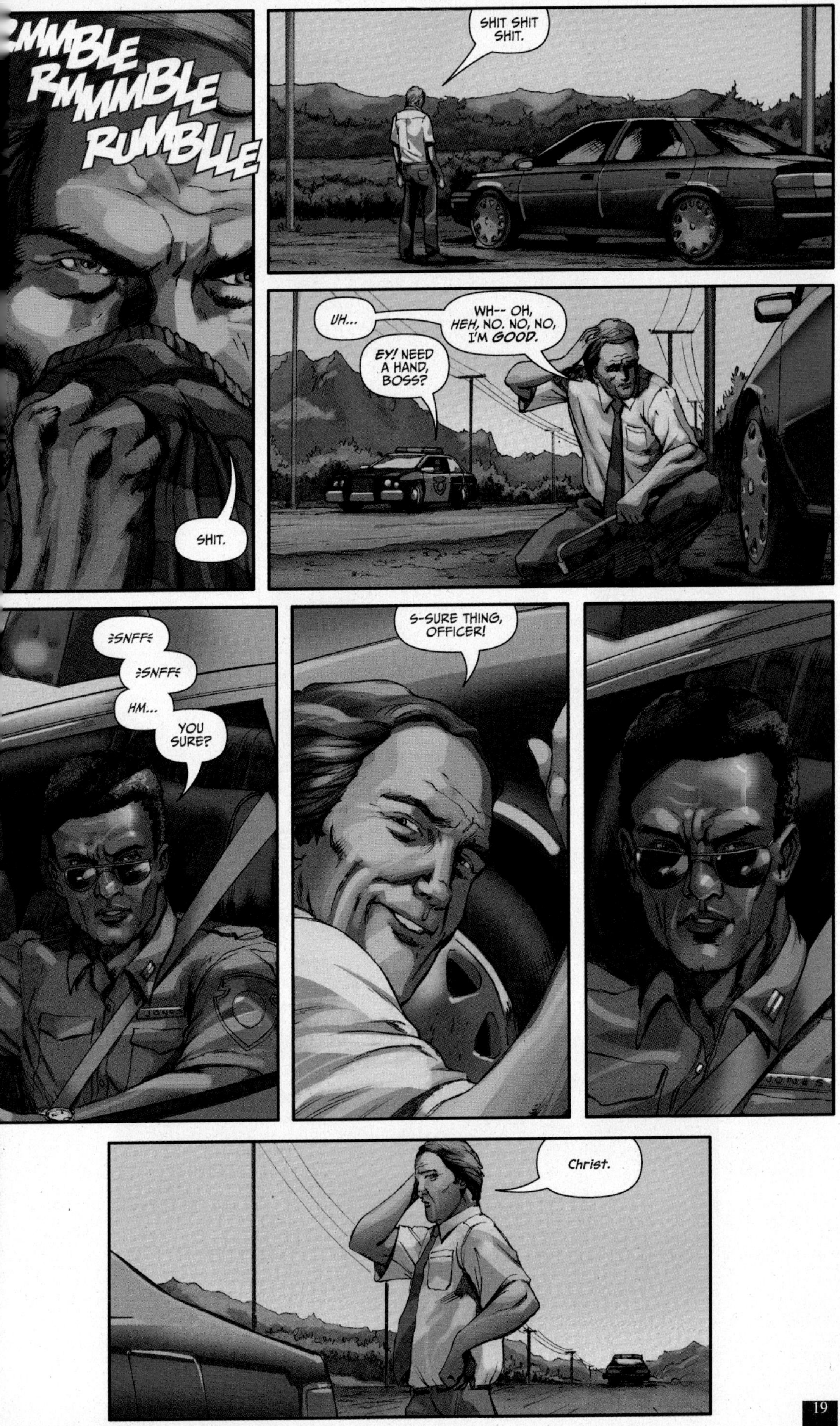

RMMBLE RMMMBLE RUMBLLE
SHIT.
SHIT SHIT SHIT.
UH...
EY! NEED A HAND, BOSS?
WH-- OH, HEH, NO. NO, NO, I'M GOOD.
SNFF
SNFF
HM...
YOU SURE?
S-SURE THING, OFFICER!
Christ.

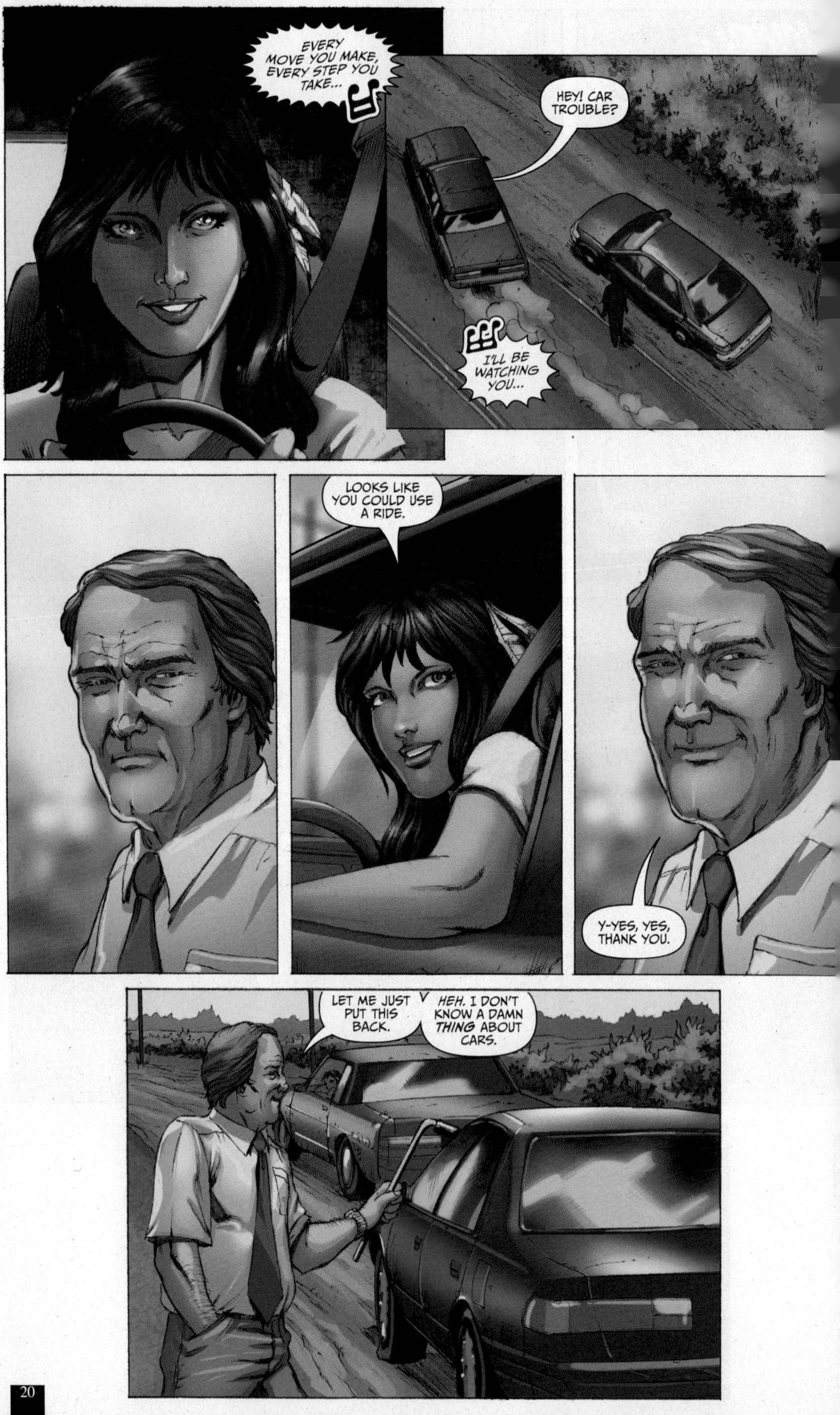
EVERY MOVE YOU MAKE, EVERY STEP YOU TAKE...
HEY! CAR TROUBLE?
I'LL BE WATCHING YOU...
LOOKS LIKE YOU COULD USE A RIDE.
Y-YES, YES, THANK YOU.
LET ME JUST PUT THIS BACK.
HEH. I DON'T KNOW A DAMN THING ABOUT CARS.

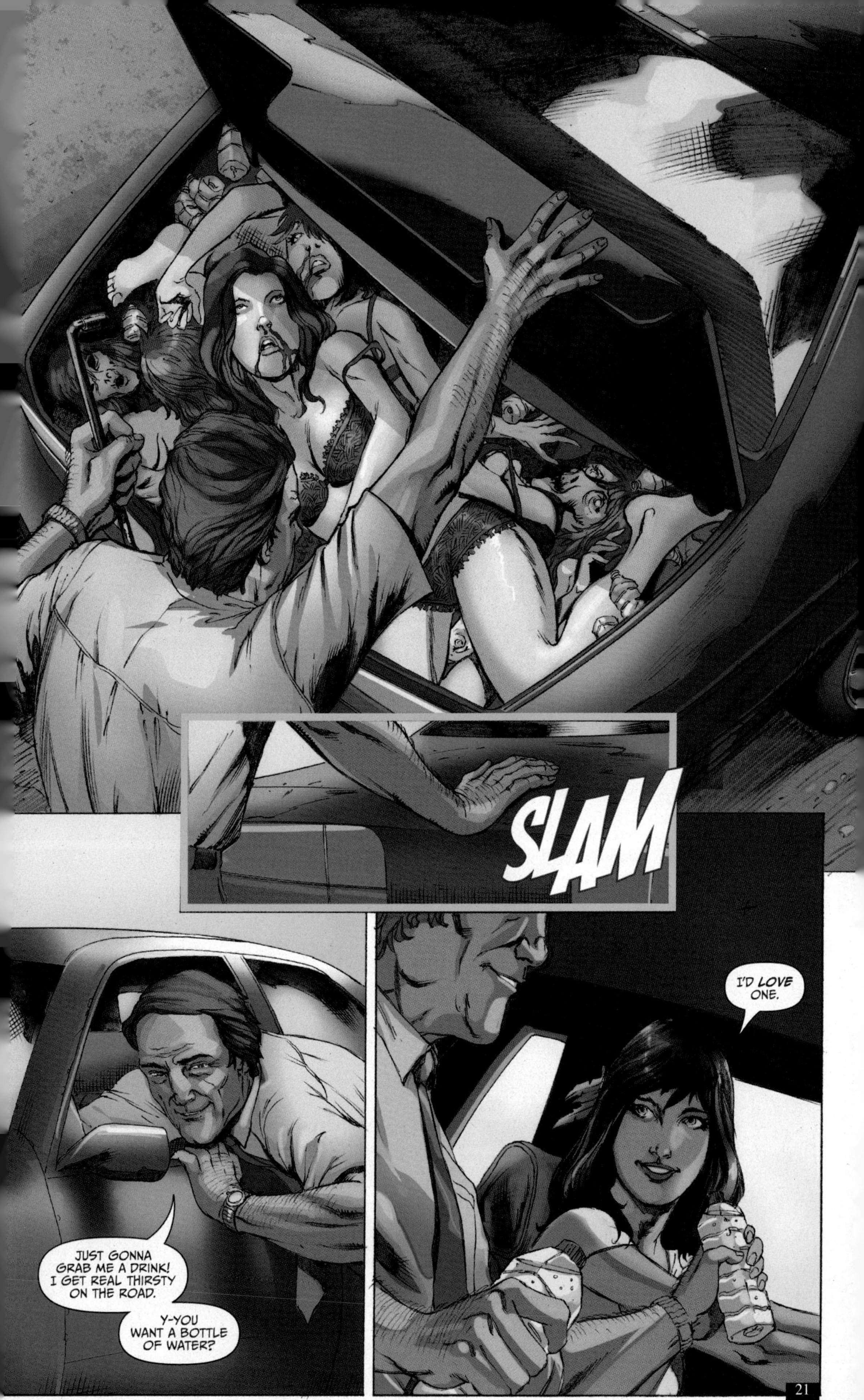
SLAM
JUST GONNA GRAB ME A DRINK! I GET REAL THIRSTY ON THE ROAD.
Y-YOU WANT A BOTTLE OF WATER?
I'D LOVE ONE.

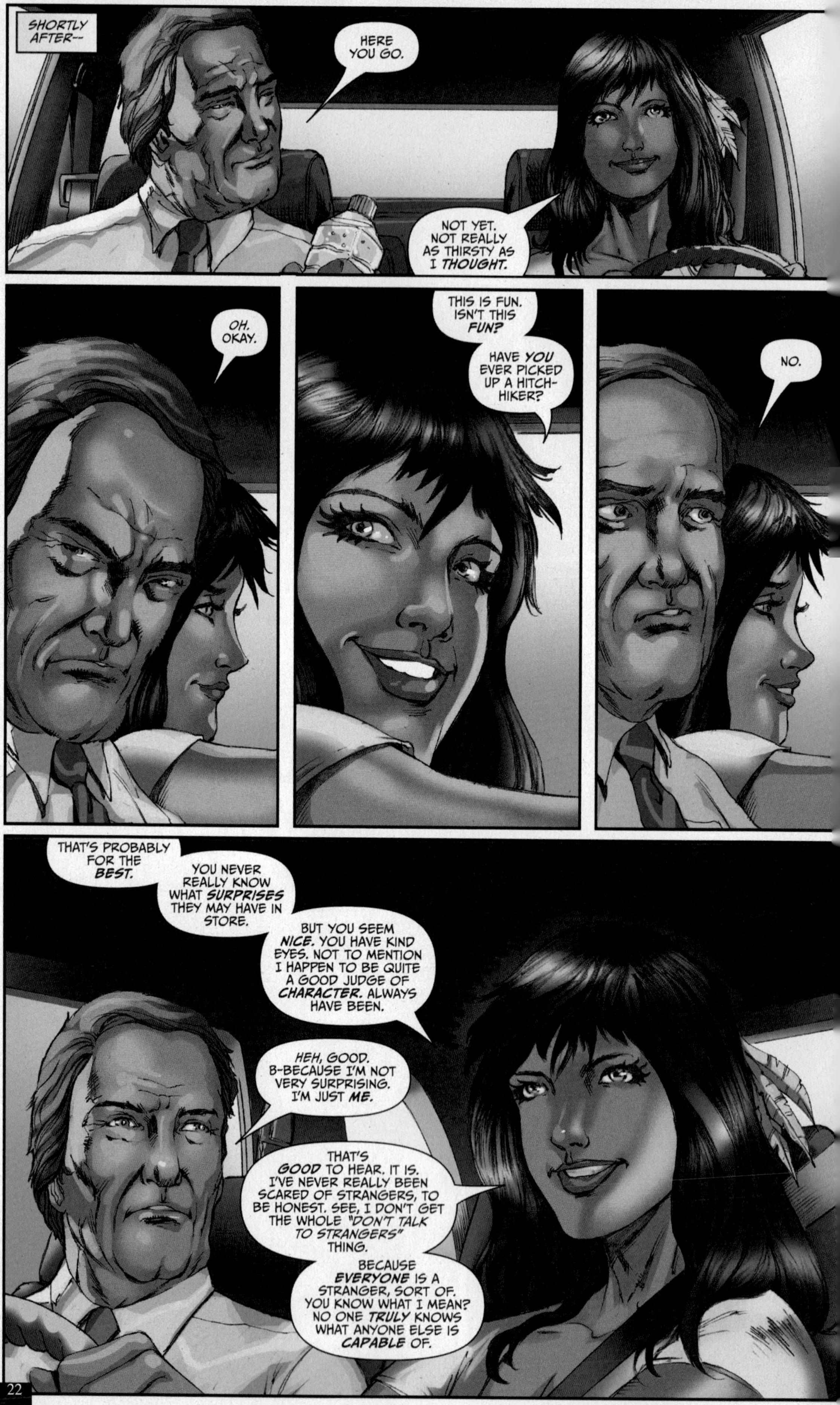

SHORTLY AFTER--
HERE YOU GO.
NOT YET. NOT REALLY AS THIRSTY AS I *THOUGHT.*
OH. OKAY.
THIS IS FUN. ISN'T THIS *FUN?*
HAVE *YOU* EVER PICKED UP A HITCH-HIKER?
NO.
THAT'S PROBABLY FOR THE *BEST.*
YOU NEVER REALLY KNOW WHAT *SURPRISES* THEY MAY HAVE IN STORE.
BUT YOU SEEM *NICE.* YOU HAVE KIND EYES. NOT TO MENTION I HAPPEN TO BE QUITE A GOOD JUDGE OF *CHARACTER.* ALWAYS HAVE BEEN.
HEH, GOOD. B-BECAUSE I'M NOT VERY SURPRISING. I'M JUST ***ME.***
THAT'S *GOOD* TO HEAR. IT IS. I'VE NEVER REALLY BEEN SCARED OF STRANGERS, TO BE HONEST. SEE, I DON'T GET THE WHOLE *"DON'T TALK TO STRANGERS"* THING.
BECAUSE *EVERYONE* IS A STRANGER, SORT OF. YOU KNOW WHAT I MEAN? NO ONE *TRULY* KNOWS WHAT ANYONE ELSE IS *CAPABLE* OF.

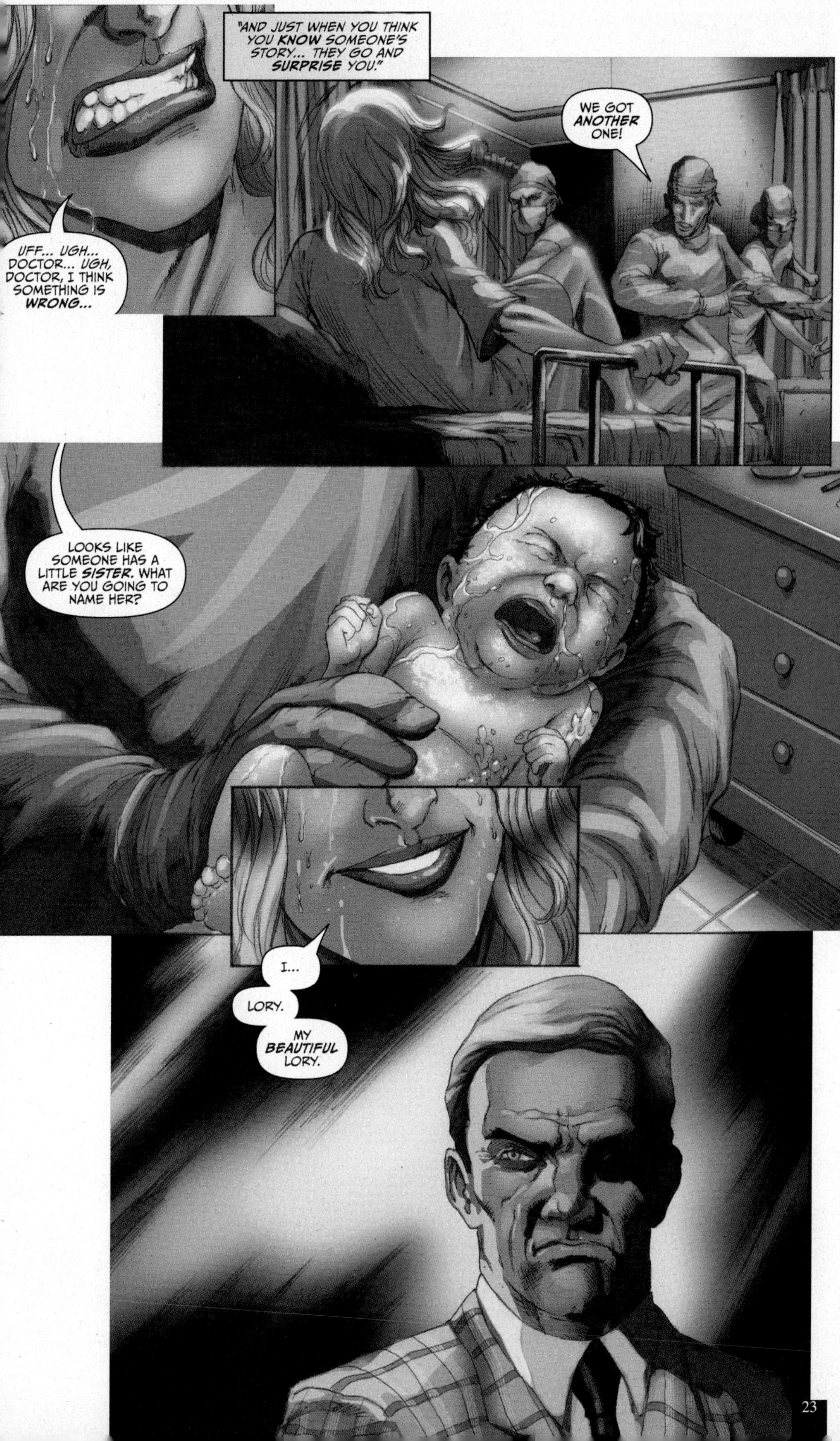
"AND JUST WHEN YOU THINK YOU KNOW SOMEONE'S STORY... THEY GO AND SURPRISE YOU."
UFF... UGH... DOCTOR... UGH, DOCTOR, I THINK SOMETHING IS WRONG...
WE GOT ANOTHER ONE!
LOOKS LIKE SOMEONE HAS A LITTLE SISTER. WHAT ARE YOU GOING TO NAME HER?
I...
LORY.
MY BEAUTIFUL LORY.

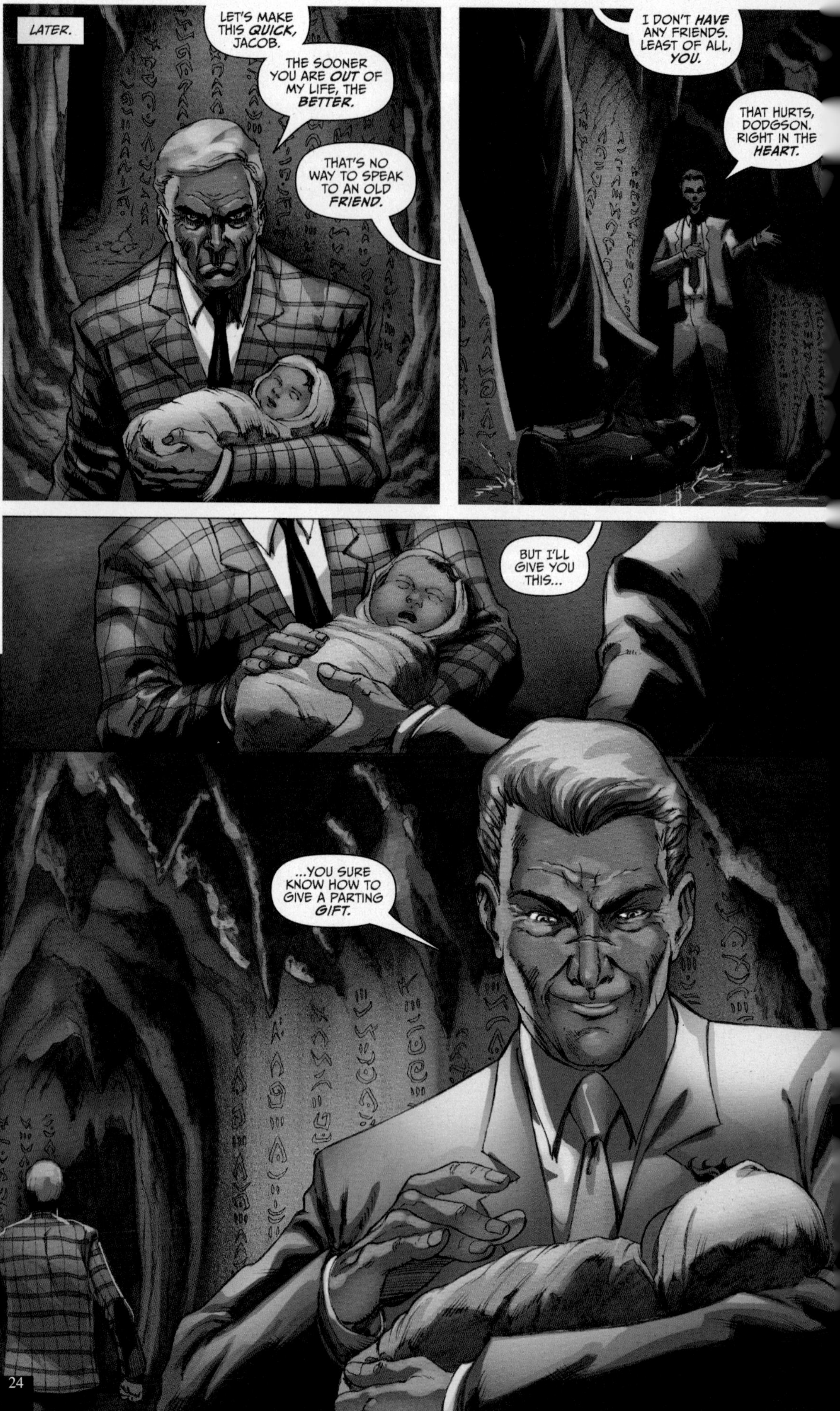
LATER.
LET'S MAKE THIS QUICK, JACOB.
THE SOONER YOU ARE OUT OF MY LIFE, THE BETTER.
THAT'S NO WAY TO SPEAK TO AN OLD FRIEND.
I DON'T HAVE ANY FRIENDS. LEAST OF ALL, YOU.
THAT HURTS, DODGSON. RIGHT IN THE HEART.
BUT I'LL GIVE YOU THIS...
...YOU SURE KNOW HOW TO GIVE A PARTING GIFT.

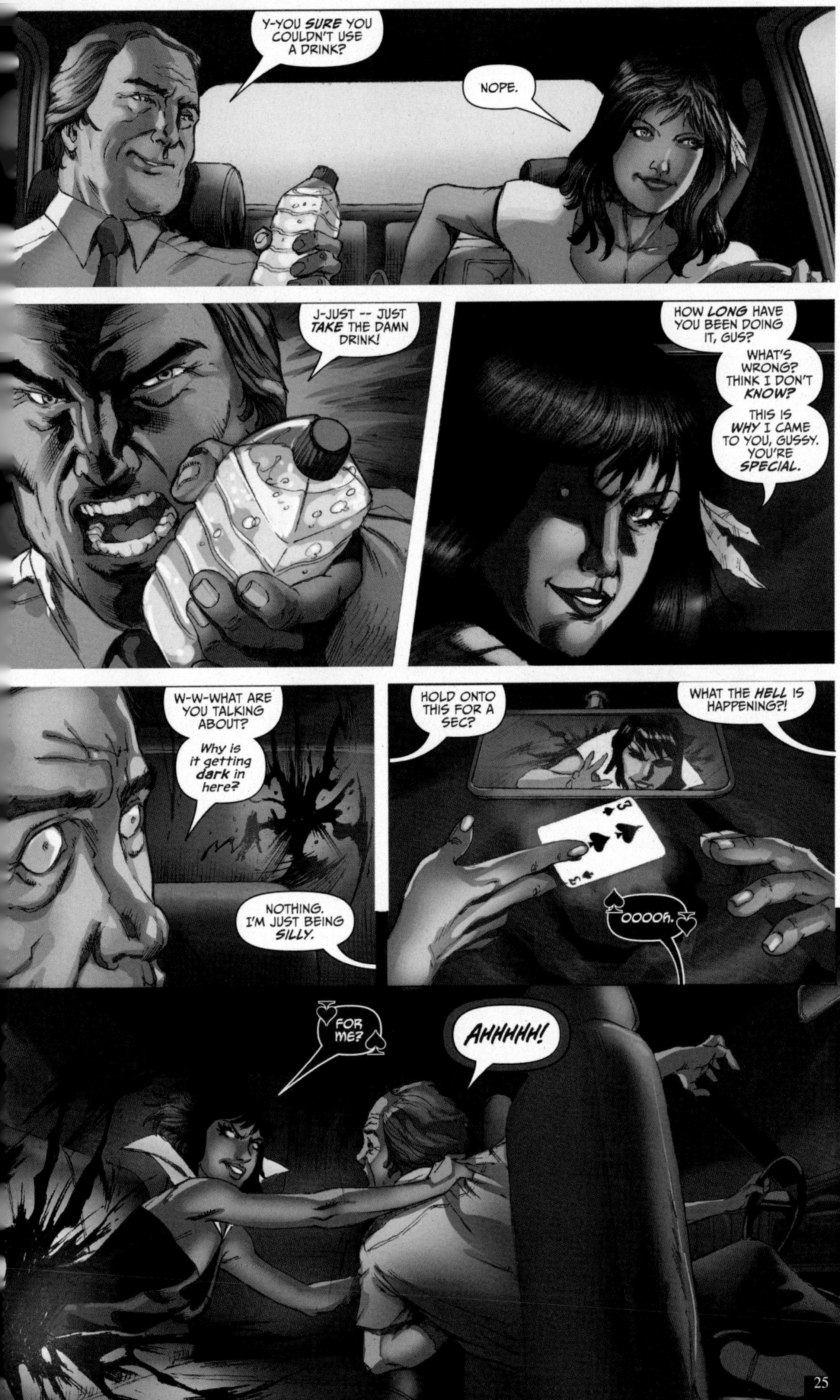
Y-YOU SURE YOU COULDN'T USE A DRINK?
NOPE.
J-JUST -- JUST TAKE THE DAMN DRINK!
HOW LONG HAVE YOU BEEN DOING IT, GUS?
WHAT'S WRONG? THINK I DON'T KNOW?
THIS IS WHY I CAME TO YOU, GUSSY. YOU'RE SPECIAL.
W-W-WHAT ARE YOU TALKING ABOUT?
Why is it getting dark in here?
NOTHING. I'M JUST BEING SILLY.
HOLD ONTO THIS FOR A SEC?
WHAT THE HELL IS HAPPENING?!
OOOOh.
FOR ME?
AHHHHH!

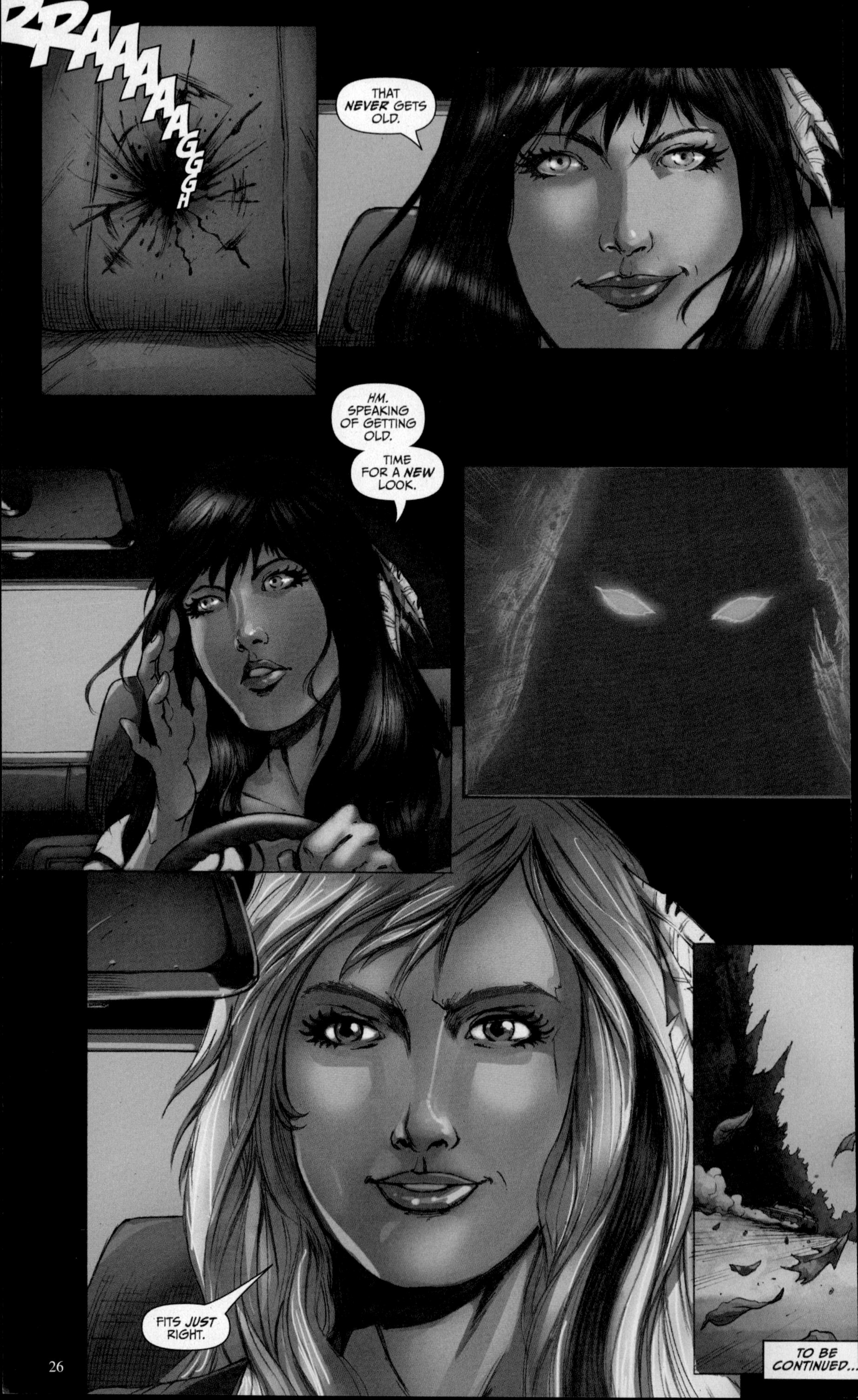
RRAAAAAAGGGH
THAT NEVER GETS OLD.
HM. SPEAKING OF GETTING OLD.
TIME FOR A NEW LOOK.
FITS JUST RIGHT.
TO BE CONTINUED...

Grimm Fairy Tales presents

Wonderland

Chapter Two

STORY RAVEN GREGORY
WRITER PAT SHAND
PENCILS SHELDON GOH AND JG MIRANDA
COLORS LEONARDO PACIAROTTI
LETTERS JIM CAMPBELL

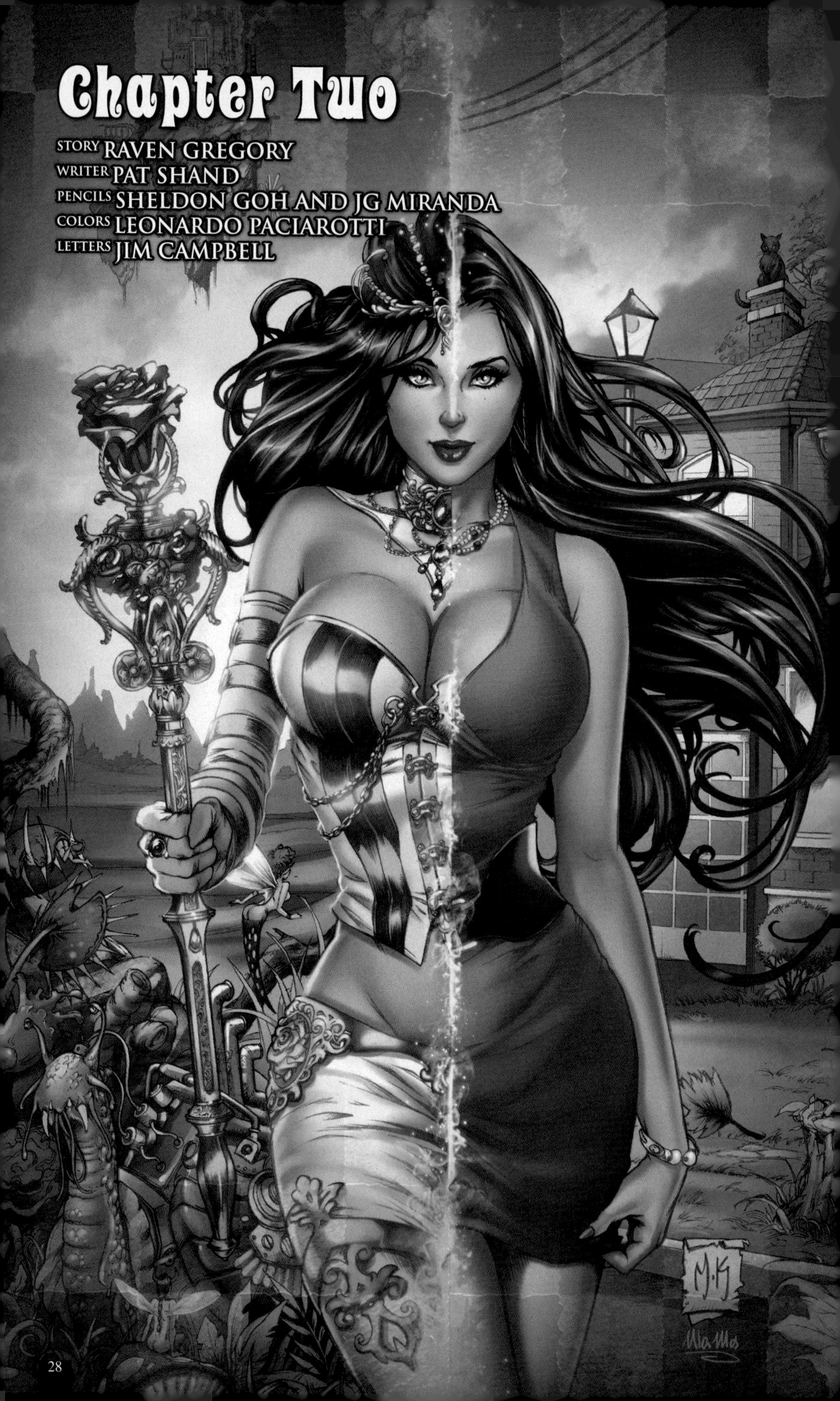

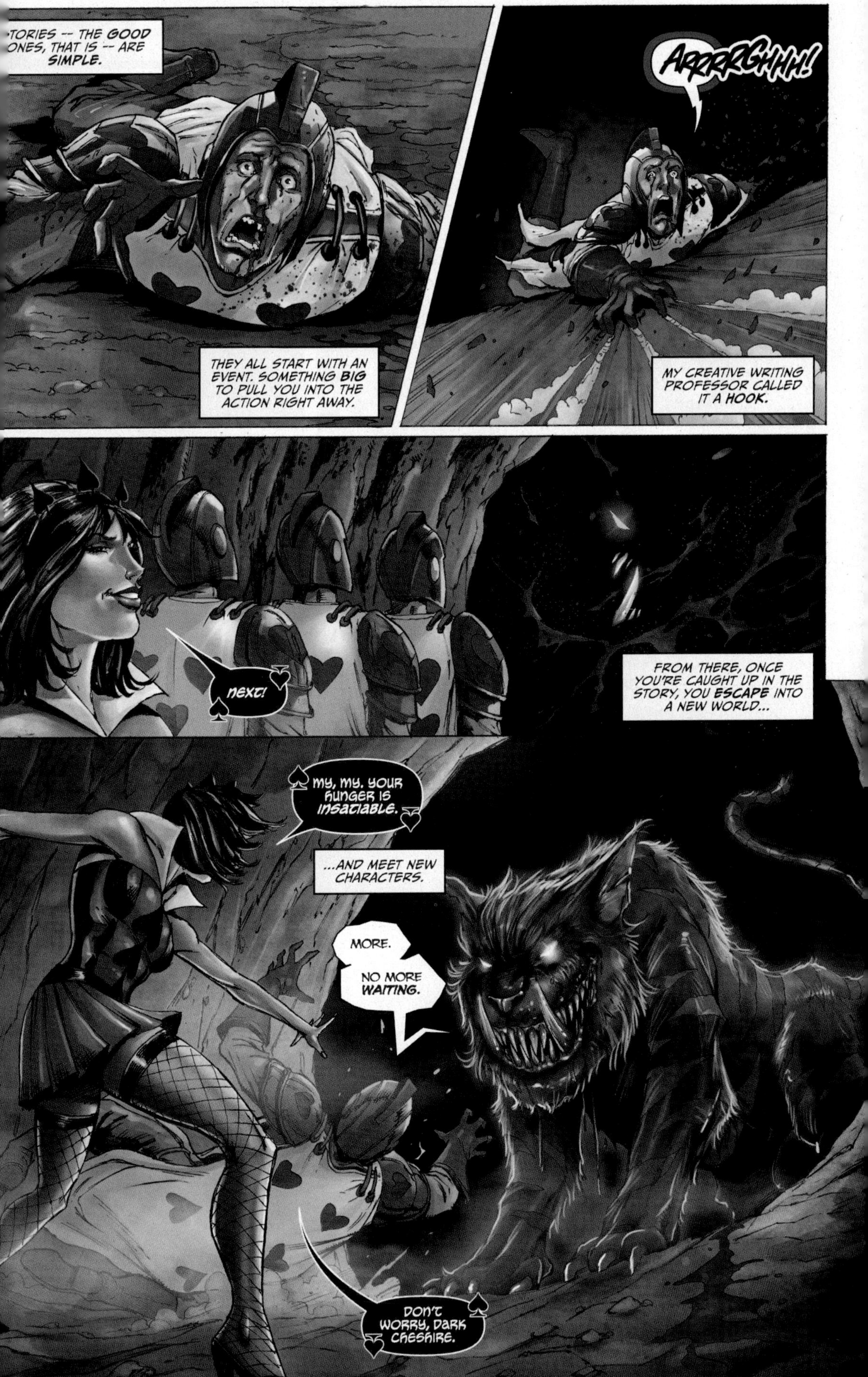
STORIES -- THE GOOD ONES, THAT IS -- ARE SIMPLE.
THEY ALL START WITH AN EVENT. SOMETHING BIG TO PULL YOU INTO THE ACTION RIGHT AWAY.
ARRRRGHHH!
MY CREATIVE WRITING PROFESSOR CALLED IT A HOOK.
next!
FROM THERE, ONCE YOU'RE CAUGHT UP IN THE STORY, YOU ESCAPE INTO A NEW WORLD...
my, my. your hunger is insatiable.
...AND MEET NEW CHARACTERS.
MORE.
NO MORE WAITING.
don't worry, dark cheshire.

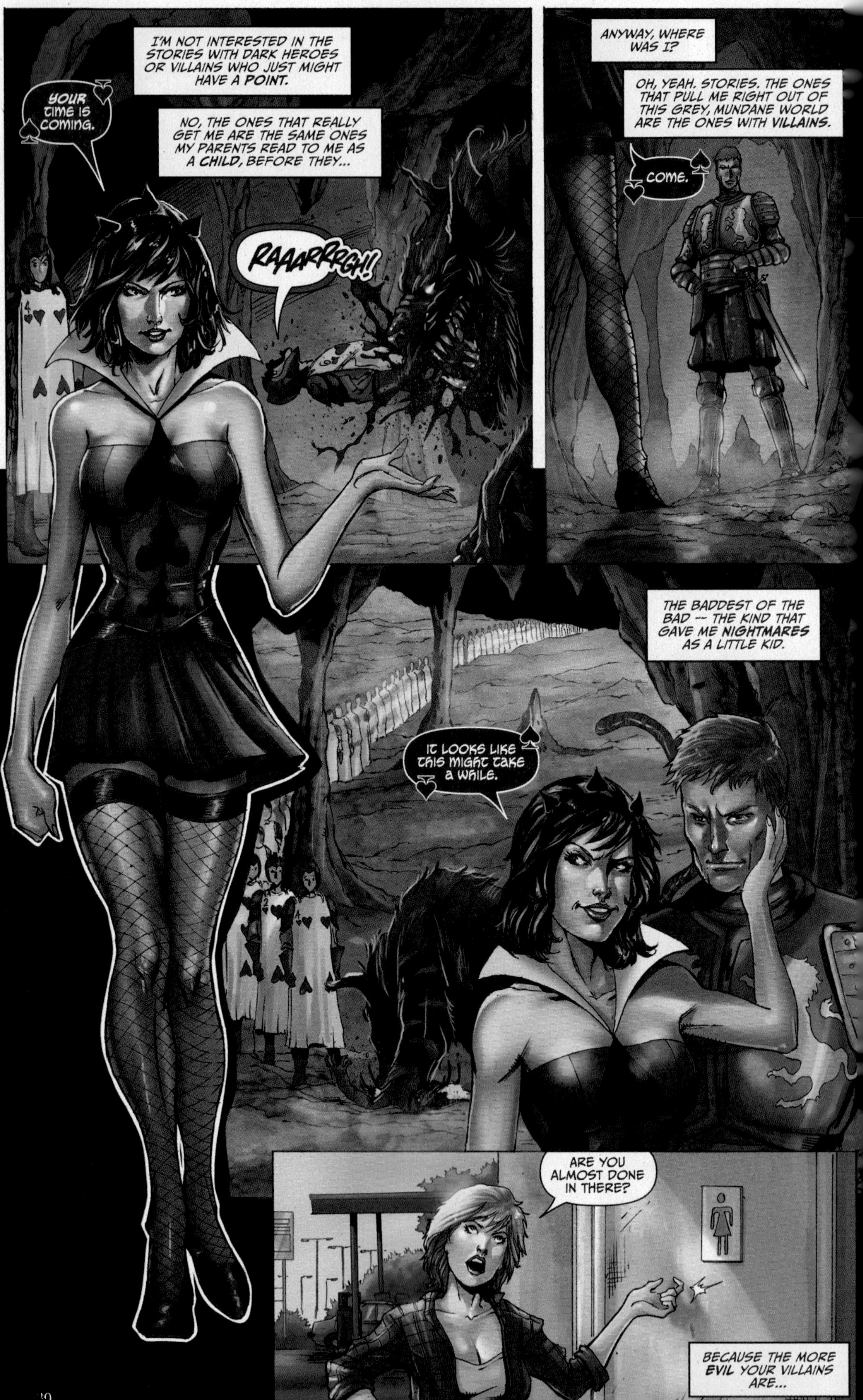
I'M NOT INTERESTED IN THE STORIES WITH DARK HEROES OR VILLAINS WHO JUST MIGHT HAVE A POINT.
YOUR TIME IS COMING.
NO, THE ONES THAT REALLY GET ME ARE THE SAME ONES MY PARENTS READ TO ME AS A CHILD, BEFORE THEY...
RAAARRRGH!!
ANYWAY, WHERE WAS I?
OH, YEAH. STORIES. THE ONES THAT PULL ME RIGHT OUT OF THIS GREY, MUNDANE WORLD ARE THE ONES WITH VILLAINS.
COME.
THE BADDEST OF THE BAD -- THE KIND THAT GAVE ME NIGHTMARES AS A LITTLE KID.
IT LOOKS LIKE THIS MIGHT TAKE A WHILE.
ARE YOU ALMOST DONE IN THERE?
BECAUSE THE MORE EVIL YOUR VILLAINS ARE...

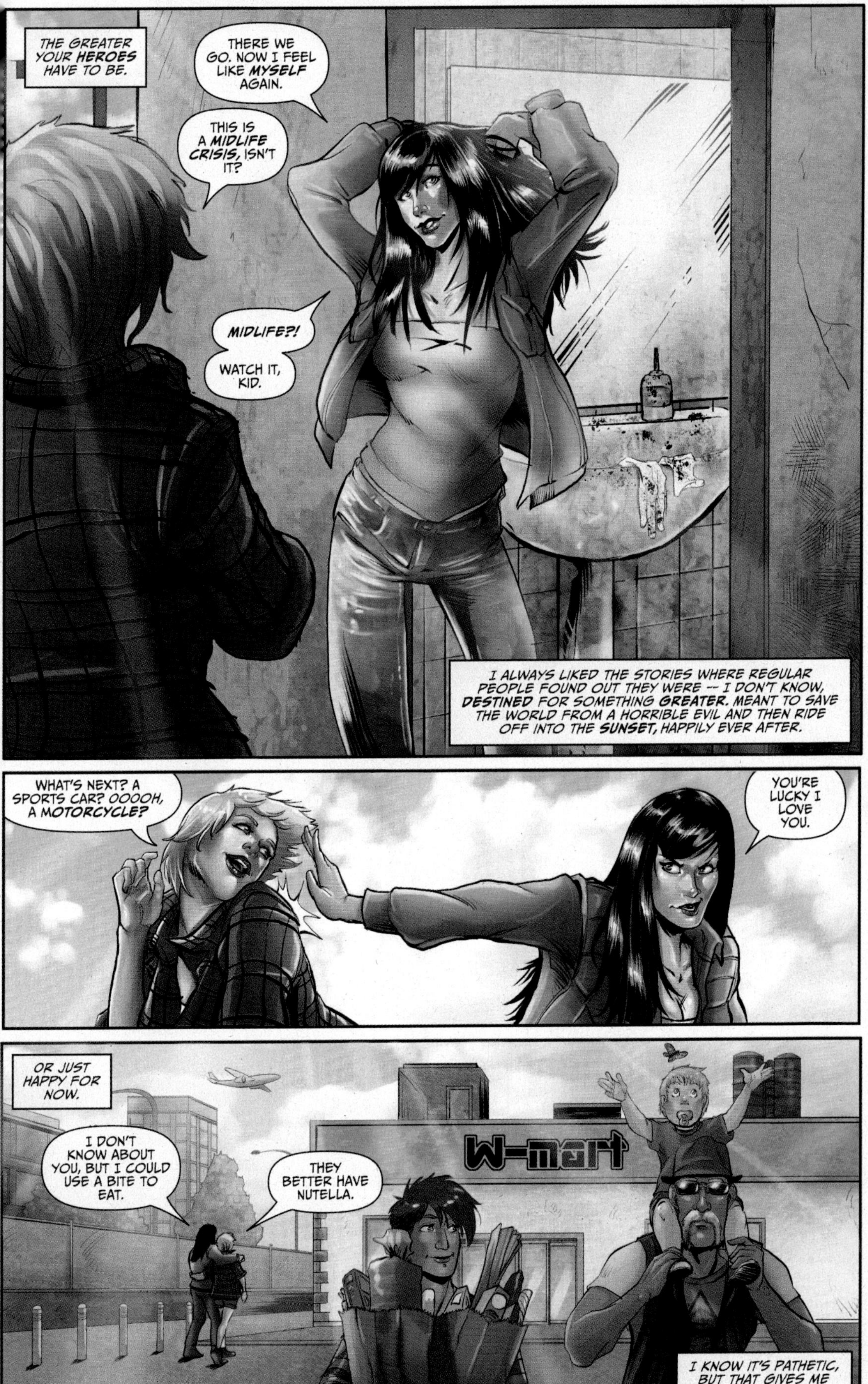
THE GREATER YOUR **HEROES** HAVE TO BE.
THERE WE GO. NOW I FEEL LIKE ***MYSELF*** AGAIN.
THIS IS A ***MIDLIFE CRISIS,*** ISN'T IT?
MIDLIFE?!
WATCH IT, KID.
I ALWAYS LIKED THE STORIES WHERE REGULAR PEOPLE FOUND OUT THEY WERE -- I DON'T KNOW, **DESTINED** FOR SOMETHING **GREATER**. MEANT TO SAVE THE WORLD FROM A HORRIBLE EVIL AND THEN RIDE OFF INTO THE **SUNSET**, HAPPILY EVER AFTER.
WHAT'S NEXT? A SPORTS CAR? OOOOH, A ***MOTORCYCLE?***
YOU'RE LUCKY I LOVE YOU.
OR JUST HAPPY FOR NOW.
W-mart
I DON'T KNOW ABOUT YOU, BUT I COULD USE A BITE TO EAT.
THEY BETTER HAVE NUTELLA.
I KNOW IT'S PATHETIC, BUT THAT GIVES ME **HOPE**.

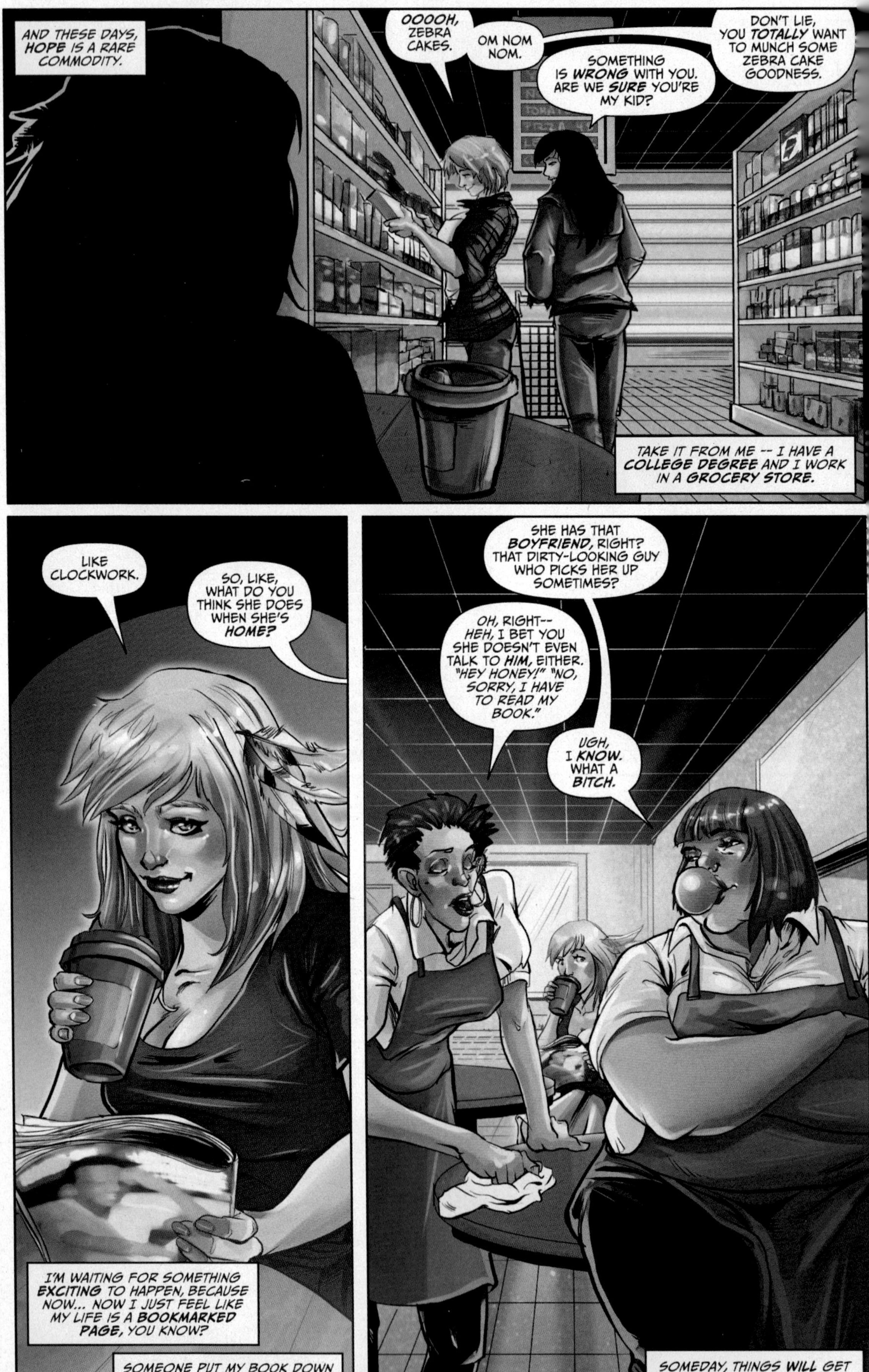
AND THESE DAYS, HOPE IS A RARE COMMODITY.
OOOOH, ZEBRA CAKES.
OM NOM NOM.
SOMETHING IS WRONG WITH YOU. ARE WE SURE YOU'RE MY KID?
DON'T LIE, YOU TOTALLY WANT TO MUNCH SOME ZEBRA CAKE GOODNESS.
TAKE IT FROM ME -- I HAVE A COLLEGE DEGREE AND I WORK IN A GROCERY STORE.
LIKE CLOCKWORK.
SO, LIKE, WHAT DO YOU THINK SHE DOES WHEN SHE'S HOME?
I'M WAITING FOR SOMETHING EXCITING TO HAPPEN, BECAUSE NOW... NOW I JUST FEEL LIKE MY LIFE IS A BOOKMARKED PAGE, YOU KNOW?
SOMEONE PUT MY BOOK DOWN IN THE MIDDLE OF THE STORY, AND I'M IN THIS... PAUSE.
SHE HAS THAT BOYFRIEND, RIGHT? THAT DIRTY-LOOKING GUY WHO PICKS HER UP SOMETIMES?
OH, RIGHT-- HEH, I BET YOU SHE DOESN'T EVEN TALK TO HIM, EITHER. "HEY HONEY!" "NO, SORRY, I HAVE TO READ MY BOOK."
UGH, I KNOW. WHAT A BITCH.
SOMEDAY, THINGS WILL GET BETTER. I'LL MOVE ONTO A BETTER CHAPTER.

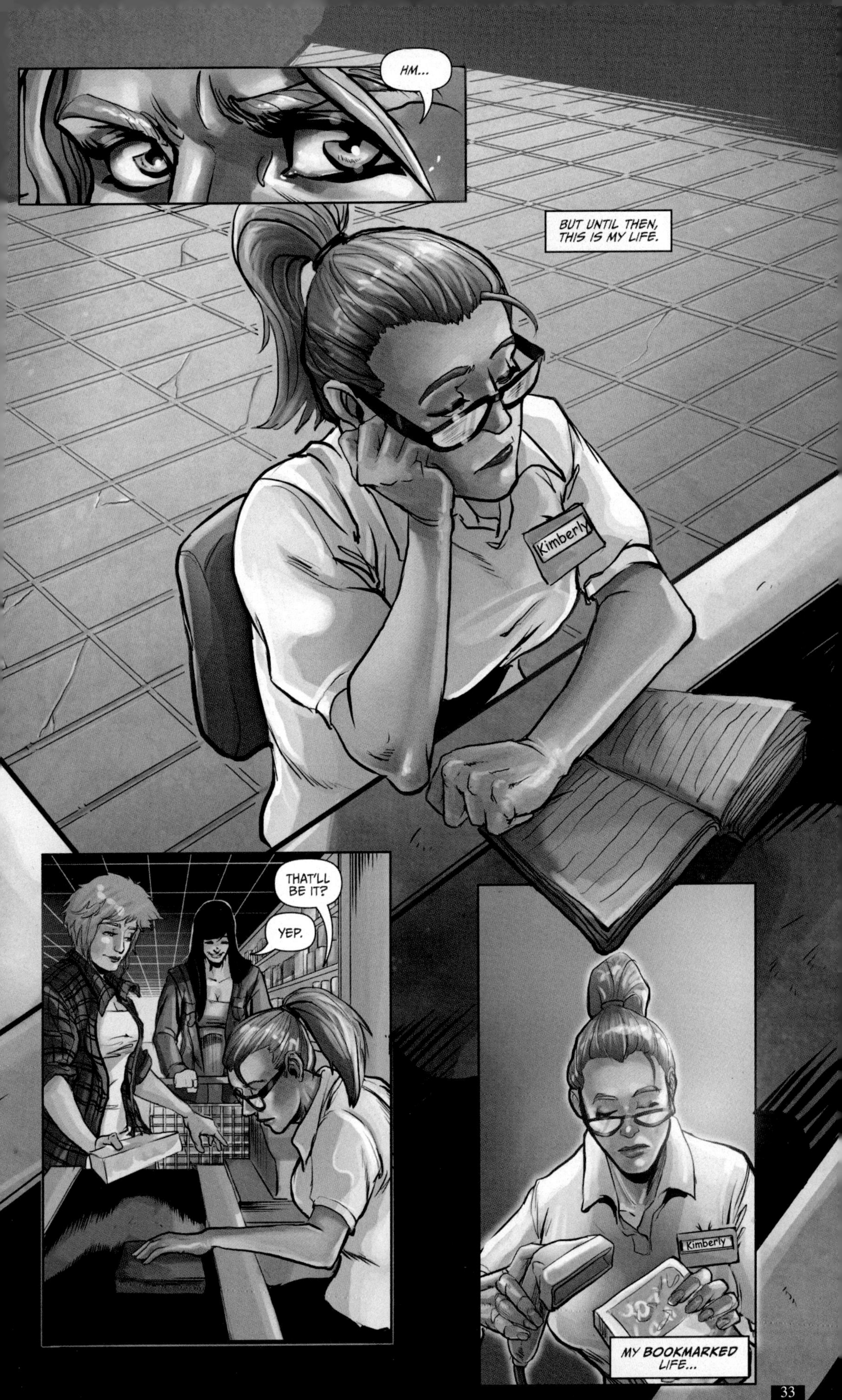
HM...
BUT UNTIL THEN, THIS IS MY LIFE.
Kimberly
THAT'LL BE IT?
YEP.
Kimberly
MY BOOKMARKED LIFE...

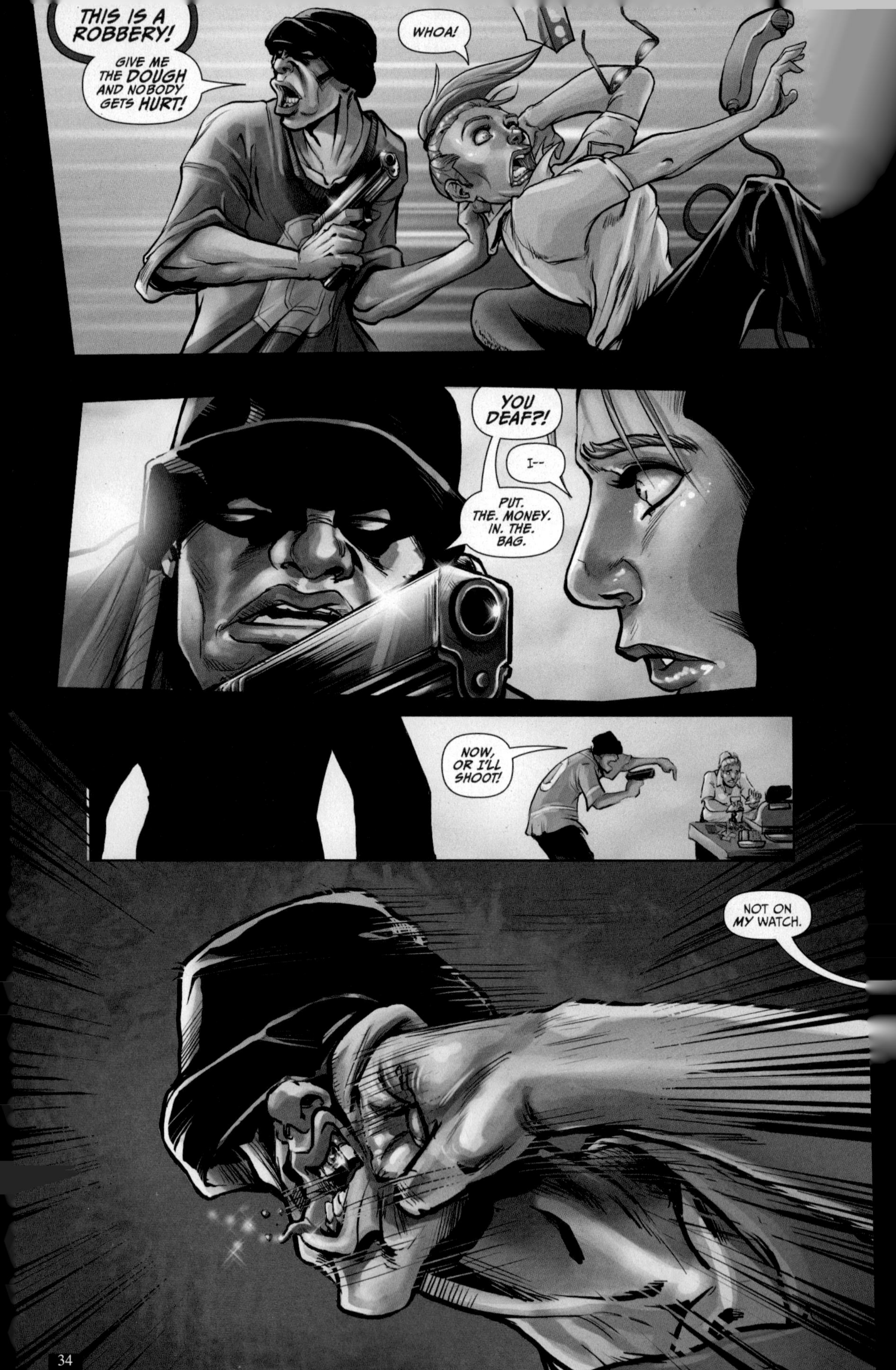
THIS IS A ROBBERY!
GIVE ME THE DOUGH AND NOBODY GETS HURT!
WHOA!
YOU DEAF?!
I--
PUT. THE. MONEY. IN. THE. BAG.
NOW, OR I'LL SHOOT!
NOT ON MY WATCH.

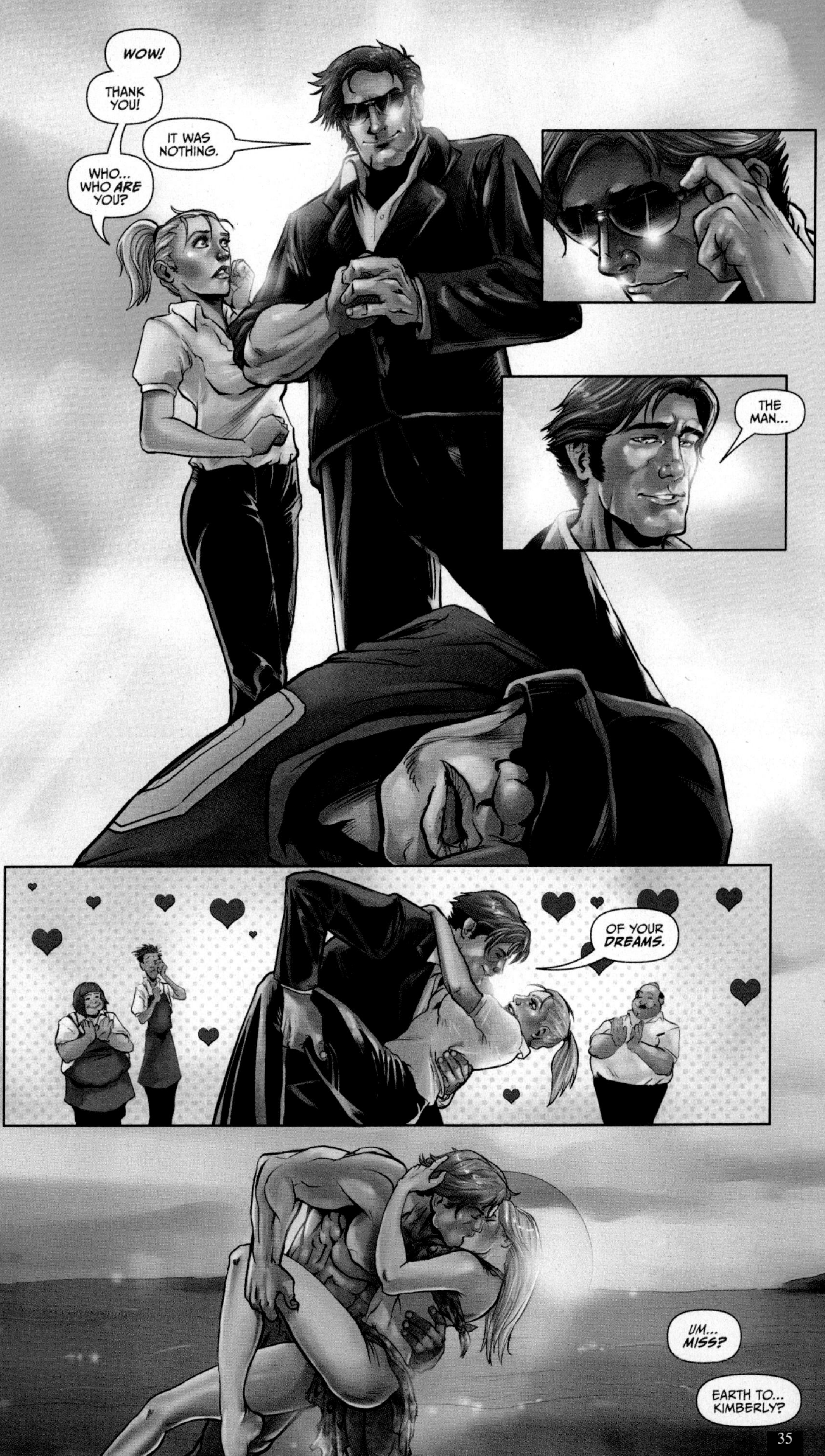
WOW!
THANK YOU!
IT WAS NOTHING.
WHO... WHO *ARE* YOU?
THE MAN...
OF YOUR *DREAMS.*
UM... *MISS?*
EARTH TO... KIMBERLY?

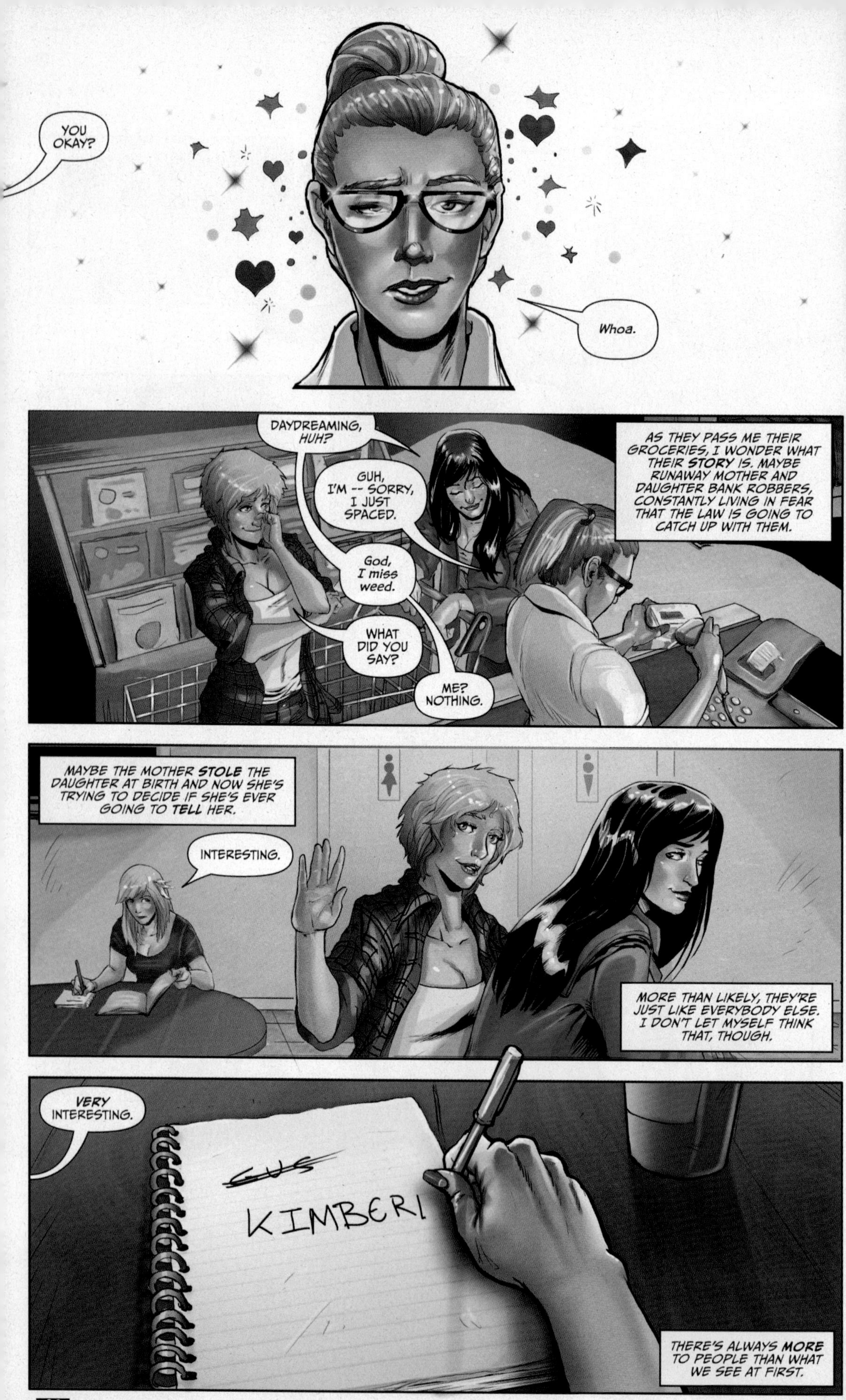
YOU OKAY?
Whoa.
DAYDREAMING, HUH?
GUH, I'M -- SORRY, I JUST SPACED.
AS THEY PASS ME THEIR GROCERIES, I WONDER WHAT THEIR STORY IS. MAYBE RUNAWAY MOTHER AND DAUGHTER BANK ROBBERS, CONSTANTLY LIVING IN FEAR THAT THE LAW IS GOING TO CATCH UP WITH THEM.
God, I miss weed.
WHAT DID YOU SAY?
ME? NOTHING.
MAYBE THE MOTHER STOLE THE DAUGHTER AT BIRTH AND NOW SHE'S TRYING TO DECIDE IF SHE'S EVER GOING TO TELL HER.
INTERESTING.
MORE THAN LIKELY, THEY'RE JUST LIKE EVERYBODY ELSE. I DON'T LET MYSELF THINK THAT, THOUGH.
VERY INTERESTING.
KIMBERI
THERE'S ALWAYS MORE TO PEOPLE THAN WHAT WE SEE AT FIRST.

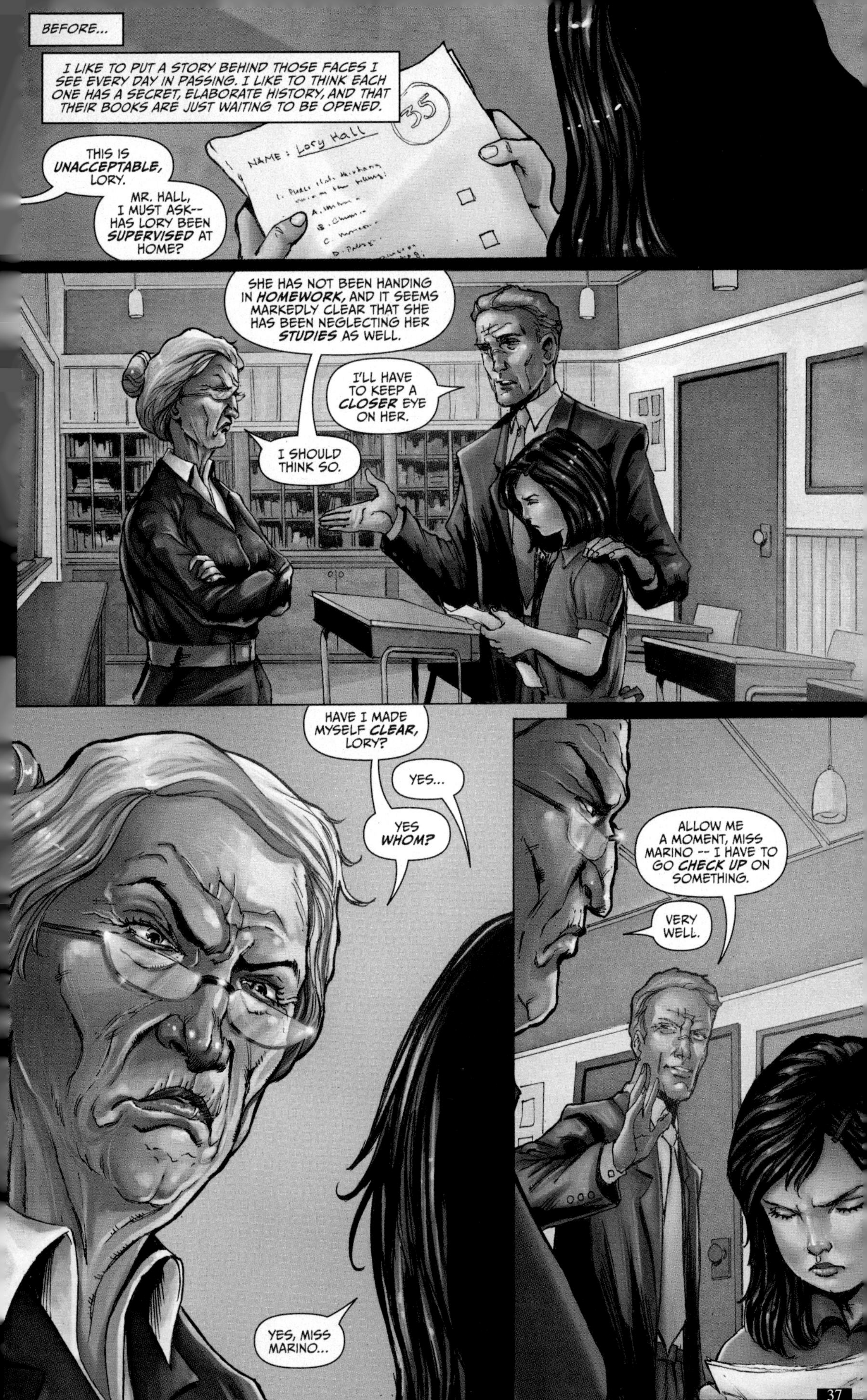

BEFORE...
I LIKE TO PUT A STORY BEHIND THOSE FACES I SEE EVERY DAY IN PASSING. I LIKE TO THINK EACH ONE HAS A SECRET, ELABORATE HISTORY, AND THAT THEIR BOOKS ARE JUST WAITING TO BE OPENED.
35
NAME: Lory Hall
THIS IS UNACCEPTABLE, LORY.
MR. HALL, I MUST ASK-- HAS LORY BEEN SUPERVISED AT HOME?
SHE HAS NOT BEEN HANDING IN HOMEWORK, AND IT SEEMS MARKEDLY CLEAR THAT SHE HAS BEEN NEGLECTING HER STUDIES AS WELL.
I'LL HAVE TO KEEP A CLOSER EYE ON HER.
I SHOULD THINK SO.
HAVE I MADE MYSELF CLEAR, LORY?
YES...
YES WHOM?
YES, MISS MARINO...
ALLOW ME A MOMENT, MISS MARINO -- I HAVE TO GO CHECK UP ON SOMETHING.
VERY WELL.

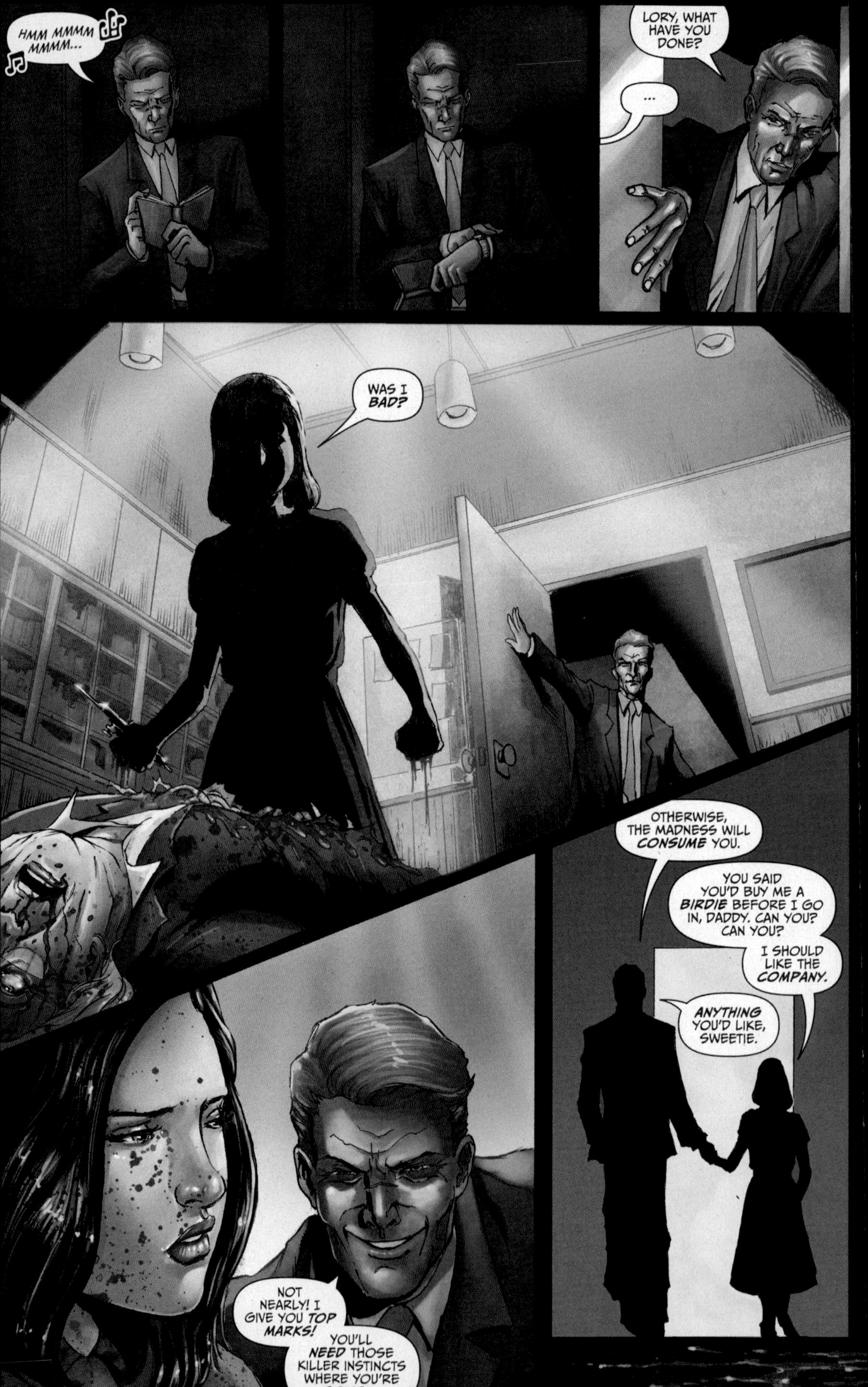
HMM MMMM MMMM...
LORY, WHAT HAVE YOU DONE?
...
WAS I BAD?
NOT NEARLY! I GIVE YOU TOP MARKS!
YOU'LL NEED THOSE KILLER INSTINCTS WHERE YOU'RE GOING...
OTHERWISE, THE MADNESS WILL CONSUME YOU.
YOU SAID YOU'D BUY ME A BIRDIE BEFORE I GO IN, DADDY. CAN YOU? CAN YOU?
I SHOULD LIKE THE COMPANY.
ANYTHING YOU'D LIKE, SWEETIE.

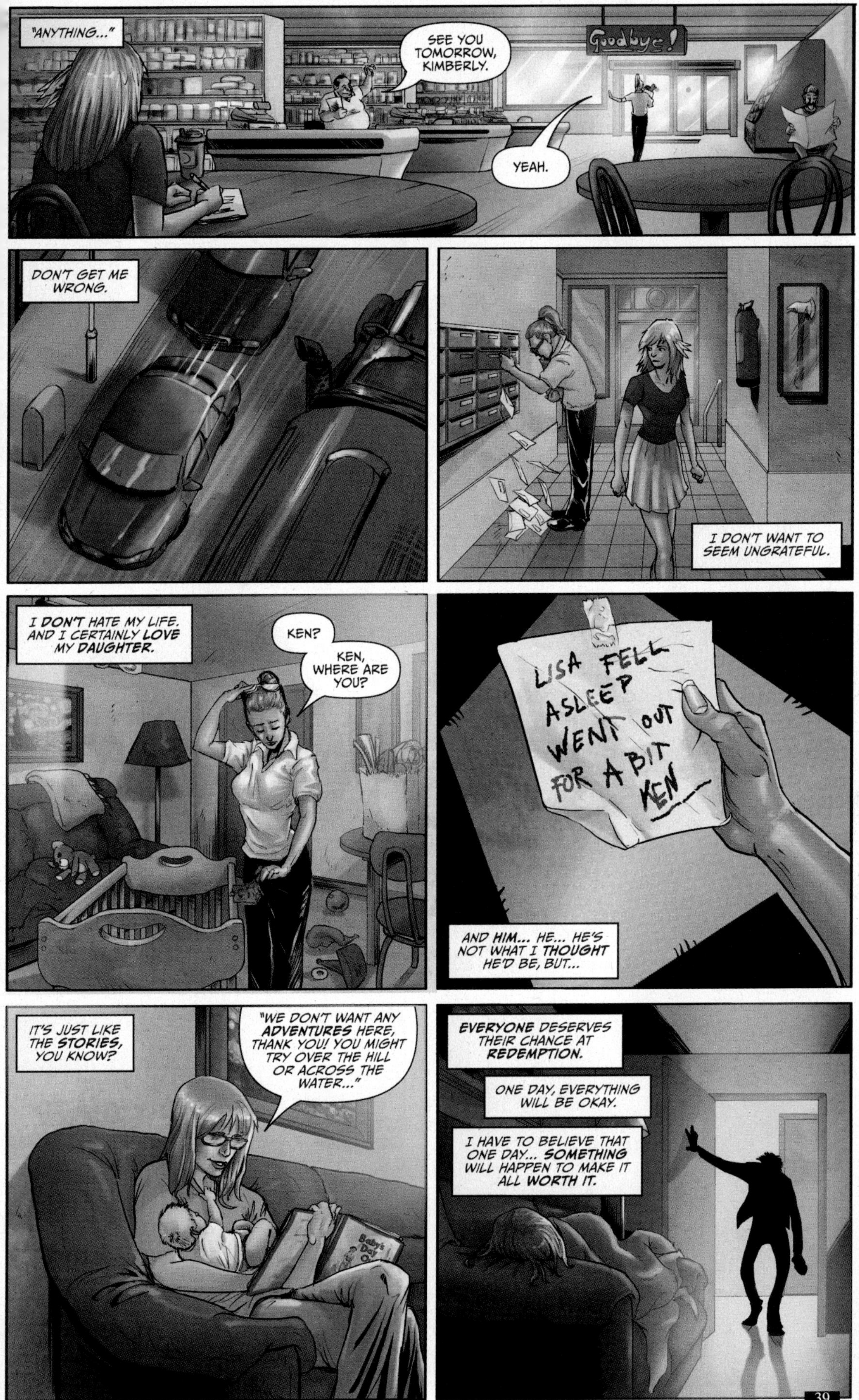
"ANYTHING..."
SEE YOU TOMORROW, KIMBERLY.
Goodbye!
YEAH.
DON'T GET ME WRONG.
I DON'T WANT TO SEEM UNGRATEFUL.
I DON'T HATE MY LIFE. AND I CERTAINLY LOVE MY DAUGHTER.
KEN?
KEN, WHERE ARE YOU?
LISA FELL ASLEEP WENT OUT FOR A BIT KEN
AND HIM... HE... HE'S NOT WHAT I THOUGHT HE'D BE, BUT...
IT'S JUST LIKE THE STORIES, YOU KNOW?
"WE DON'T WANT ANY ADVENTURES HERE, THANK YOU! YOU MIGHT TRY OVER THE HILL OR ACROSS THE WATER..."
EVERYONE DESERVES THEIR CHANCE AT REDEMPTION.
ONE DAY, EVERYTHING WILL BE OKAY.
I HAVE TO BELIEVE THAT ONE DAY... SOMETHING WILL HAPPEN TO MAKE IT ALL WORTH IT.

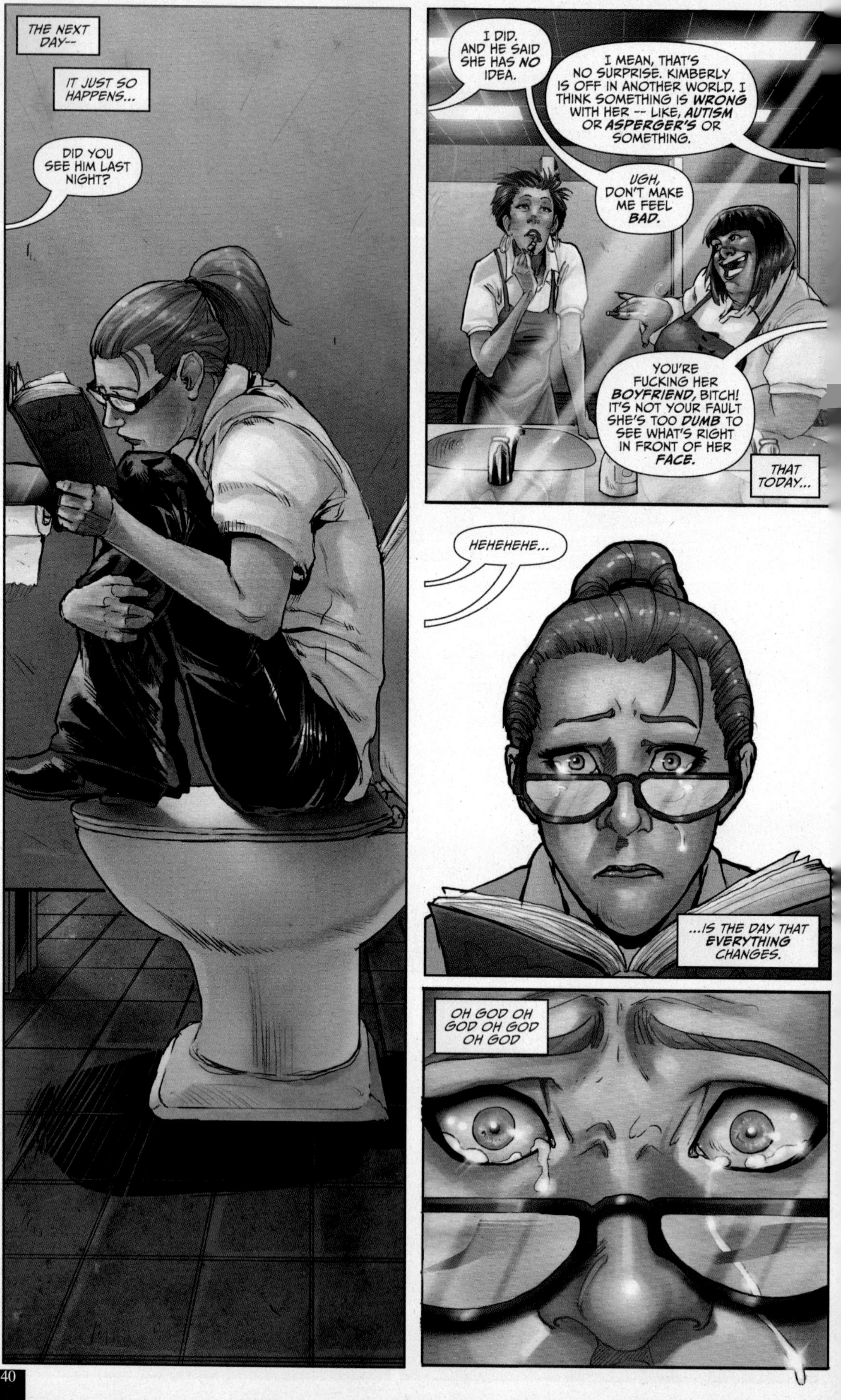
THE NEXT DAY--
IT JUST SO HAPPENS...
DID YOU SEE HIM LAST NIGHT?
I DID. AND HE SAID SHE HAS NO IDEA.
I MEAN, THAT'S NO SURPRISE. KIMBERLY IS OFF IN ANOTHER WORLD. I THINK SOMETHING IS WRONG WITH HER -- LIKE, AUTISM OR ASPERGER'S OR SOMETHING.
UGH, DON'T MAKE ME FEEL BAD.
YOU'RE FUCKING HER BOYFRIEND, BITCH! IT'S NOT YOUR FAULT SHE'S TOO DUMB TO SEE WHAT'S RIGHT IN FRONT OF HER FACE.
THAT TODAY...
HEHEHEHE...
...IS THE DAY THAT EVERYTHING CHANGES.
OH GOD OH GOD OH GOD OH GOD

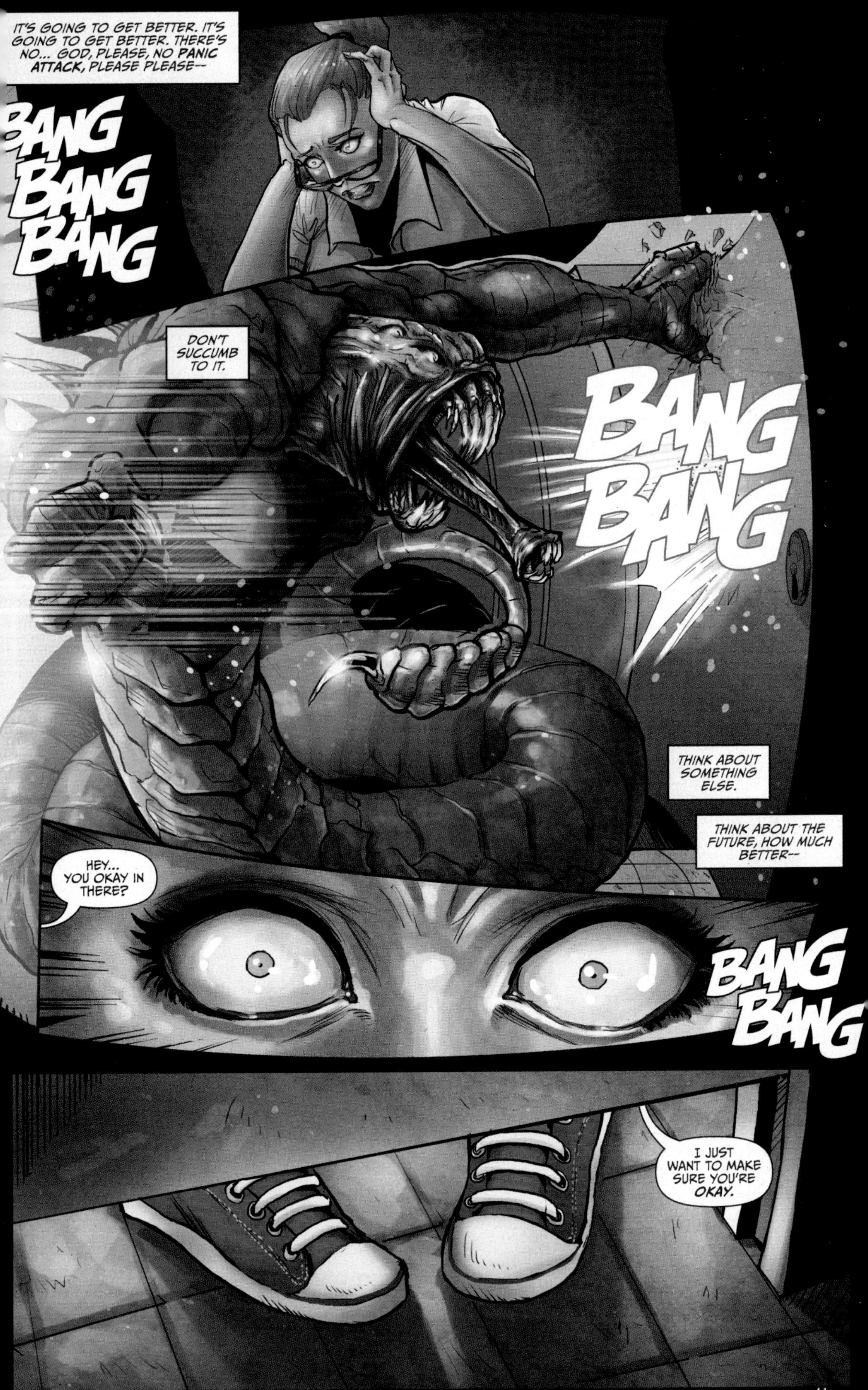
IT'S GOING TO GET BETTER. IT'S GOING TO GET BETTER. THERE'S NO... GOD, PLEASE, NO PANIC ATTACK, PLEASE PLEASE--
BANG BANG BANG
DON'T SUCCUMB TO IT.
BANG BANG
THINK ABOUT SOMETHING ELSE.
THINK ABOUT THE FUTURE, HOW MUCH BETTER--
HEY... YOU OKAY IN THERE?
BANG BANG
I JUST WANT TO MAKE SURE YOU'RE OKAY.

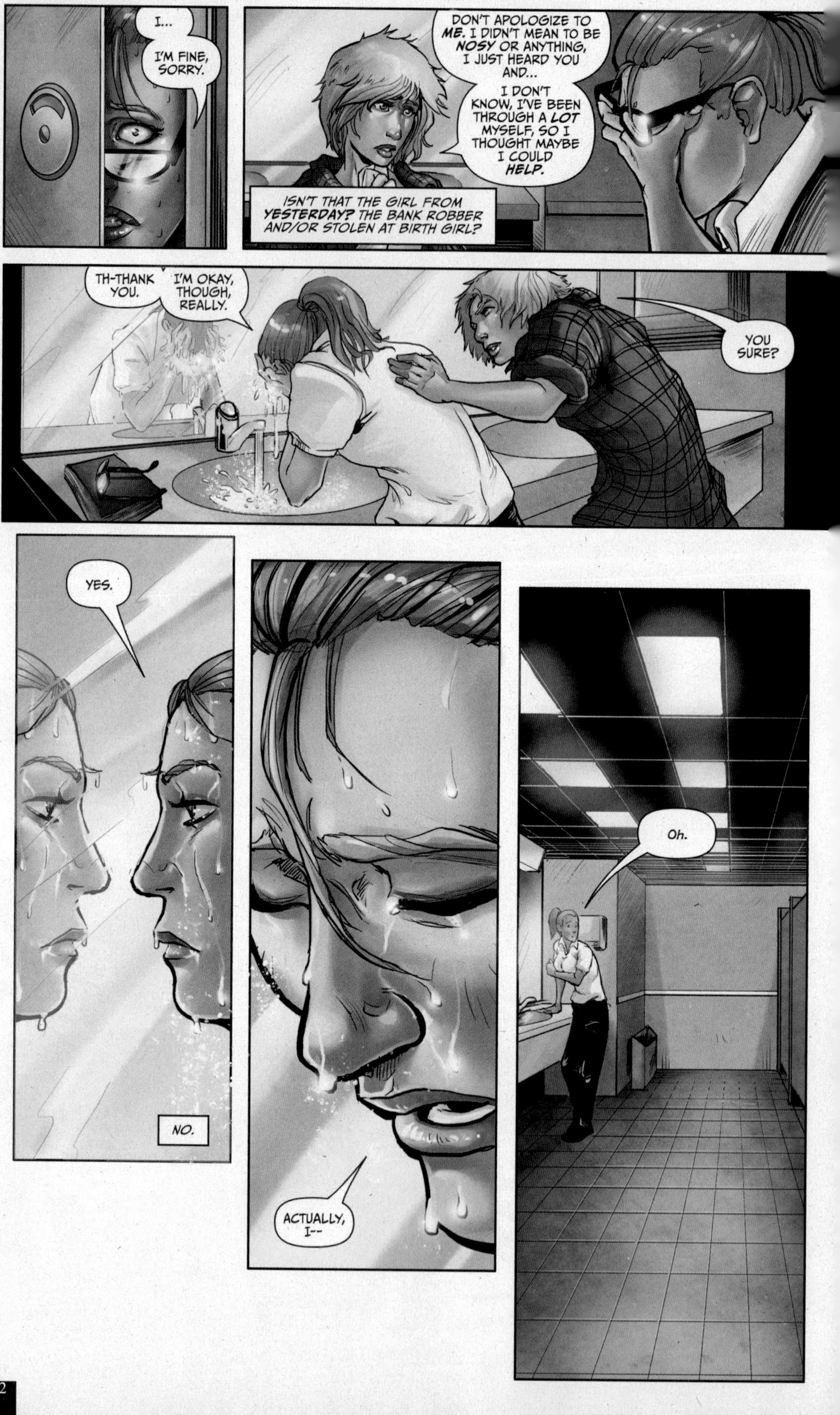
I...
I'M FINE, SORRY.
DON'T APOLOGIZE TO ME. I DIDN'T MEAN TO BE NOSY OR ANYTHING, I JUST HEARD YOU AND...
I DON'T KNOW, I'VE BEEN THROUGH A LOT MYSELF, SO I THOUGHT MAYBE I COULD HELP.
ISN'T THAT THE GIRL FROM YESTERDAY? THE BANK ROBBER AND/OR STOLEN AT BIRTH GIRL?
TH-THANK YOU.
I'M OKAY, THOUGH, REALLY.
YOU SURE?
YES.
NO.
ACTUALLY, I--
Oh.

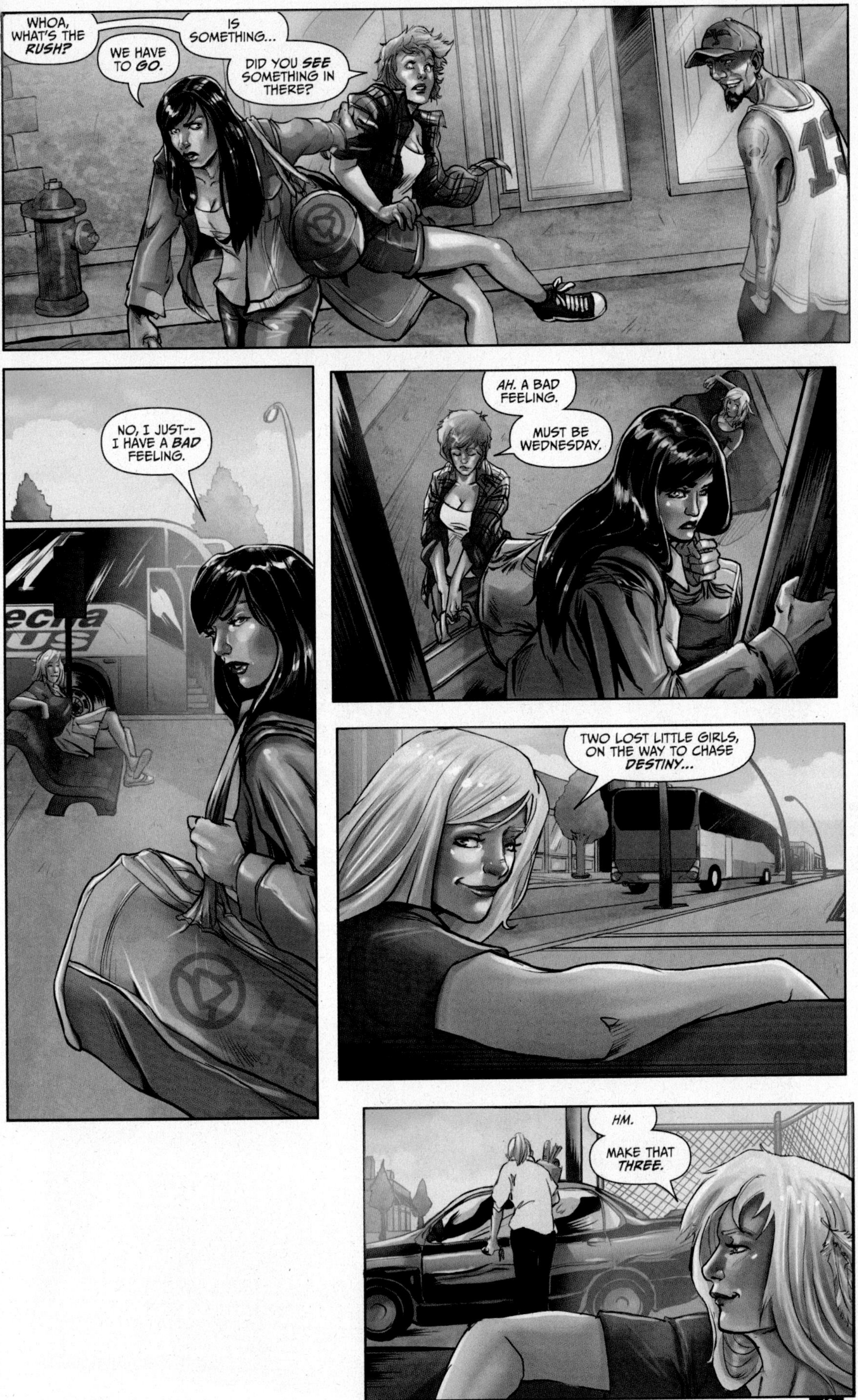
WHOA, WHAT'S THE *RUSH?*
WE HAVE TO *GO.*
IS SOMETHING...
DID YOU *SEE* SOMETHING IN THERE?
NO, I JUST-- I HAVE A *BAD* FEELING.
AH. A BAD FEELING.
MUST BE WEDNESDAY.
TWO LOST LITTLE GIRLS, ON THE WAY TO CHASE *DESTINY...*
HM.
MAKE THAT *THREE.*

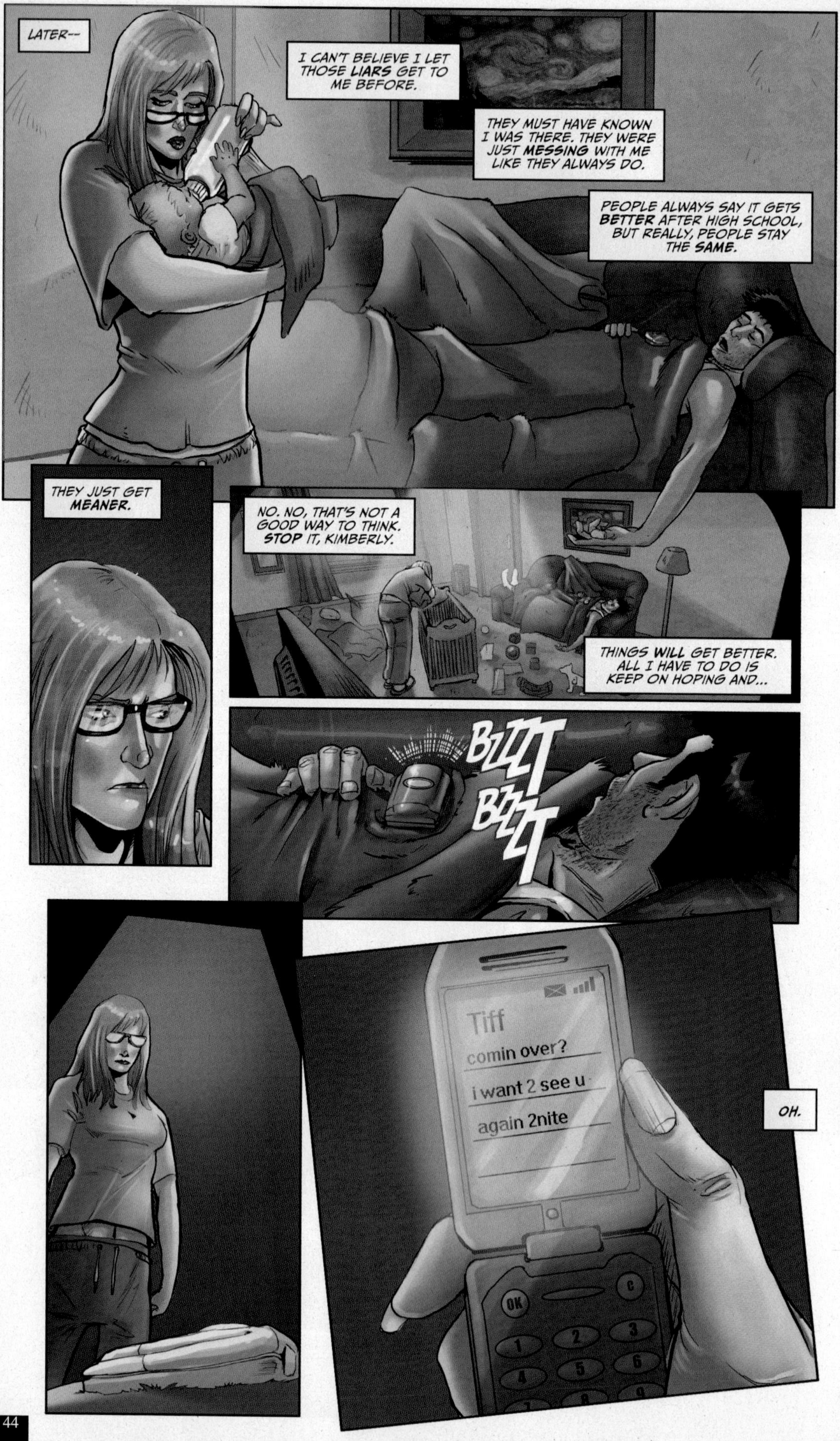
LATER--
I CAN'T BELIEVE I LET THOSE LIARS GET TO ME BEFORE.
THEY MUST HAVE KNOWN I WAS THERE. THEY WERE JUST MESSING WITH ME LIKE THEY ALWAYS DO.
PEOPLE ALWAYS SAY IT GETS BETTER AFTER HIGH SCHOOL, BUT REALLY, PEOPLE STAY THE SAME.
THEY JUST GET MEANER.
NO. NO, THAT'S NOT A GOOD WAY TO THINK. STOP IT, KIMBERLY.
THINGS WILL GET BETTER. ALL I HAVE TO DO IS KEEP ON HOPING AND...
BZZZT BZZZT
Tiff
comin over?
i want 2 see u
again 2nite
OH.

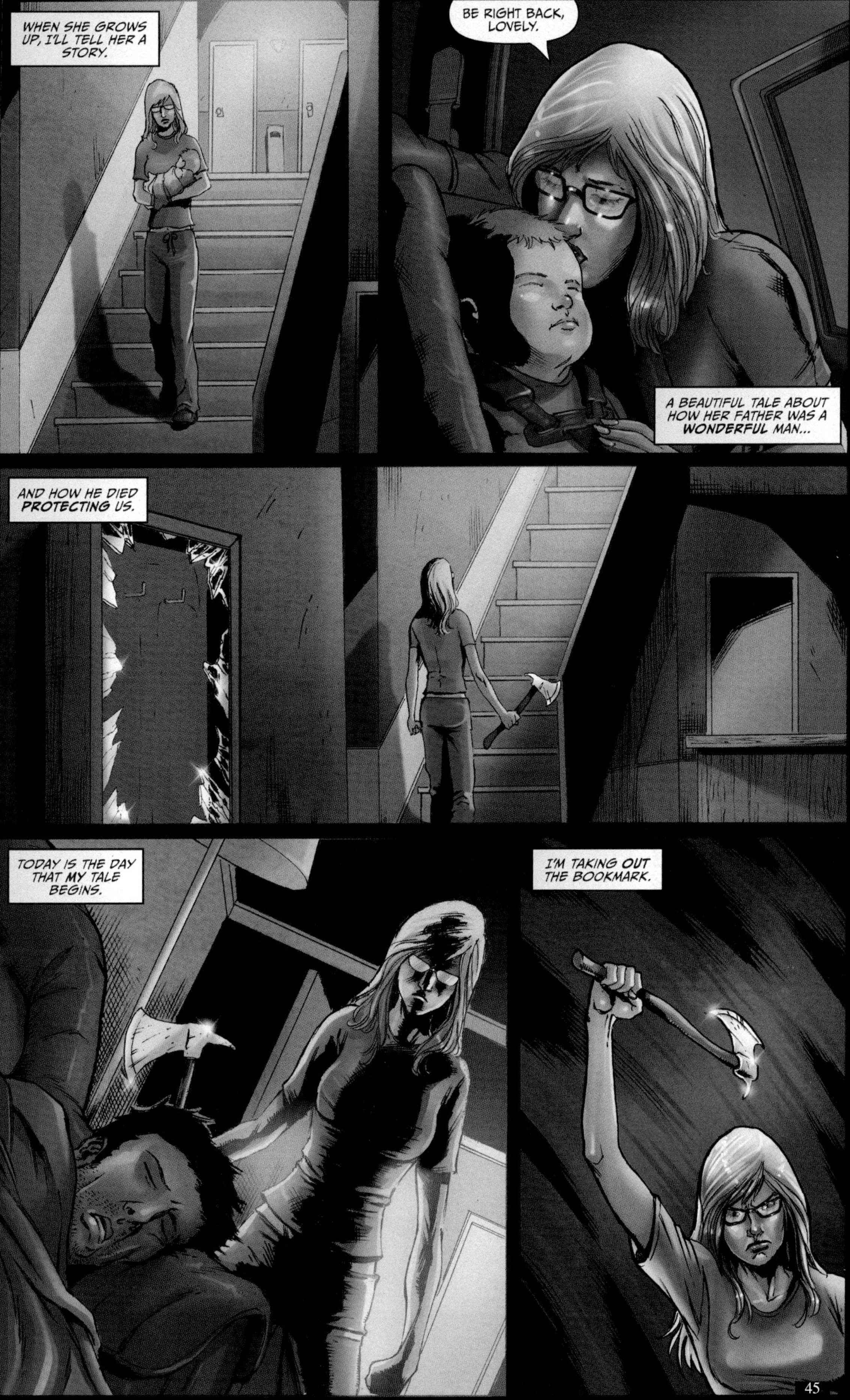

WHEN SHE GROWS UP, I'LL TELL HER A STORY.
BE RIGHT BACK, LOVELY.
A BEAUTIFUL TALE ABOUT HOW HER FATHER WAS A **WONDERFUL** MAN...
AND HOW HE DIED **PROTECTING** US.
TODAY IS THE DAY THAT **MY** TALE BEGINS.
I'M TAKING **OUT** THE BOOKMARK.

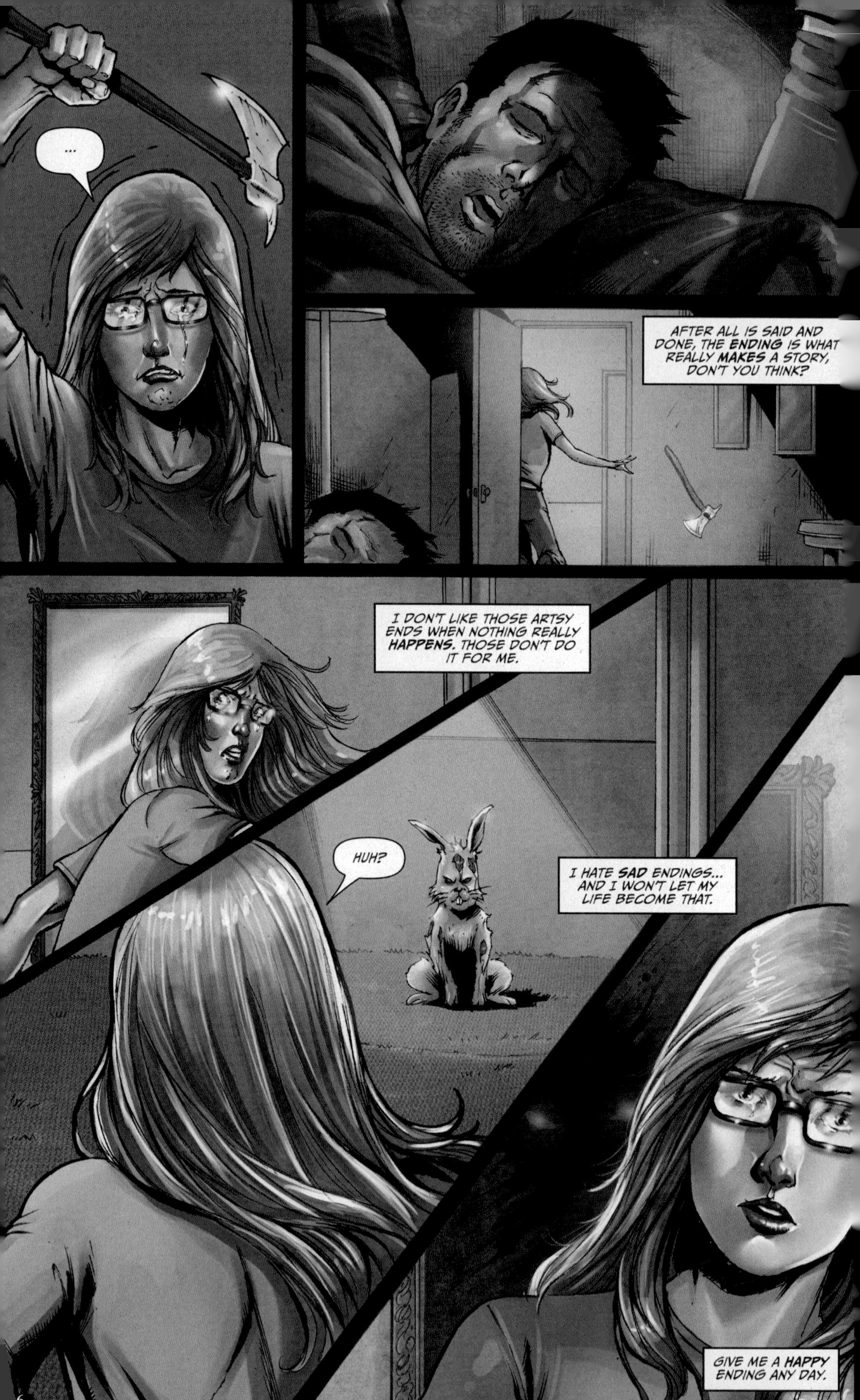

...
AFTER ALL IS SAID AND DONE, THE ENDING IS WHAT REALLY MAKES A STORY, DON'T YOU THINK?
I DON'T LIKE THOSE ARTSY ENDS WHEN NOTHING REALLY HAPPENS. THOSE DON'T DO IT FOR ME.
HUH?
I HATE SAD ENDINGS... AND I WON'T LET MY LIFE BECOME THAT.
GIVE ME A HAPPY ENDING ANY DAY.

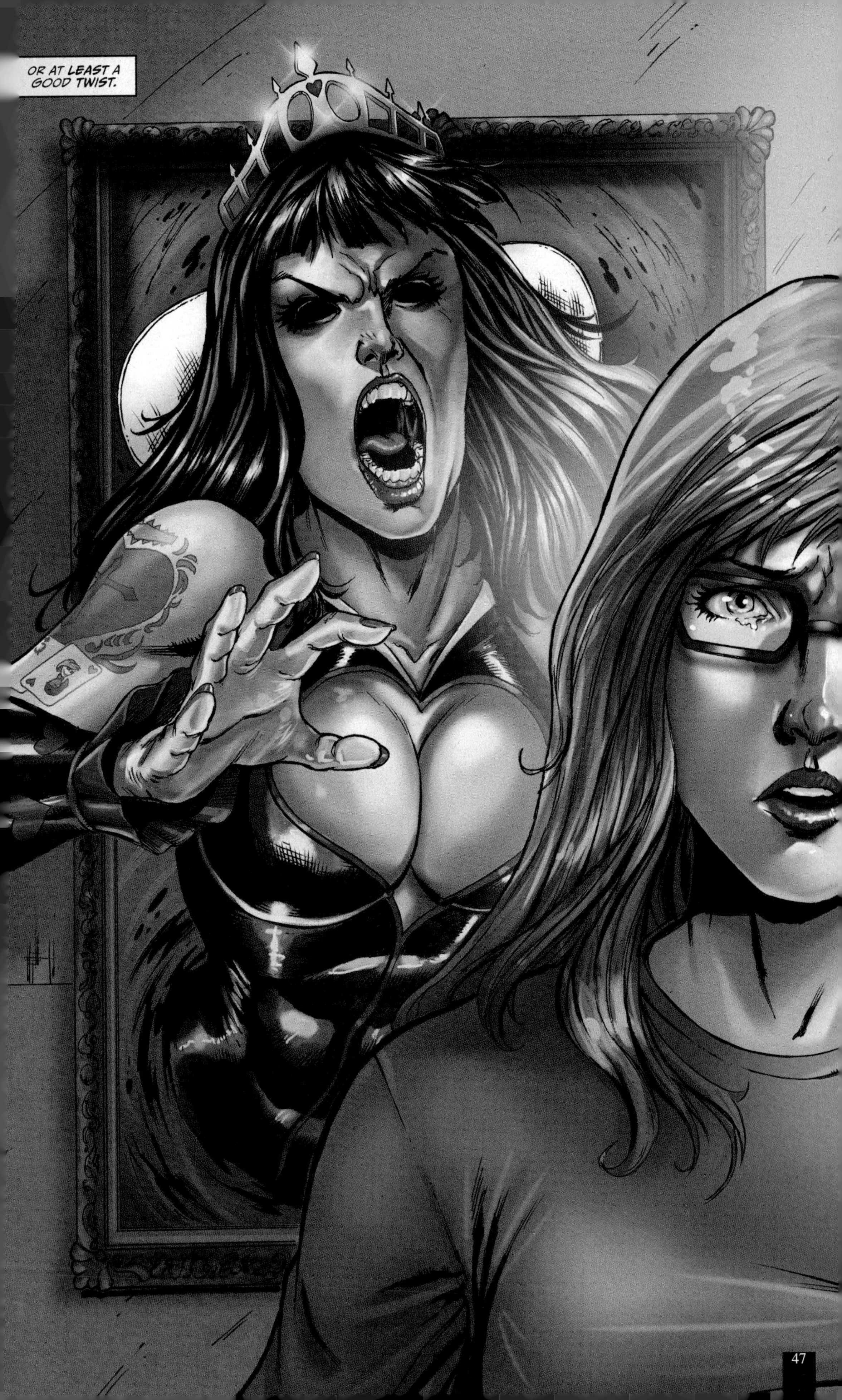
OR AT LEAST A GOOD TWIST.

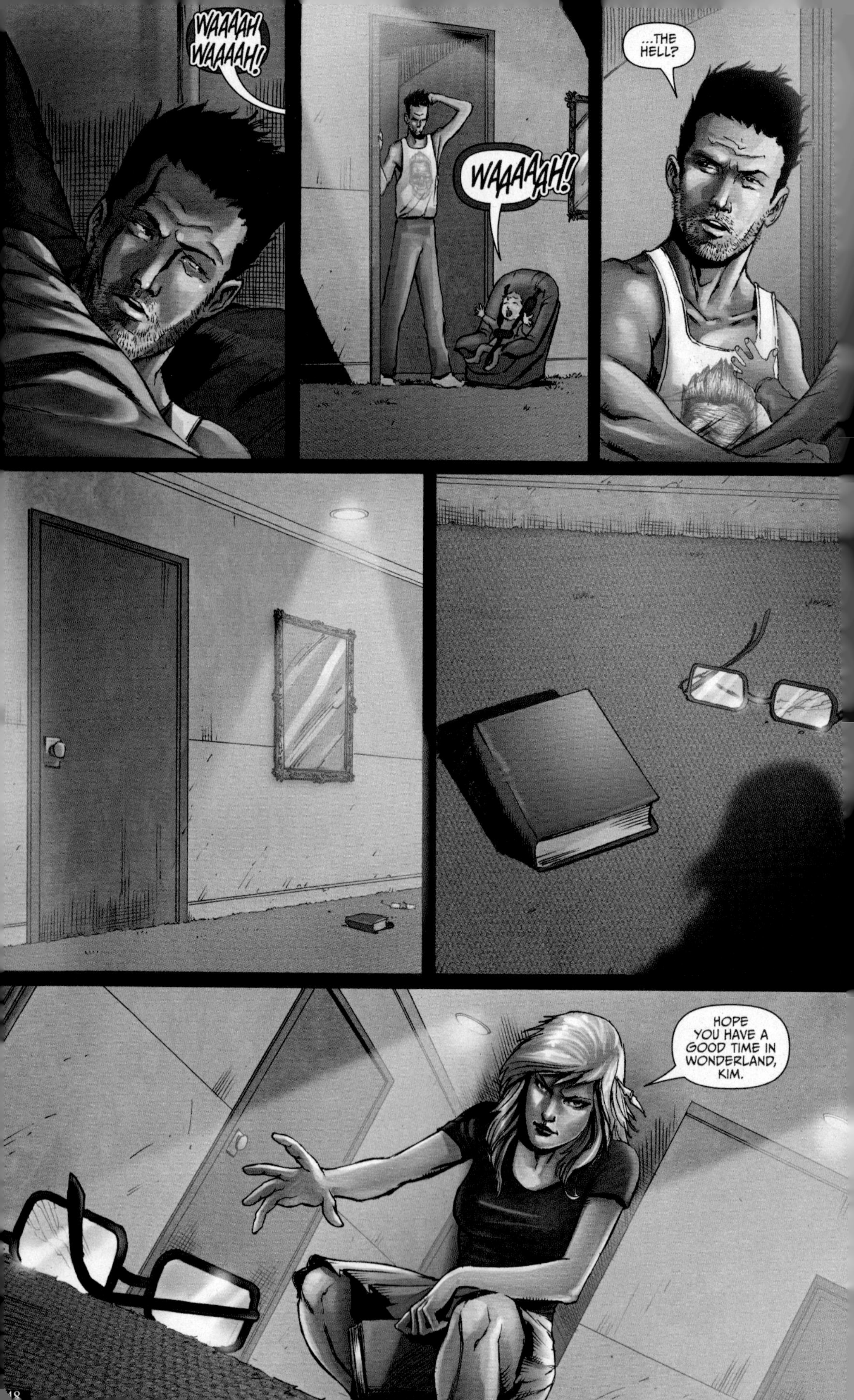
WAAAAH WAAAAH!
WAAAAAAH!
...THE HELL?
HOPE YOU HAVE A GOOD TIME IN WONDERLAND, KIM.

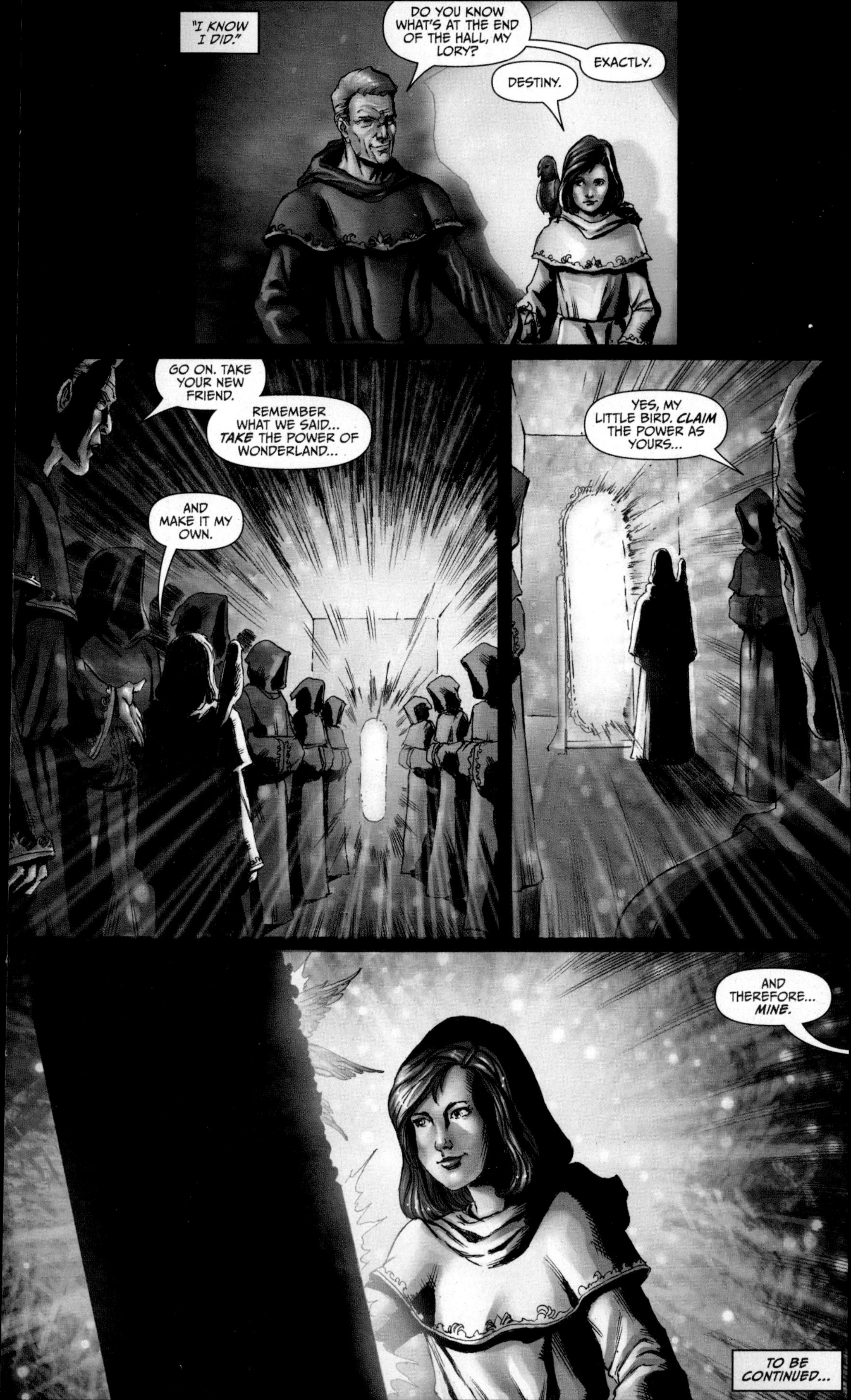
"I KNOW I DID."
DO YOU KNOW WHAT'S AT THE END OF THE HALL, MY LORY?
DESTINY.
EXACTLY.
GO ON. TAKE YOUR NEW FRIEND.
REMEMBER WHAT WE SAID... TAKE THE POWER OF WONDERLAND...
AND MAKE IT MY OWN.
YES, MY LITTLE BIRD. CLAIM THE POWER AS YOURS...
AND THEREFORE... MINE.
TO BE CONTINUED...

Chapter Three

STORY RAVEN GREGORY
WRITERS PAT SHAND AND RAVEN GREGORY
PENCILS ANTONIO BIFULCO
COLORS LEONARDO PACIAROTTI
LETTERS JIM CAMPBELL

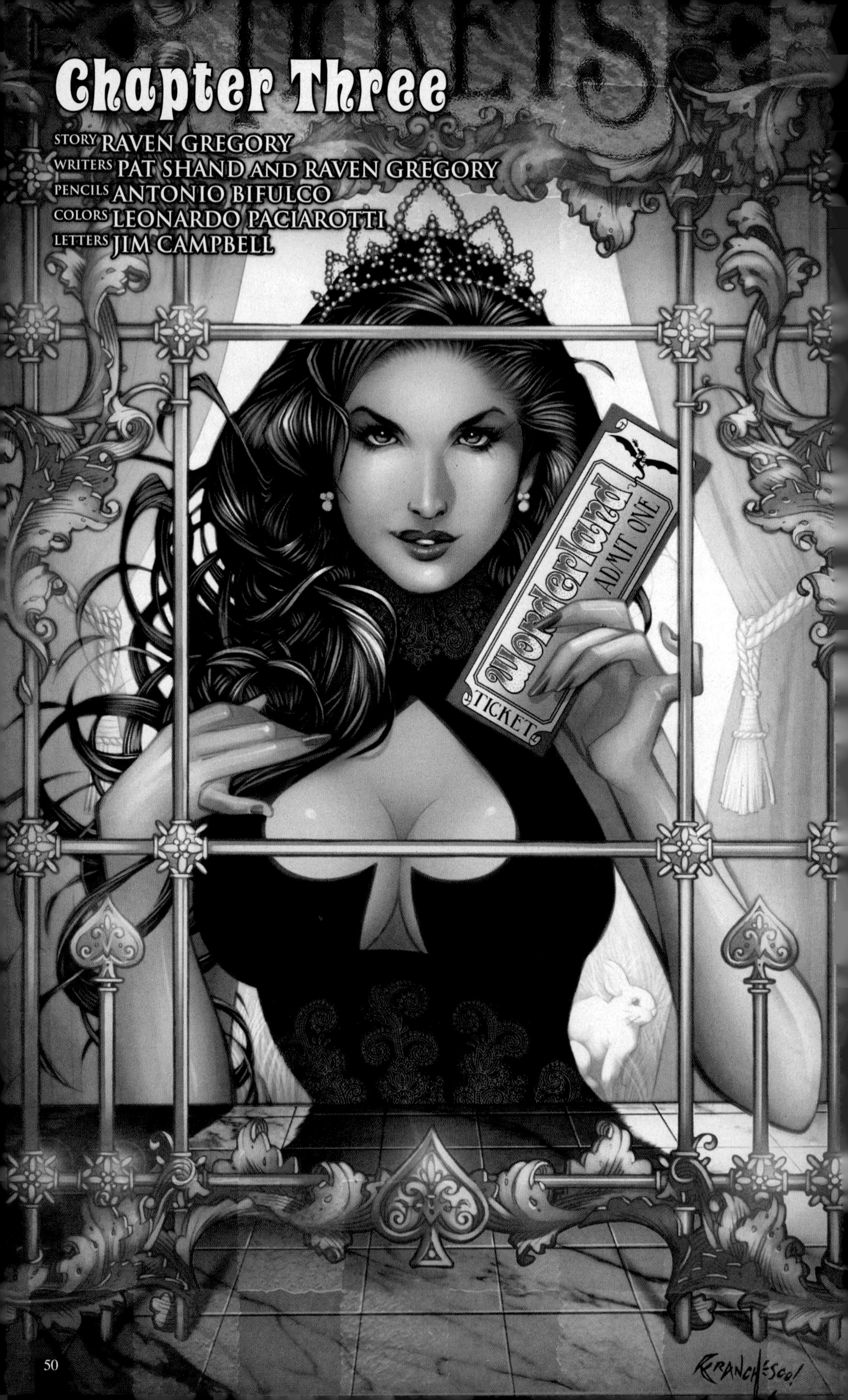
Wonderland
ADMIT ONE
TICKET

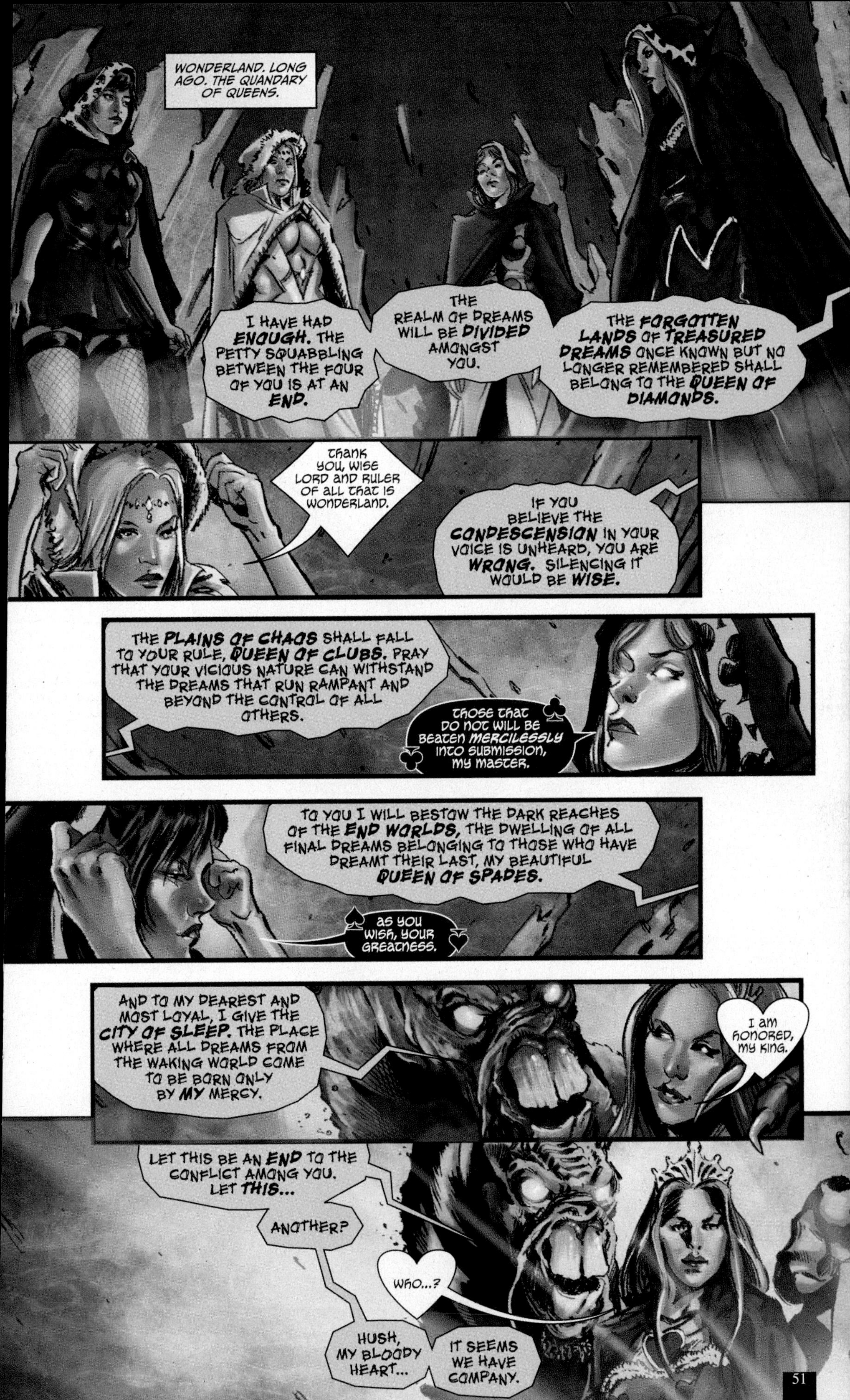

WONDERLAND. LONG AGO. THE QUANDARY OF QUEENS.
I HAVE HAD ENOUGH. THE PETTY SQUABBLING BETWEEN THE FOUR OF YOU IS AT AN END.
THE REALM OF DREAMS WILL BE DIVIDED AMONGST YOU.
THE FORGOTTEN LANDS OF TREASURED DREAMS ONCE KNOWN BUT NO LONGER REMEMBERED SHALL BELONG TO THE QUEEN OF DIAMONDS.
THANK YOU, WISE LORD AND RULER OF ALL THAT IS WONDERLAND.
IF YOU BELIEVE THE CONDESCENSION IN YOUR VOICE IS UNHEARD, YOU ARE WRONG. SILENCING IT WOULD BE WISE.
THE PLAINS OF CHAOS SHALL FALL TO YOUR RULE, QUEEN OF CLUBS. PRAY THAT YOUR VICIOUS NATURE CAN WITHSTAND THE DREAMS THAT RUN RAMPANT AND BEYOND THE CONTROL OF ALL OTHERS.
THOSE THAT DO NOT WILL BE BEATEN MERCILESSLY INTO SUBMISSION, MY MASTER.
TO YOU I WILL BESTOW THE DARK REACHES OF THE END WORLDS, THE DWELLING OF ALL FINAL DREAMS BELONGING TO THOSE WHO HAVE DREAMT THEIR LAST, MY BEAUTIFUL QUEEN OF SPADES.
AS YOU WISH, YOUR GREATNESS.
AND TO MY DEAREST AND MOST LOYAL, I GIVE THE CITY OF SLEEP. THE PLACE WHERE ALL DREAMS FROM THE WAKING WORLD COME TO BE BORN ONLY BY MY MERCY.
I AM HONORED, MY KING.
LET THIS BE AN END TO THE CONFLICT AMONG YOU. LET THIS...
ANOTHER?
WHO...?
HUSH, MY BLOODY HEART...
IT SEEMS WE HAVE COMPANY.

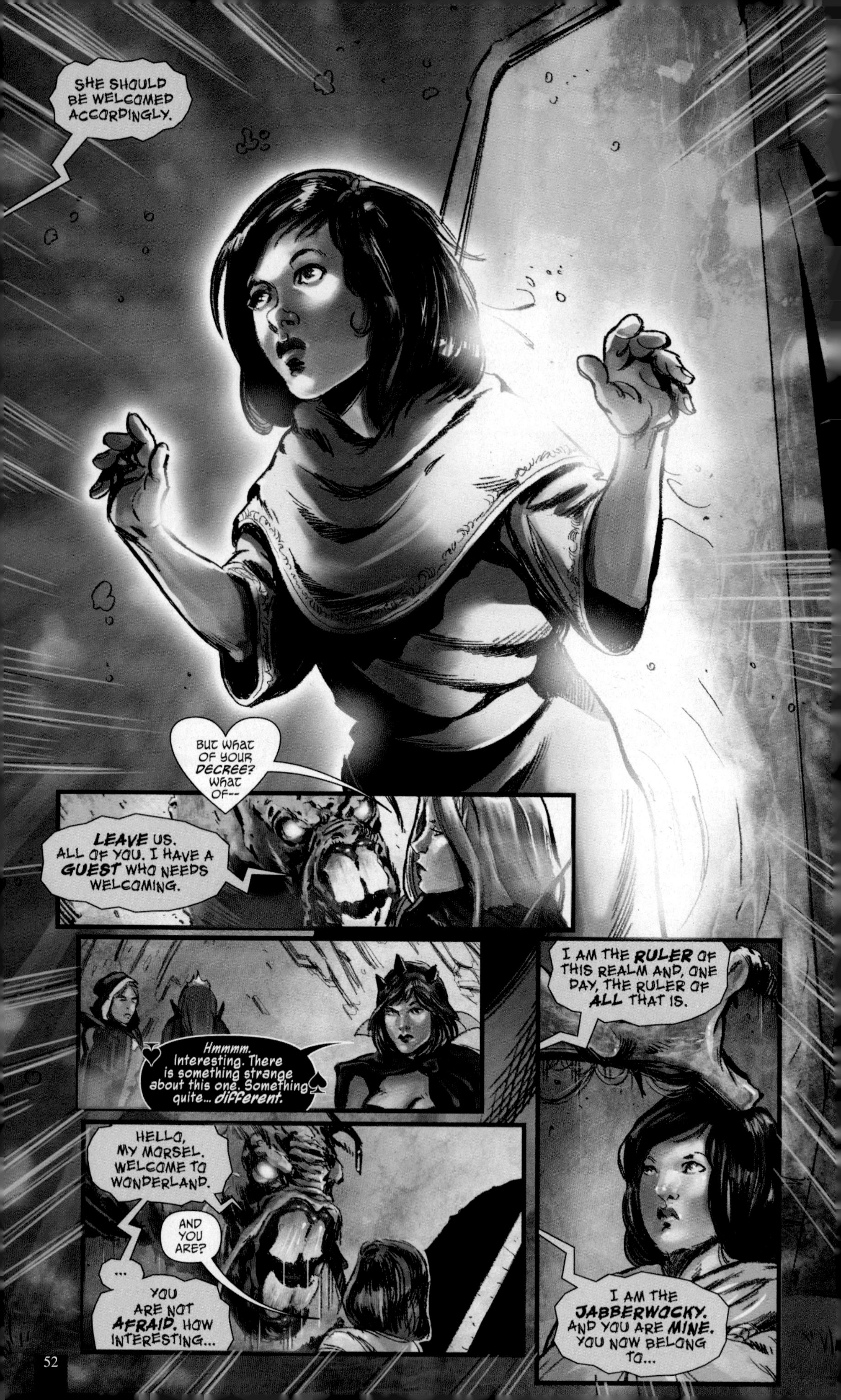
SHE SHOULD BE WELCOMED ACCORDINGLY.
BUT WHAT OF YOUR DECREE? WHAT OF--
LEAVE US. ALL OF YOU. I HAVE A GUEST WHO NEEDS WELCOMING.
Hmmmm. Interesting. There is something strange about this one. Something quite... different.
I AM THE RULER OF THIS REALM AND, ONE DAY, THE RULER OF ALL THAT IS.
HELLO, MY MORSEL. WELCOME TO WONDERLAND.
AND YOU ARE?
...
YOU ARE NOT AFRAID. HOW INTERESTING...
I AM THE JABBERWOCKY. AND YOU ARE MINE. YOU NOW BELONG TO...

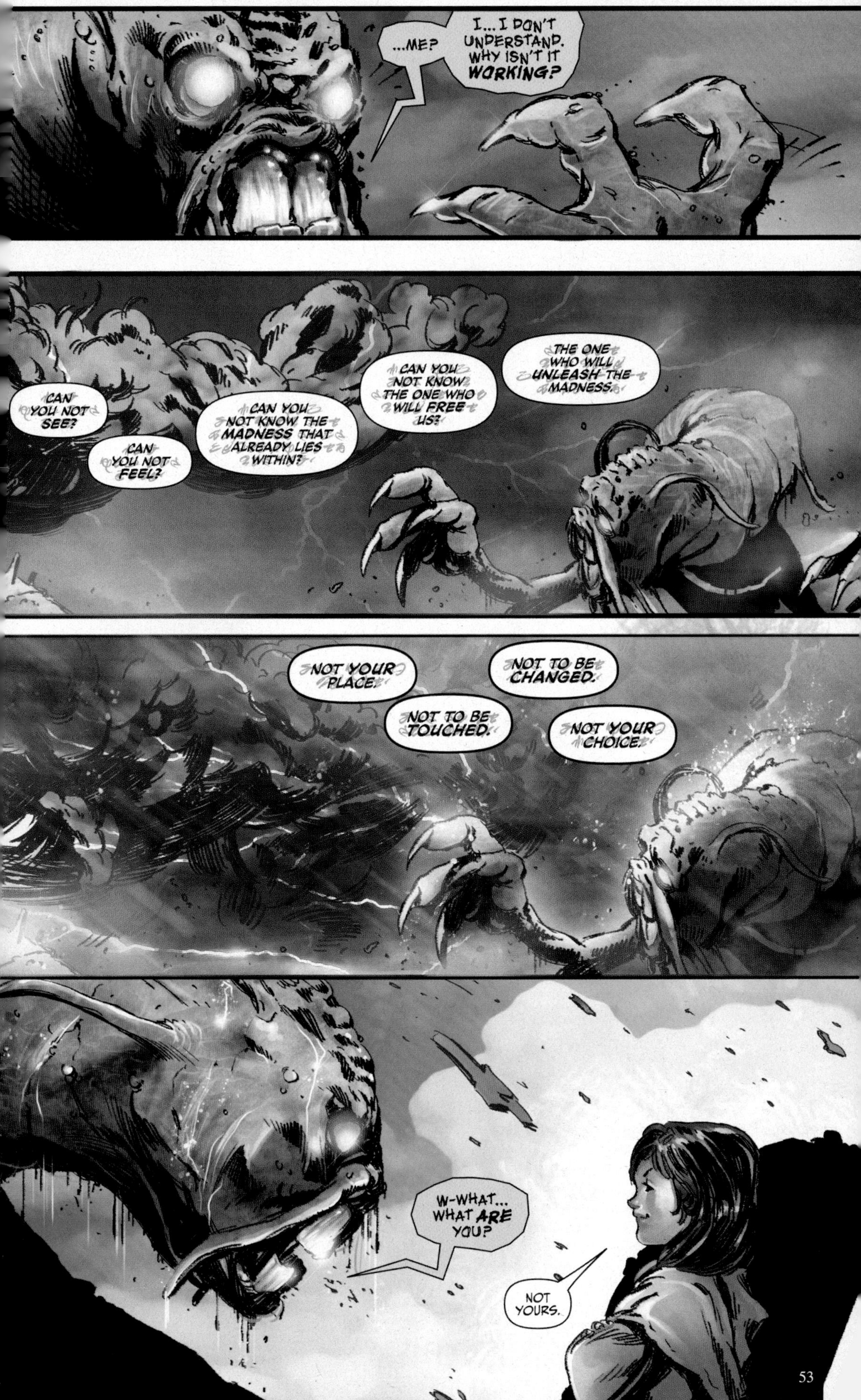
...ME?
I... I DON'T UNDERSTAND. WHY ISN'T IT WORKING?
CAN YOU NOT SEE?
CAN YOU NOT FEEL?
CAN YOU NOT KNOW THE MADNESS THAT ALREADY LIES WITHIN?
CAN YOU NOT KNOW THE ONE WHO WILL FREE US?
THE ONE WHO WILL UNLEASH THE MADNESS.
NOT YOUR PLACE.
NOT TO BE TOUCHED.
NOT TO BE CHANGED.
NOT YOUR CHOICE.
W-WHAT... WHAT ARE YOU?
NOT YOURS.

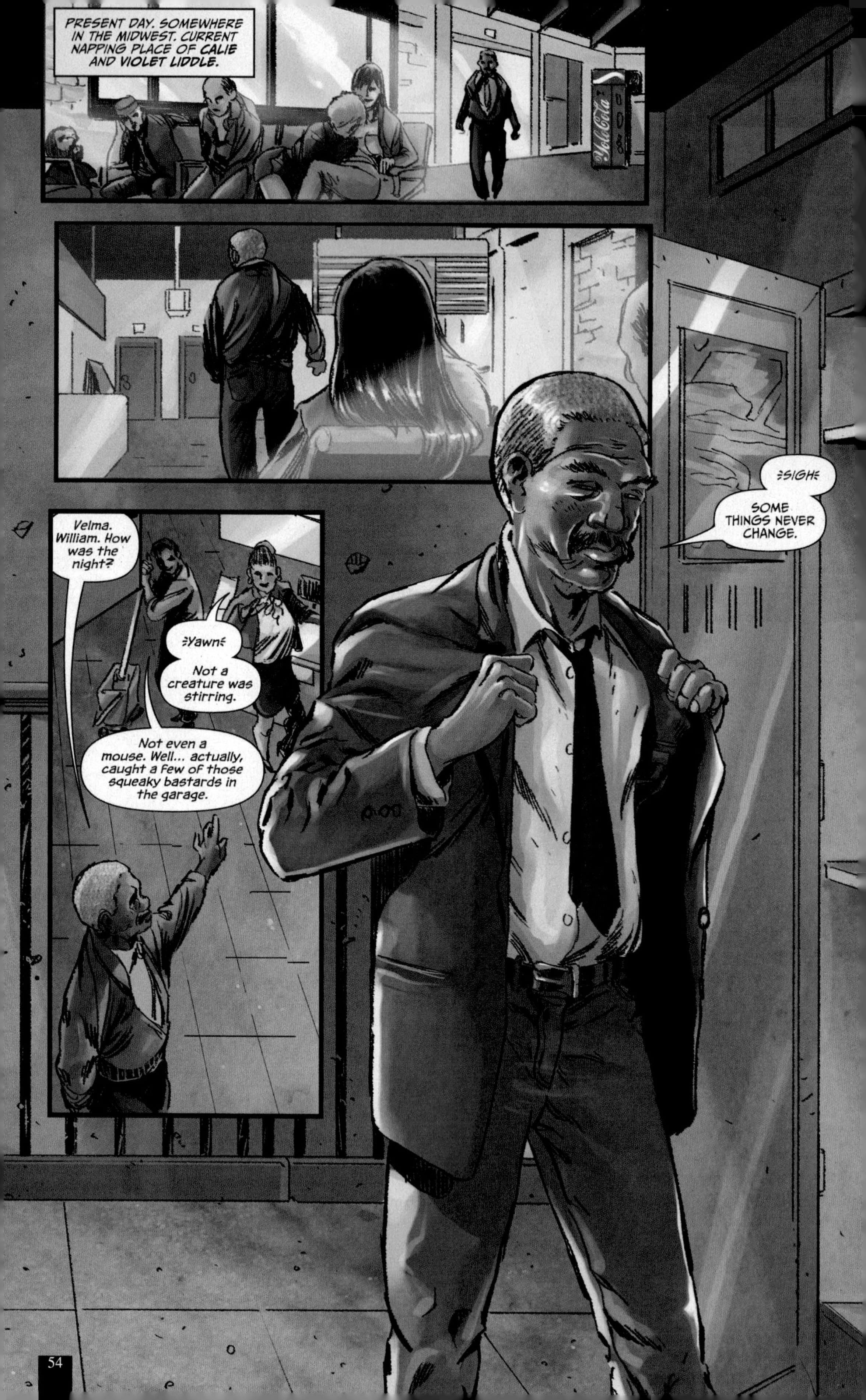
PRESENT DAY. SOMEWHERE IN THE MIDWEST. CURRENT NAPPING PLACE OF CALIE AND VIOLET LIDDLE.
Velma. William. How was the night?
Yawn
Not a creature was stirring.
Not even a mouse. Well... actually, caught a few of those squeaky bastards in the garage.
SIGH
SOME THINGS NEVER CHANGE.

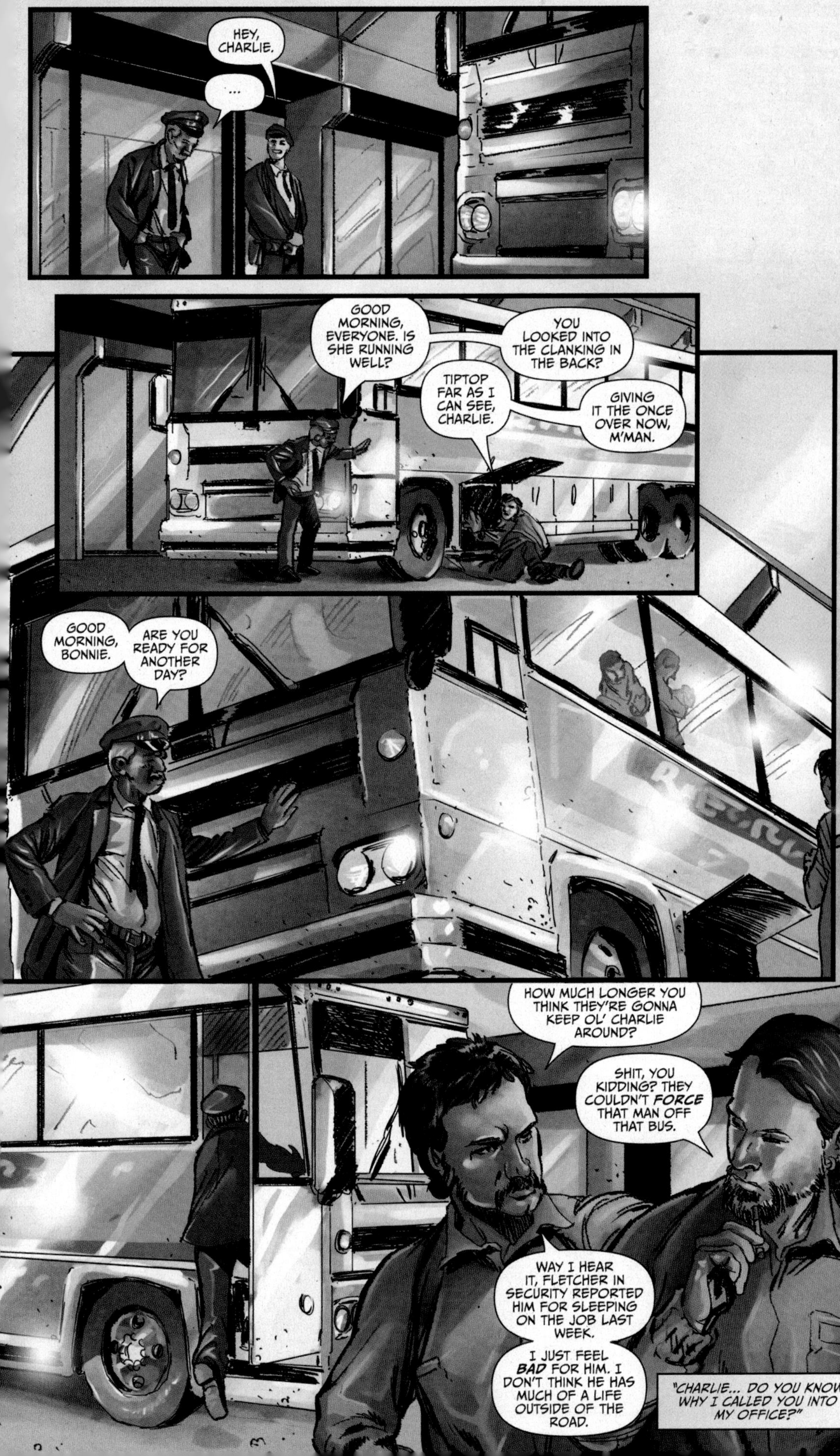
HEY, CHARLIE.
...
GOOD MORNING, EVERYONE. IS SHE RUNNING WELL?
TIPTOP FAR AS I CAN SEE, CHARLIE.
YOU LOOKED INTO THE CLANKING IN THE BACK?
GIVING IT THE ONCE OVER NOW, M'MAN.
GOOD MORNING, BONNIE.
ARE YOU READY FOR ANOTHER DAY?
HOW MUCH LONGER YOU THINK THEY'RE GONNA KEEP OL' CHARLIE AROUND?
SHIT, YOU KIDDING? THEY COULDN'T FORCE THAT MAN OFF THAT BUS.
WAY I HEAR IT, FLETCHER IN SECURITY REPORTED HIM FOR SLEEPING ON THE JOB LAST WEEK.
I JUST FEEL BAD FOR HIM. I DON'T THINK HE HAS MUCH OF A LIFE OUTSIDE OF THE ROAD.
"CHARLIE... DO YOU KNOW WHY I CALLED YOU INTO MY OFFICE?"

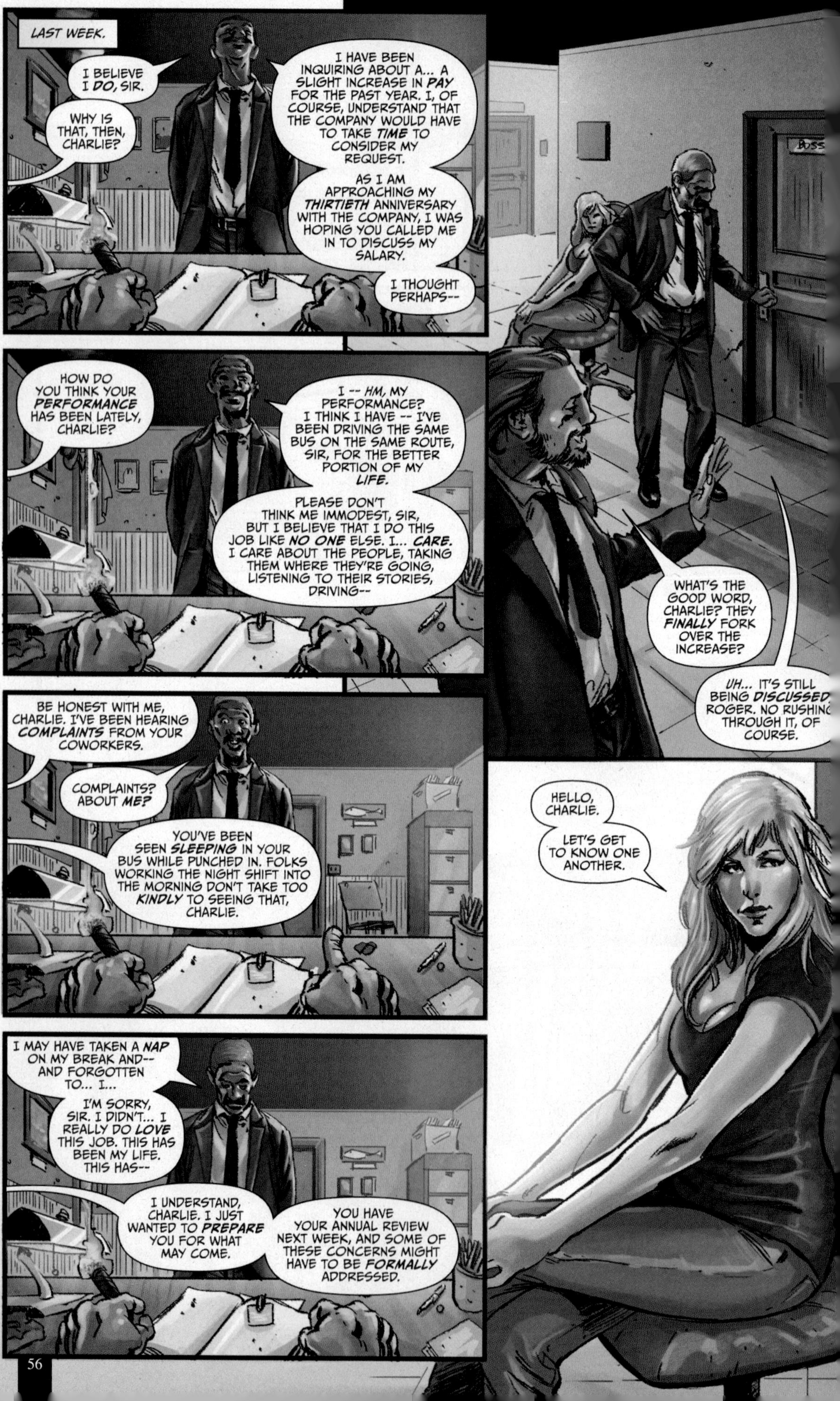
LAST WEEK.
I BELIEVE I DO, SIR.
WHY IS THAT, THEN, CHARLIE?
I HAVE BEEN INQUIRING ABOUT A... A SLIGHT INCREASE IN PAY FOR THE PAST YEAR. I, OF COURSE, UNDERSTAND THAT THE COMPANY WOULD HAVE TO TAKE TIME TO CONSIDER MY REQUEST.
AS I AM APPROACHING MY THIRTIETH ANNIVERSARY WITH THE COMPANY, I WAS HOPING YOU CALLED ME IN TO DISCUSS MY SALARY.
I THOUGHT PERHAPS--
HOW DO YOU THINK YOUR PERFORMANCE HAS BEEN LATELY, CHARLIE?
I -- HM, MY PERFORMANCE? I THINK I HAVE -- I'VE BEEN DRIVING THE SAME BUS ON THE SAME ROUTE, SIR, FOR THE BETTER PORTION OF MY LIFE.
PLEASE DON'T THINK ME IMMODEST, SIR, BUT I BELIEVE THAT I DO THIS JOB LIKE NO ONE ELSE. I... CARE. I CARE ABOUT THE PEOPLE, TAKING THEM WHERE THEY'RE GOING, LISTENING TO THEIR STORIES, DRIVING--
BE HONEST WITH ME, CHARLIE. I'VE BEEN HEARING COMPLAINTS FROM YOUR COWORKERS.
COMPLAINTS? ABOUT ME?
YOU'VE BEEN SEEN SLEEPING IN YOUR BUS WHILE PUNCHED IN. FOLKS WORKING THE NIGHT SHIFT INTO THE MORNING DON'T TAKE TOO KINDLY TO SEEING THAT, CHARLIE.
I MAY HAVE TAKEN A NAP ON MY BREAK AND-- AND FORGOTTEN TO... I...
I'M SORRY, SIR. I DIDN'T... I REALLY DO LOVE THIS JOB. THIS HAS BEEN MY LIFE. THIS HAS--
I UNDERSTAND, CHARLIE. I JUST WANTED TO PREPARE YOU FOR WHAT MAY COME.
YOU HAVE YOUR ANNUAL REVIEW NEXT WEEK, AND SOME OF THESE CONCERNS MIGHT HAVE TO BE FORMALLY ADDRESSED.
BOSS
WHAT'S THE GOOD WORD, CHARLIE? THEY FINALLY FORK OVER THE INCREASE?
UH... IT'S STILL BEING DISCUSSED, ROGER. NO RUSHING THROUGH IT, OF COURSE.
HELLO, CHARLIE.
LET'S GET TO KNOW ONE ANOTHER.

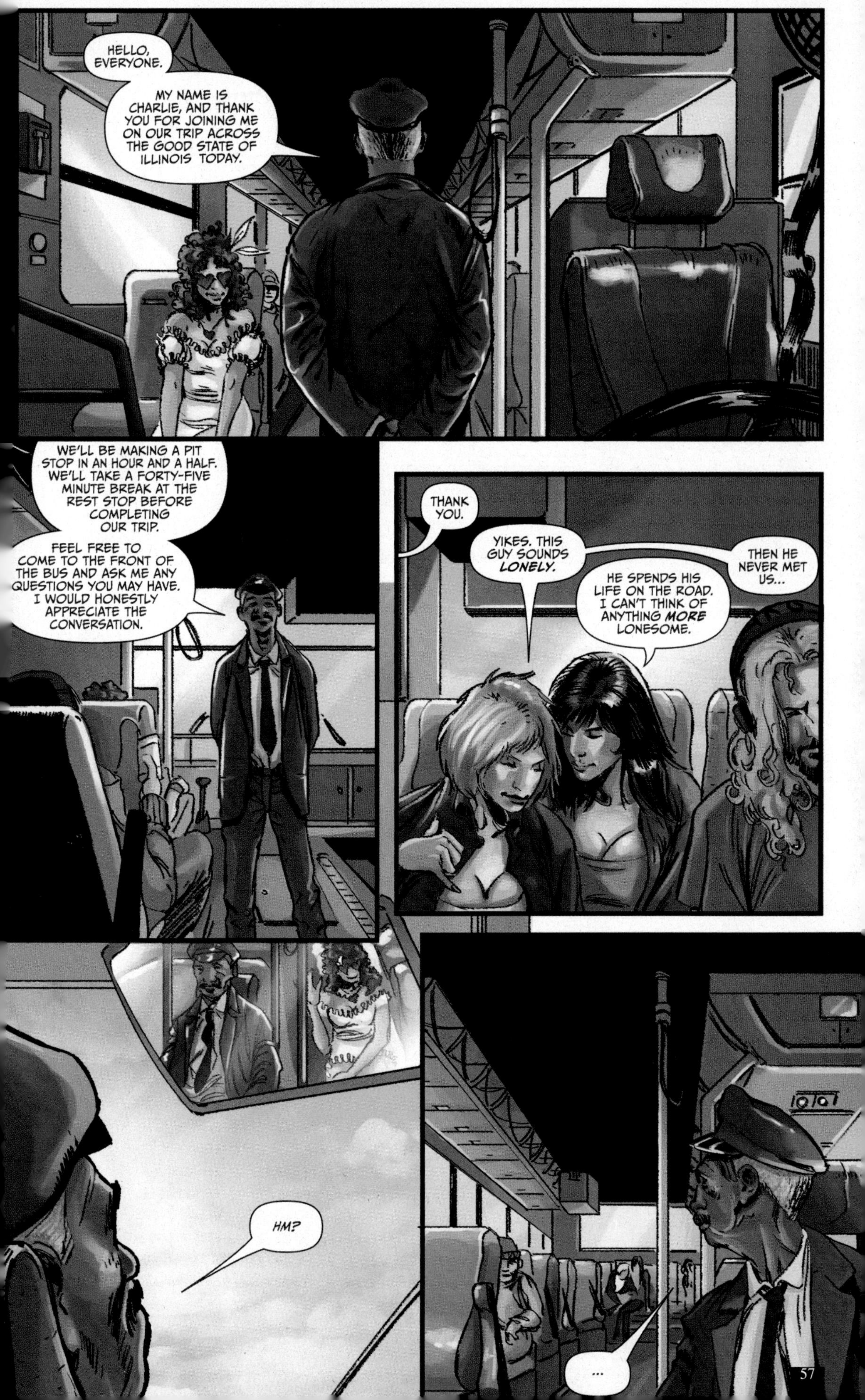
HELLO, EVERYONE.
MY NAME IS CHARLIE, AND THANK YOU FOR JOINING ME ON OUR TRIP ACROSS THE GOOD STATE OF ILLINOIS TODAY.
WE'LL BE MAKING A PIT STOP IN AN HOUR AND A HALF. WE'LL TAKE A FORTY-FIVE MINUTE BREAK AT THE REST STOP BEFORE COMPLETING OUR TRIP.
FEEL FREE TO COME TO THE FRONT OF THE BUS AND ASK ME ANY QUESTIONS YOU MAY HAVE. I WOULD HONESTLY APPRECIATE THE CONVERSATION.
THANK YOU.
YIKES. THIS GUY SOUNDS *LONELY.*
HE SPENDS HIS LIFE ON THE ROAD. I CAN'T THINK OF ANYTHING *MORE* LONESOME.
THEN HE NEVER MET US...
HM?
...

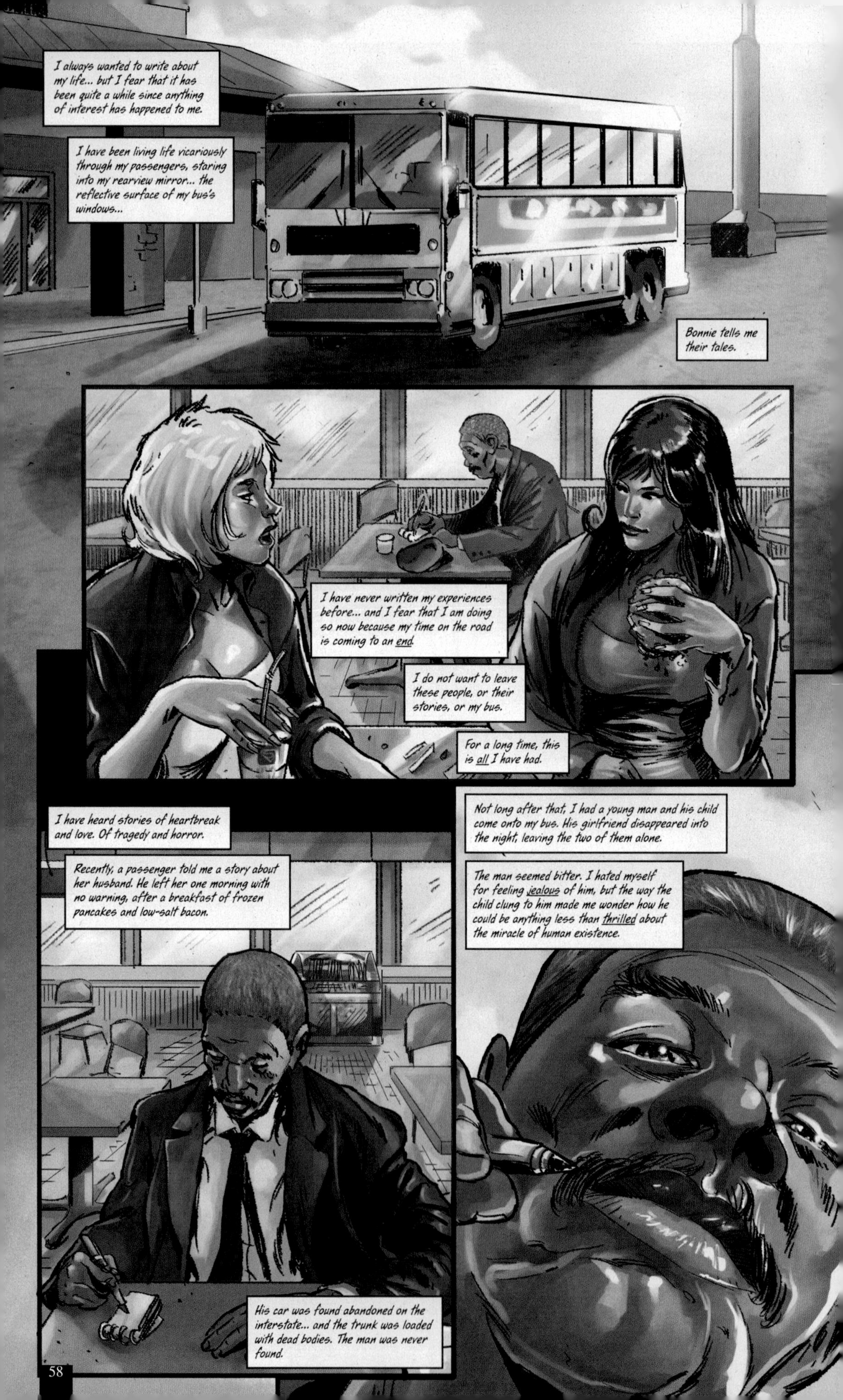
I always wanted to write about my life... but I fear that it has been quite a while since anything of interest has happened to me.
I have been living life vicariously through my passengers, staring into my rearview mirror... the reflective surface of my bus's windows...
Bonnie tells me their tales.
I have never written my experiences before... and I fear that I am doing so now because my time on the road is coming to an end.
I do not want to leave these people, or their stories, or my bus.
For a long time, this is all I have had.
I have heard stories of heartbreak and love. Of tragedy and horror.
Recently, a passenger told me a story about her husband. He left her one morning with no warning, after a breakfast of frozen pancakes and low-salt bacon.
His car was found abandoned on the interstate... and the trunk was loaded with dead bodies. The man was never found.
Not long after that, I had a young man and his child come onto my bus. His girlfriend disappeared into the night, leaving the two of them alone.
The man seemed bitter. I hated myself for feeling jealous of him, but the way the child clung to him made me wonder how he could be anything less than thrilled about the miracle of human existence.

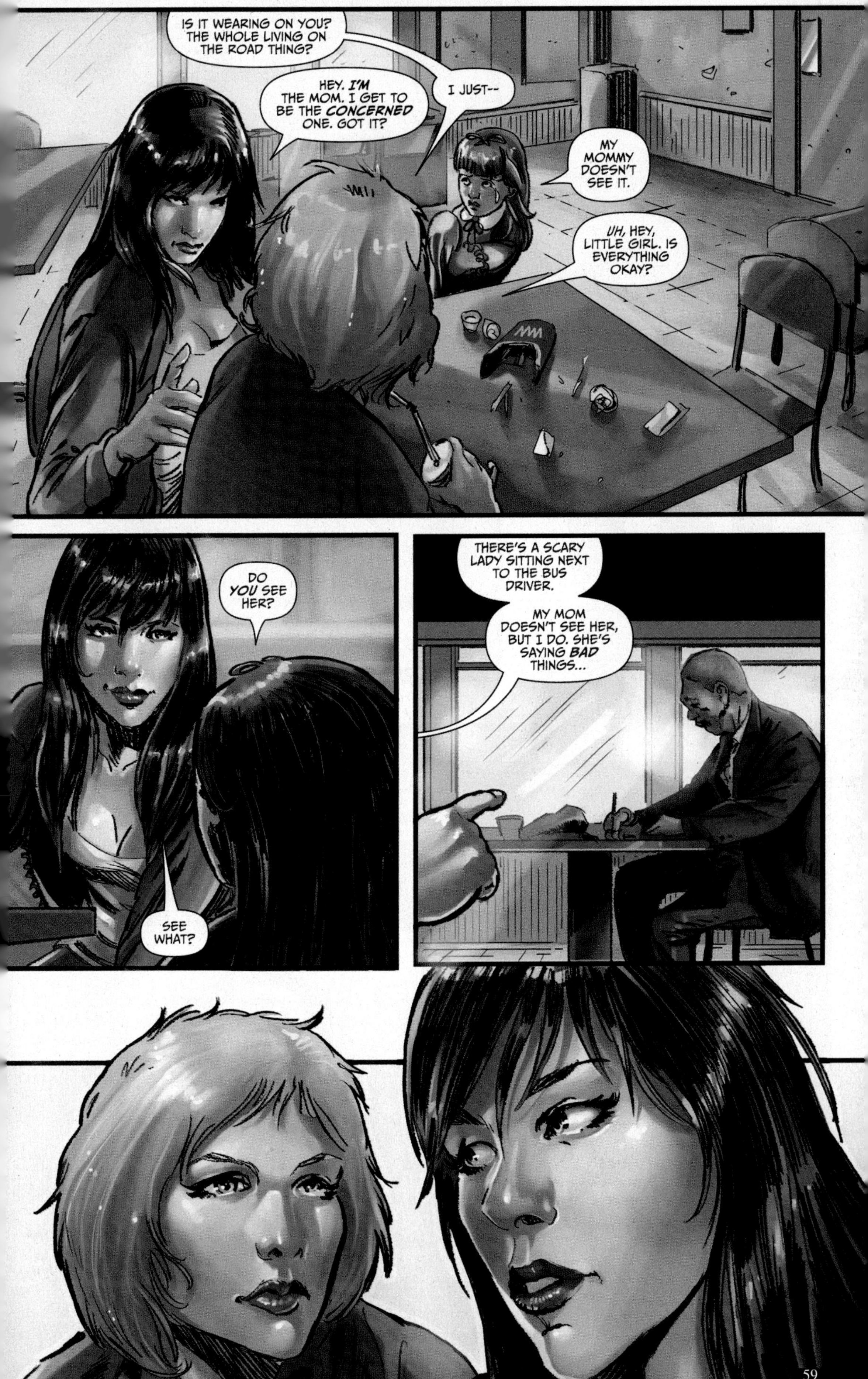
IS IT WEARING ON YOU? THE WHOLE LIVING ON THE ROAD THING?
HEY. *I'M* THE MOM. I GET TO BE THE *CONCERNED* ONE. GOT IT?
I JUST--
MY MOMMY DOESN'T SEE IT.
UH, HEY, LITTLE GIRL. IS EVERYTHING OKAY?
DO *YOU* SEE HER?
SEE WHAT?
THERE'S A SCARY LADY SITTING NEXT TO THE BUS DRIVER.
MY MOM DOESN'T SEE HER, BUT I DO. SHE'S SAYING *BAD* THINGS...

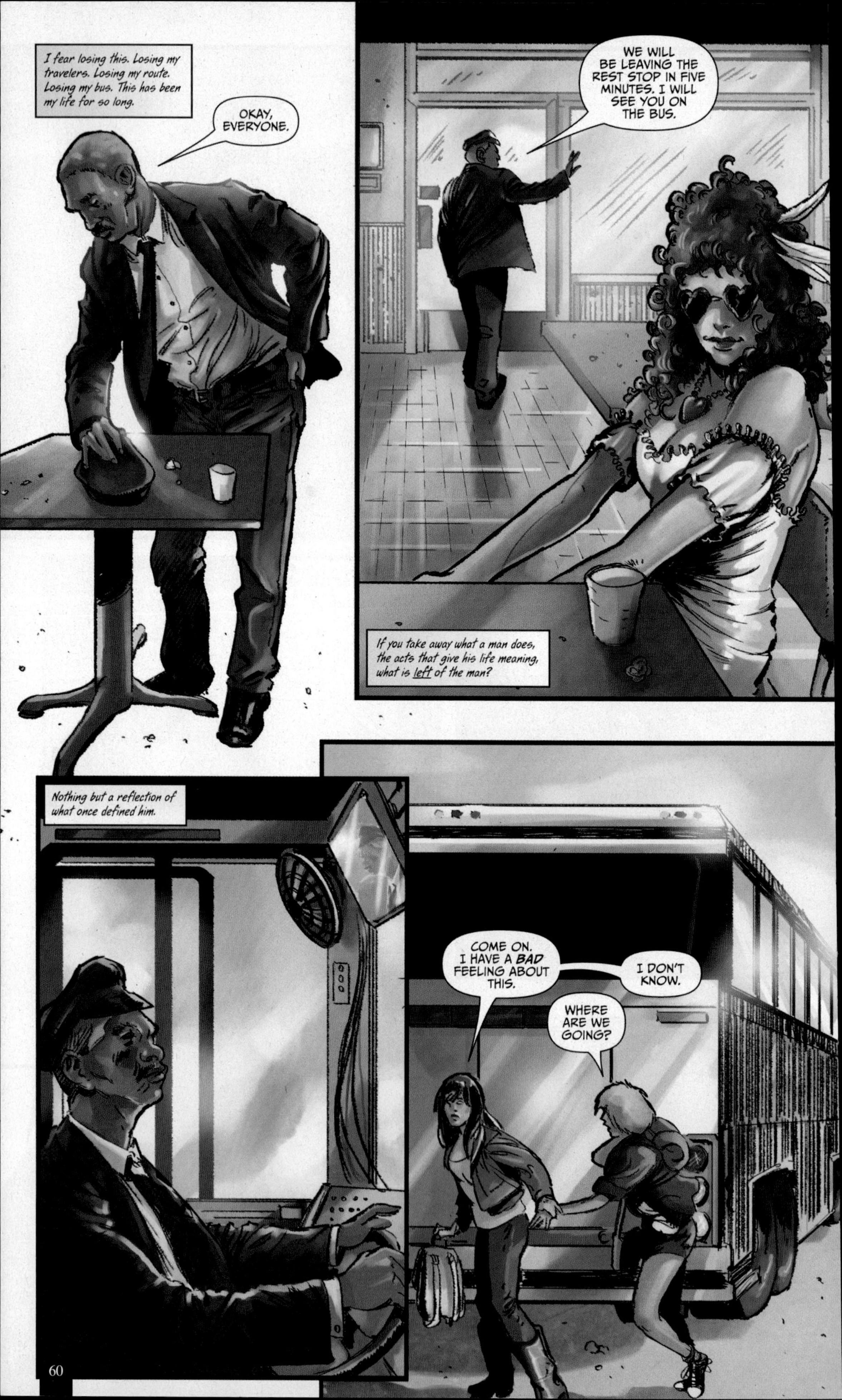
I fear losing this. Losing my travelers. Losing my route. Losing my bus. This has been my life for so long.
OKAY, EVERYONE.
WE WILL BE LEAVING THE REST STOP IN FIVE MINUTES. I WILL SEE YOU ON THE BUS.
If you take away what a man does, the acts that give his life meaning, what is left of the man?
Nothing but a reflection of what once defined him.
COME ON. I HAVE A BAD FEELING ABOUT THIS.
I DON'T KNOW.
WHERE ARE WE GOING?

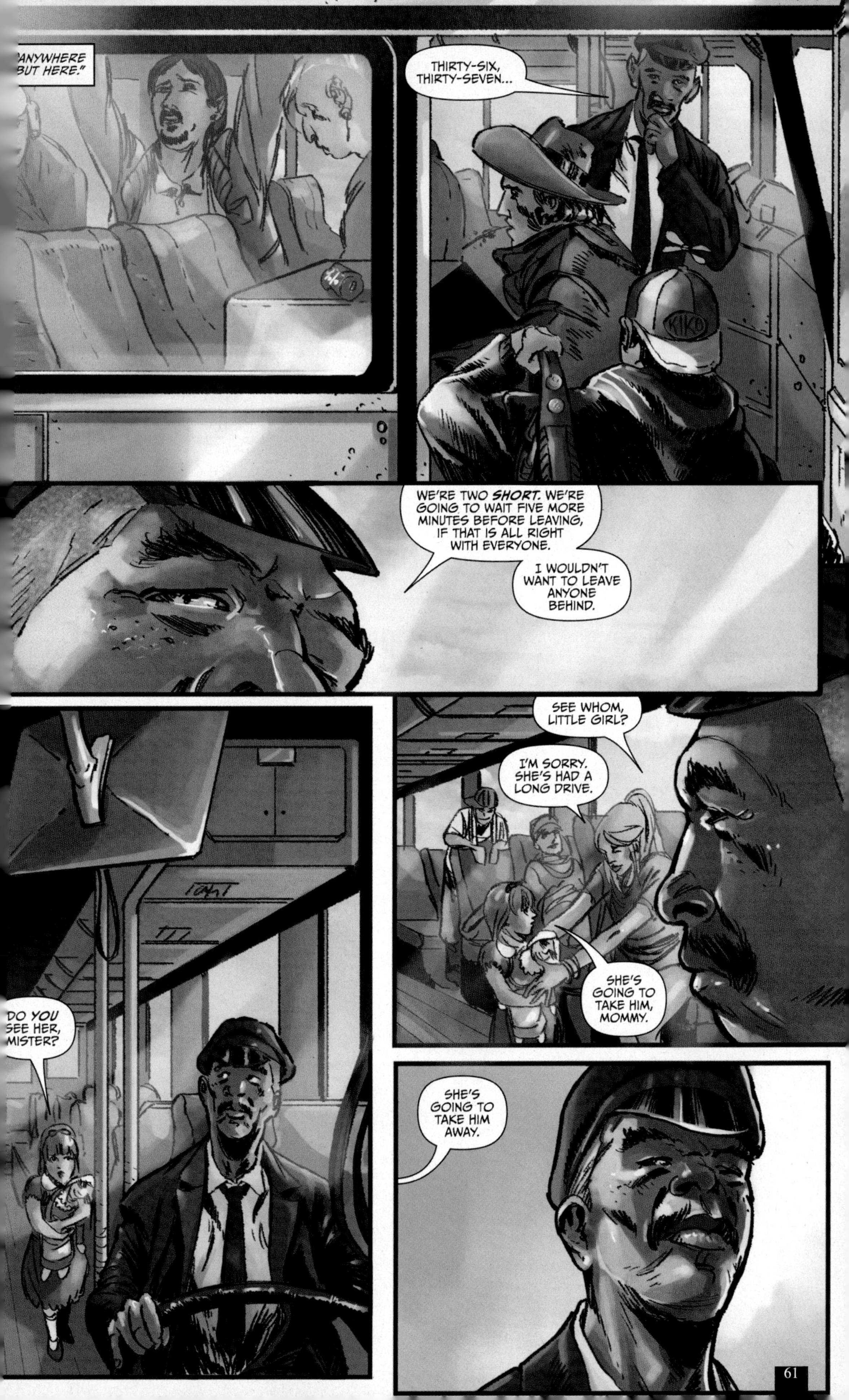
"ANYWHERE BUT HERE."
THIRTY-SIX, THIRTY-SEVEN...
KIKO
WE'RE TWO *SHORT.* WE'RE GOING TO WAIT FIVE MORE MINUTES BEFORE LEAVING, IF THAT IS ALL RIGHT WITH EVERYONE.
I WOULDN'T WANT TO LEAVE ANYONE BEHIND.
DO *YOU* SEE HER, MISTER?
SEE WHOM, LITTLE GIRL?
I'M SORRY. SHE'S HAD A LONG DRIVE.
SHE'S GOING TO TAKE HIM, MOMMY.
SHE'S GOING TO TAKE HIM AWAY.

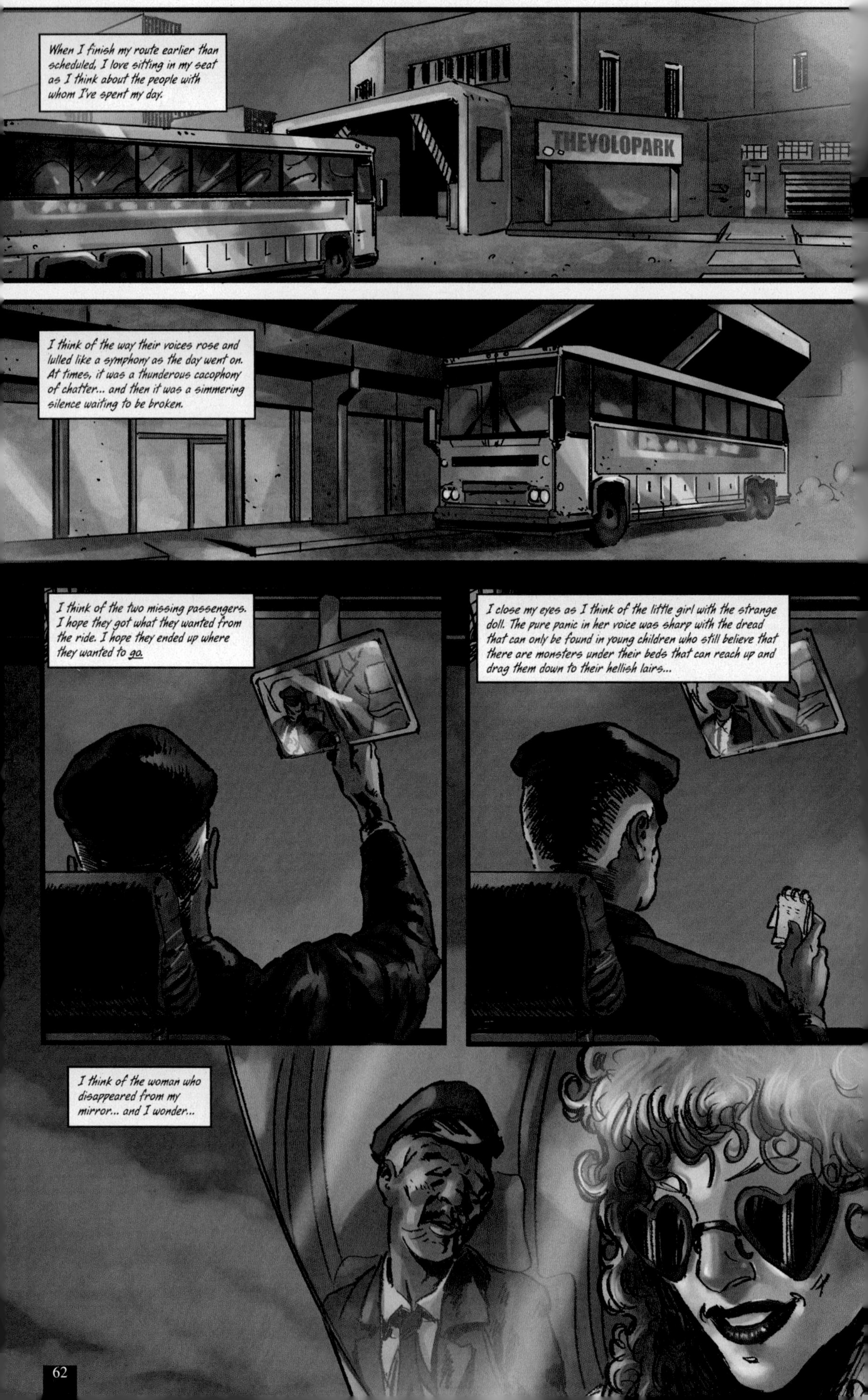

When I finish my route earlier than scheduled, I love sitting in my seat as I think about the people with whom I've spent my day.
THEYOLOPARK
I think of the way their voices rose and lulled like a symphony as the day went on. At times, it was a thunderous cacophony of chatter... and then it was a simmering silence waiting to be broken.
I think of the two missing passengers. I hope they got what they wanted from the ride. I hope they ended up where they wanted to go.
I close my eyes as I think of the little girl with the strange doll. The pure panic in her voice was sharp with the dread that can only be found in young children who still believe that there are monsters under their beds that can reach up and drag them down to their hellish lairs...
I think of the woman who disappeared from my mirror... and I wonder...

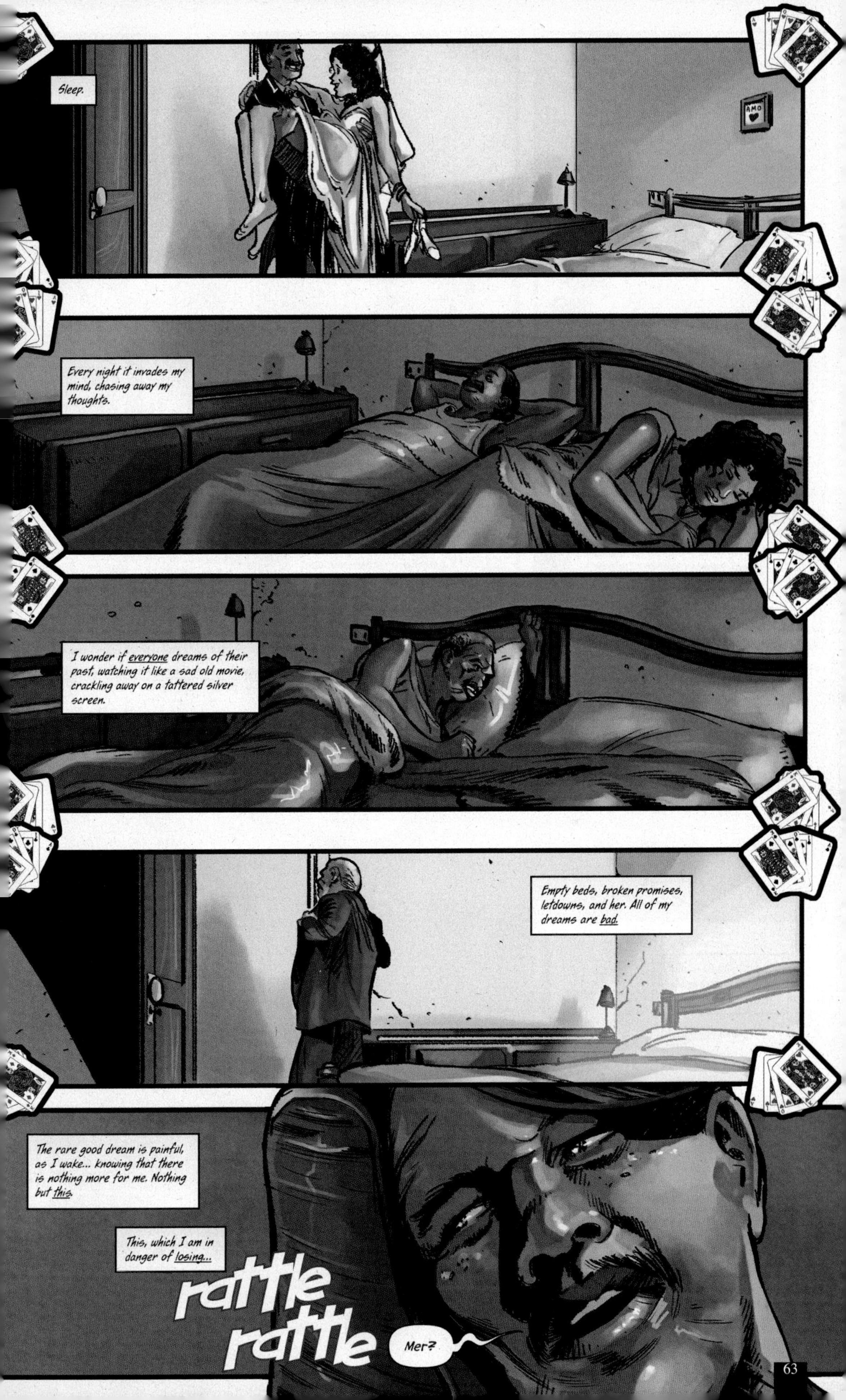

Sleep.
AMO
Every night it invades my mind, chasing away my thoughts.
I wonder if everyone dreams of their past, watching it like a sad old movie, crackling away on a tattered silver screen.
Empty beds, broken promises, letdowns, and her. All of my dreams are bad.
The rare good dream is painful, as I wake... knowing that there is nothing more for me. Nothing but this.
This, which I am in danger of losing...
rattle rattle
Mer?

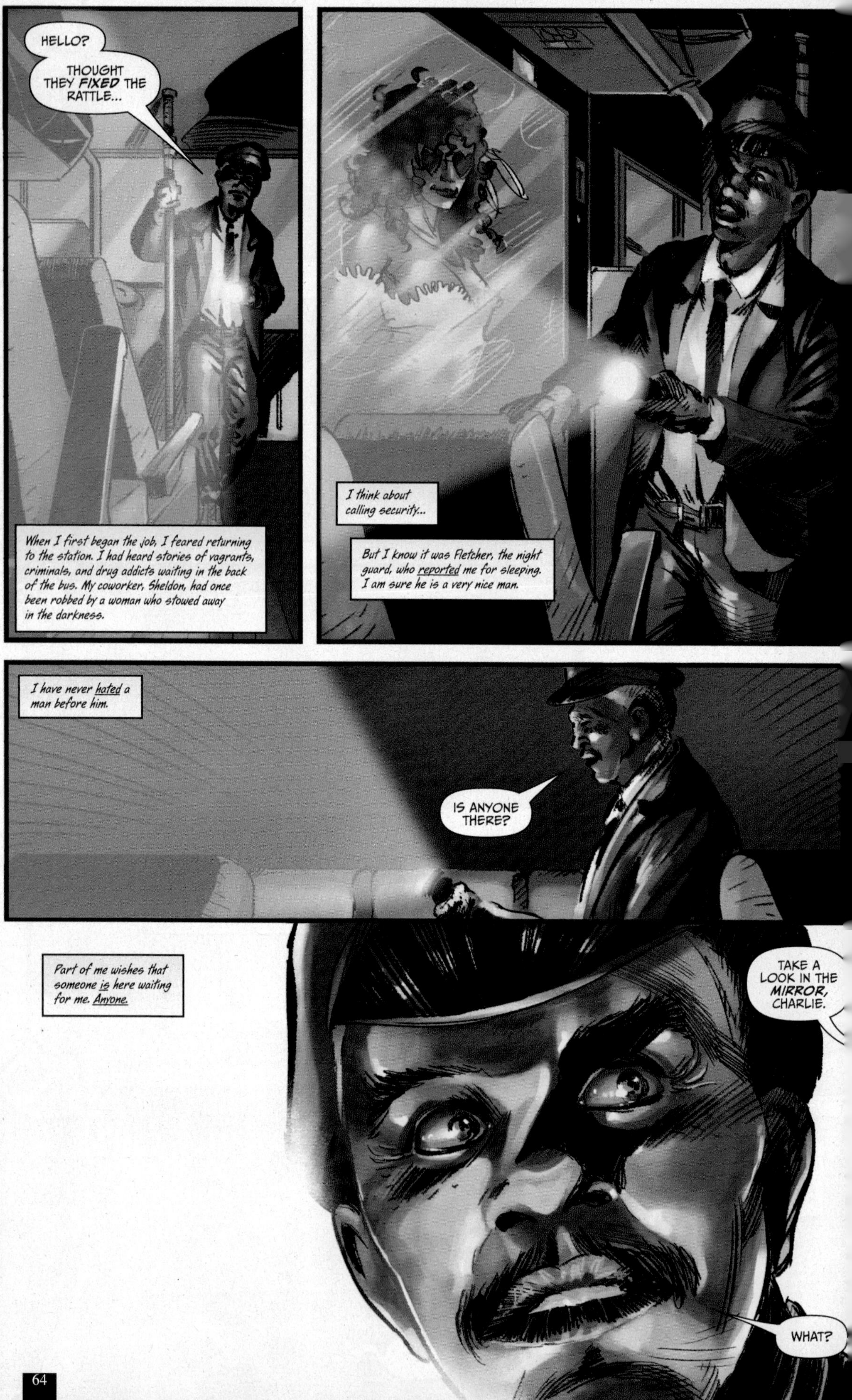
HELLO?
THOUGHT THEY *FIXED* THE RATTLE...
When I first began the job, I feared returning to the station. I had heard stories of vagrants, criminals, and drug addicts waiting in the back of the bus. My coworker, Sheldon, had once been robbed by a woman who stowed away in the darkness.
I think about calling security...
But I know it was Fletcher, the night guard, who reported me for sleeping. I am sure he is a very nice man.
I have never hated a man before him.
IS ANYONE THERE?
Part of me wishes that someone is here waiting for me. Anyone.
TAKE A LOOK IN THE *MIRROR,* CHARLIE.
WHAT?

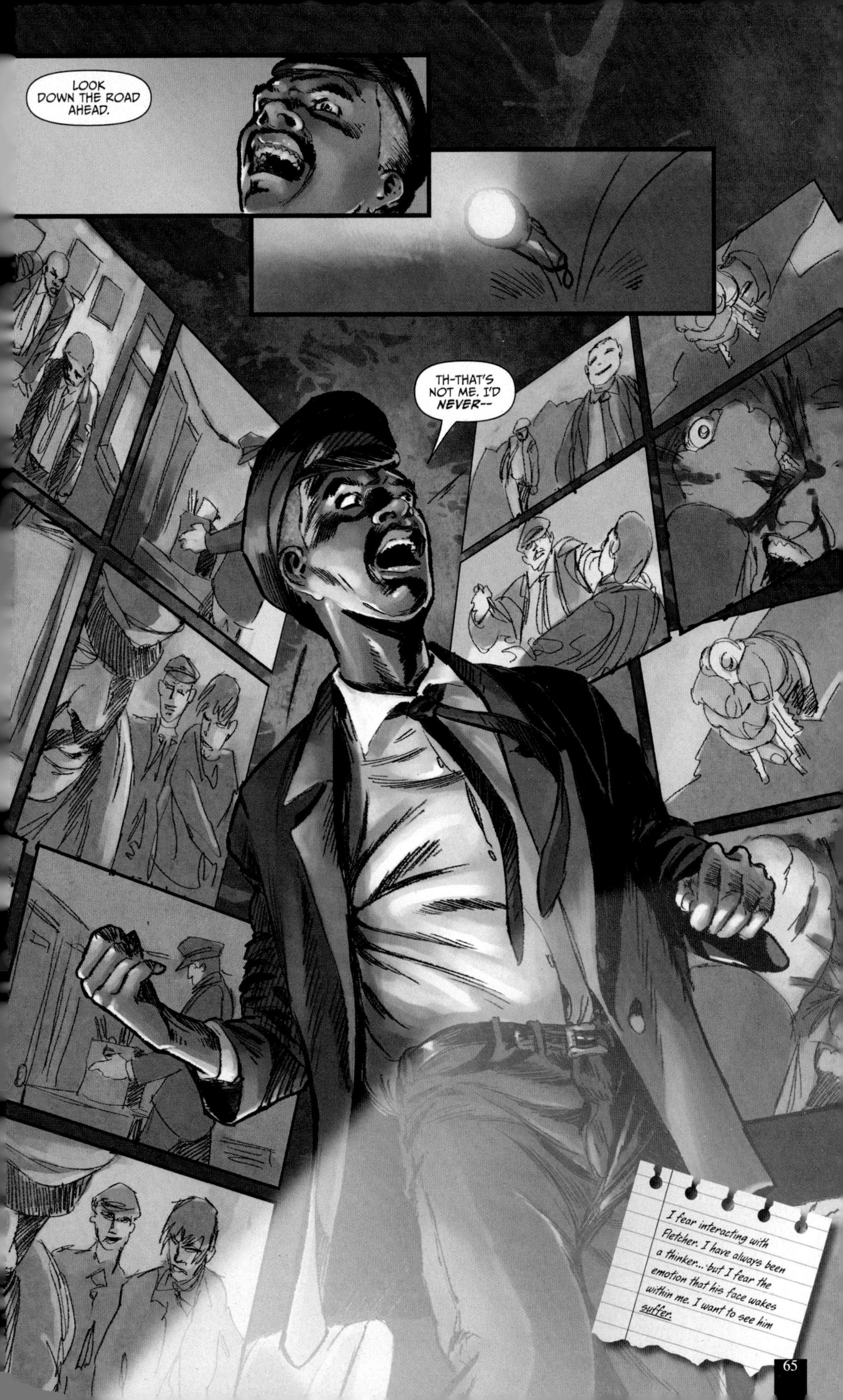
LOOK DOWN THE ROAD AHEAD.
TH-THAT'S NOT ME. I'D NEVER--
I fear interacting with Fletcher. I have always been a thinker...but I fear the emotion that his face wakes within me. I want to see him suffer.

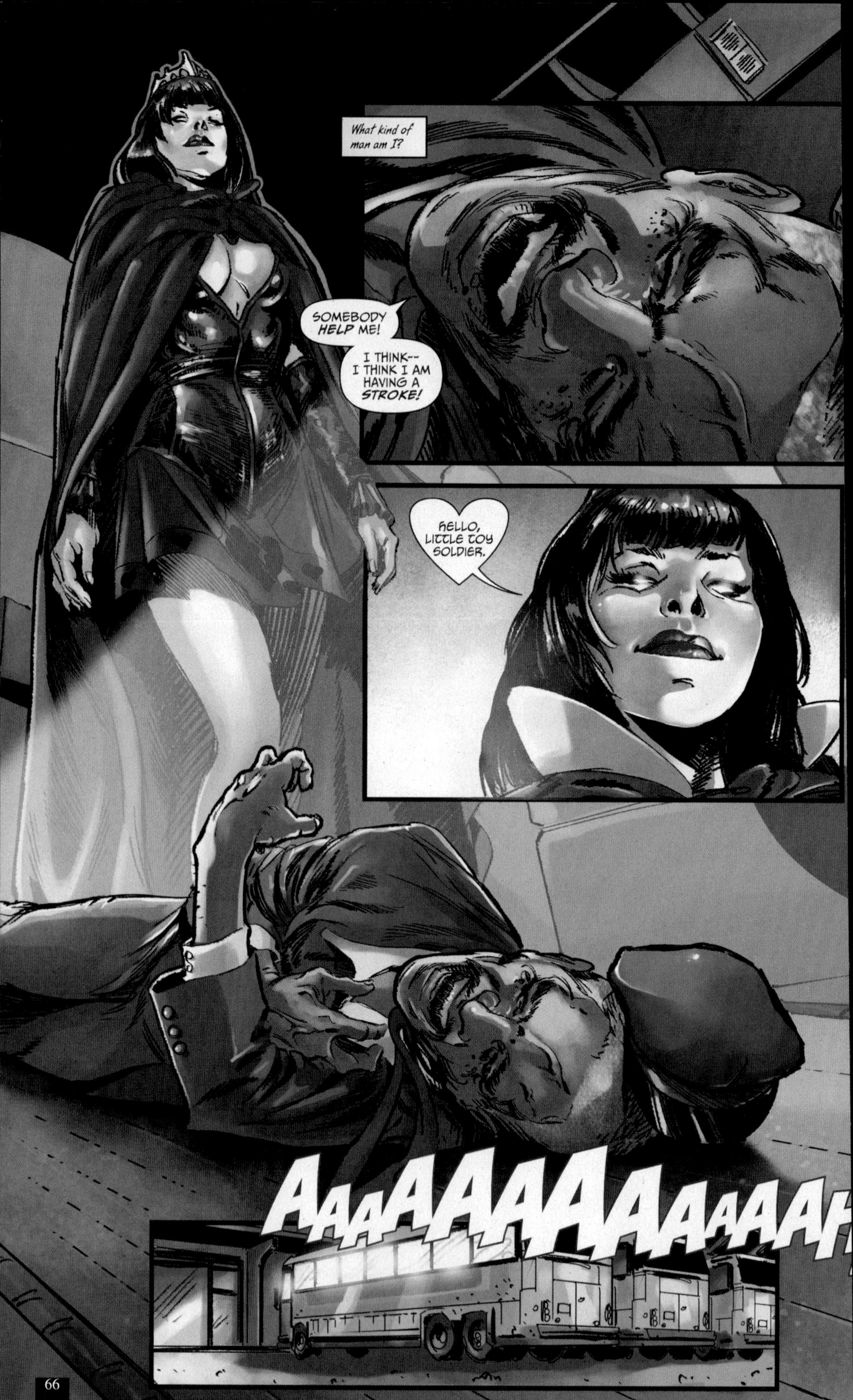
What kind of man am I?
SOMEBODY HELP ME!
I THINK-- I THINK I AM HAVING A STROKE!
HELLO, LITTLE TOY SOLDIER.
AAAAAAAAAAAAH

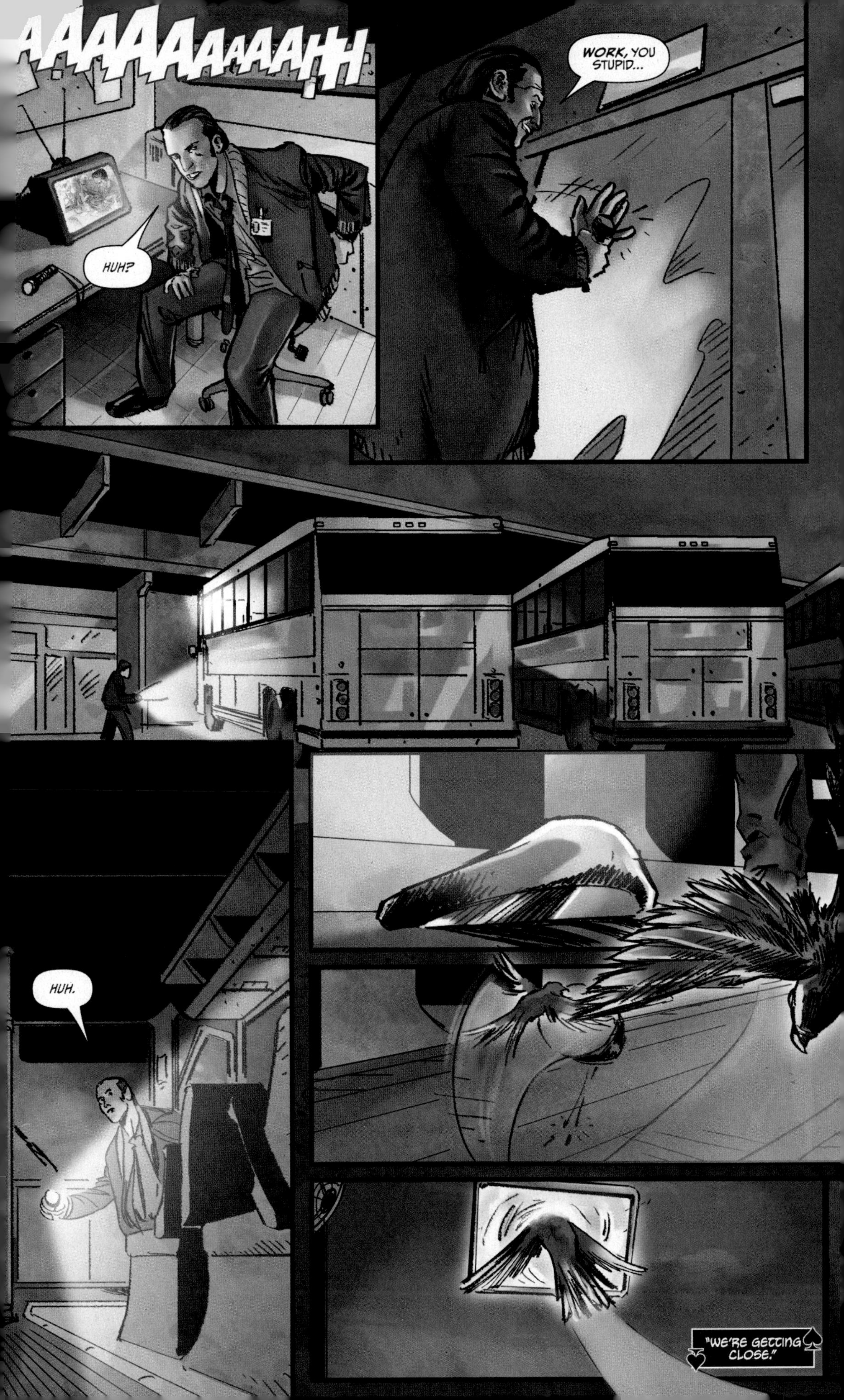
AAAAAAAAAHH
HUH?
WORK, YOU STUPID...
HUH.
"WE'RE GETTING CLOSE."

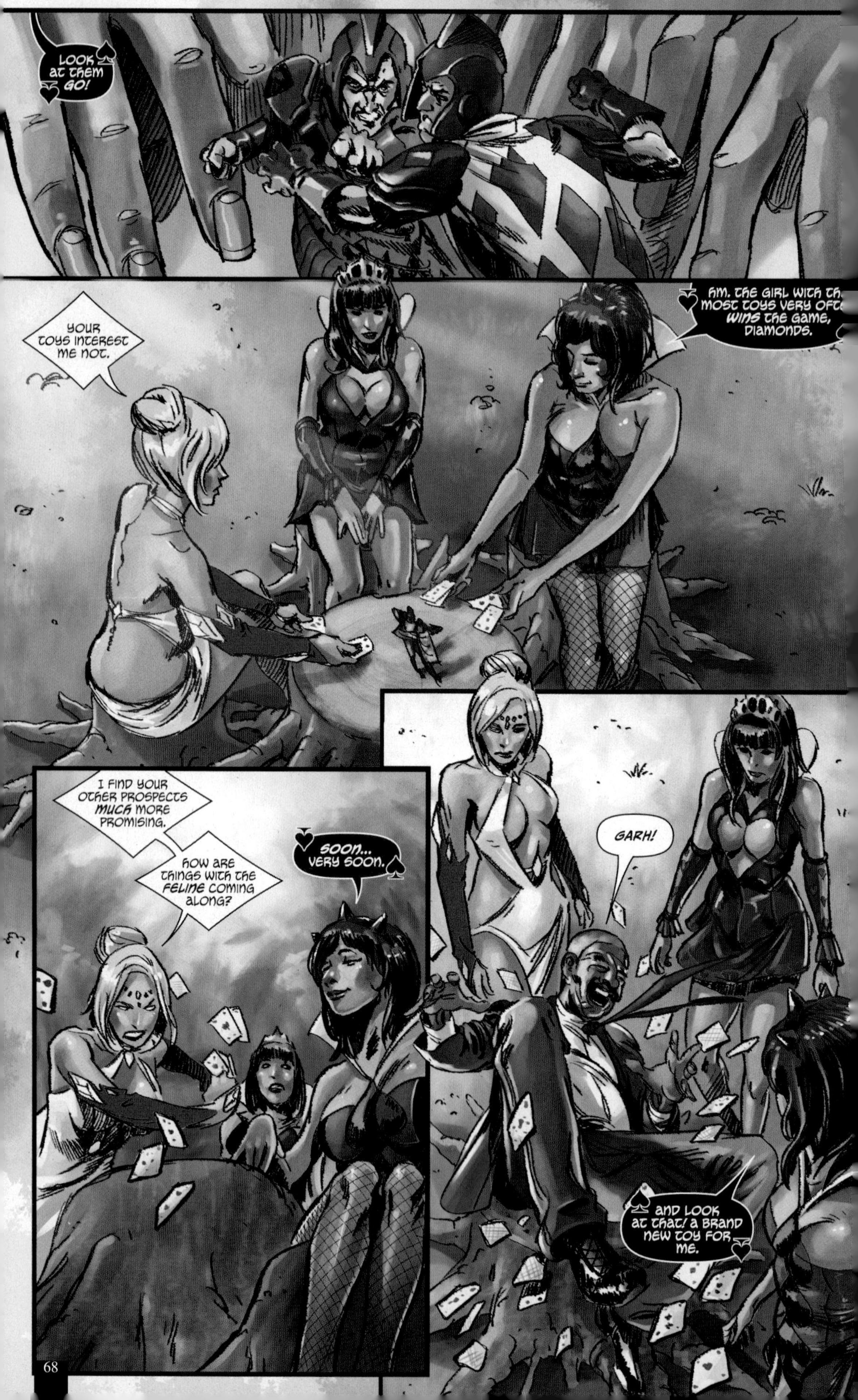
LOOK AT THEM GO!
YOUR TOYS INTEREST ME NOT.
HM. THE GIRL WITH THE MOST TOYS VERY OFTEN WINS THE GAME, DIAMONDS.
I FIND YOUR OTHER PROSPECTS MUCH MORE PROMISING.
HOW ARE THINGS WITH THE FELINE COMING ALONG?
SOON... VERY SOON.
GARH!
AND LOOK AT THAT! A BRAND NEW TOY FOR ME.

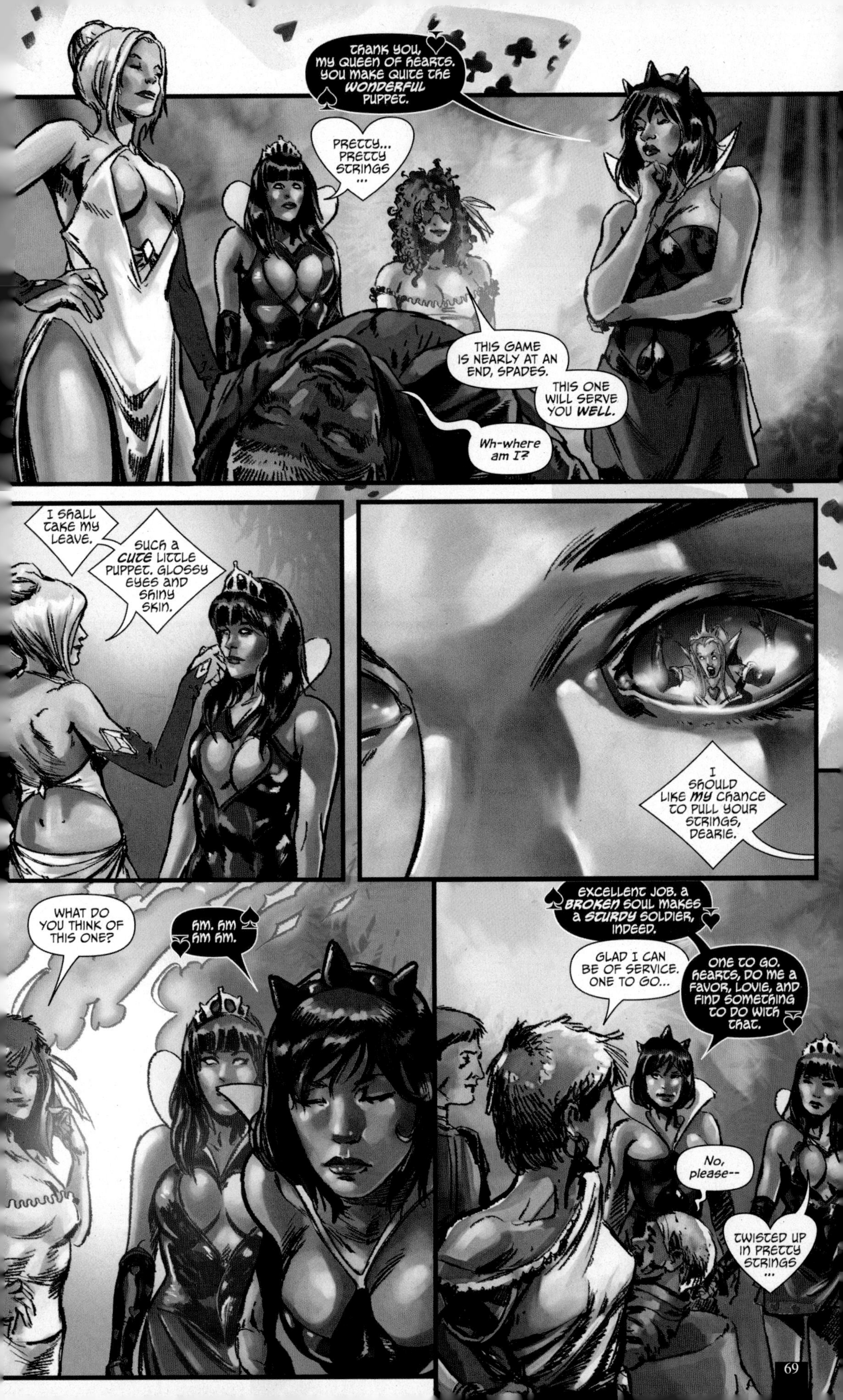

THANK YOU, MY QUEEN OF HEARTS. YOU MAKE QUITE THE WONDERFUL PUPPET.
PRETTY... PRETTY STRINGS ...
THIS GAME IS NEARLY AT AN END, SPADES.
THIS ONE WILL SERVE YOU WELL.
Wh-where am I?
I SHALL TAKE MY LEAVE.
SUCH A CUTE LITTLE PUPPET. GLOSSY EYES AND SHINY SKIN.
I SHOULD LIKE MY CHANCE TO PULL YOUR STRINGS, DEARIE.
WHAT DO YOU THINK OF THIS ONE?
HM. HM HM HM.
EXCELLENT JOB. A BROKEN SOUL MAKES A STURDY SOLDIER, INDEED.
GLAD I CAN BE OF SERVICE. ONE TO GO...
ONE TO GO. HEARTS, DO ME A FAVOR, LOVIE, AND FIND SOMETHING TO DO WITH THAT.
No, please--
TWISTED UP IN PRETTY STRINGS ...

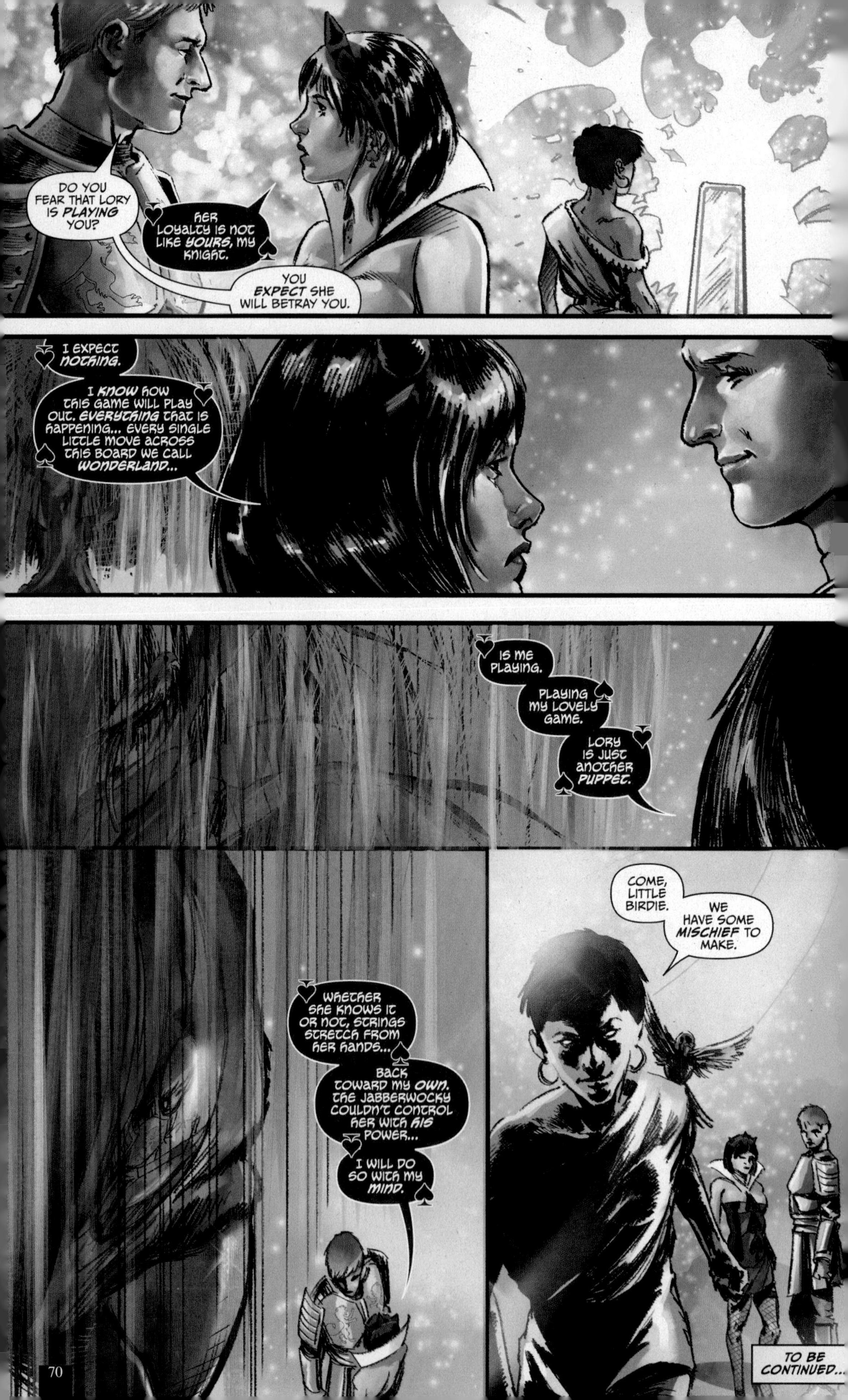
DO YOU FEAR THAT LORY IS PLAYING YOU?
HER LOYALTY IS NOT LIKE YOURS, MY KNIGHT.
YOU EXPECT SHE WILL BETRAY YOU.
I EXPECT NOTHING.
I KNOW HOW THIS GAME WILL PLAY OUT. EVERYTHING THAT IS HAPPENING... EVERY SINGLE LITTLE MOVE ACROSS THIS BOARD WE CALL WONDERLAND...
IS ME PLAYING.
PLAYING MY LOVELY GAME.
LORY IS JUST ANOTHER PUPPET.
WHETHER SHE KNOWS IT OR NOT, STRINGS STRETCH FROM HER HANDS...
BACK TOWARD MY OWN. THE JABBERWOCKY COULDN'T CONTROL HER WITH HIS POWER...
I WILL DO SO WITH MY MIND.
COME, LITTLE BIRDIE.
WE HAVE SOME MISCHIEF TO MAKE.
TO BE CONTINUED...

Grimm Fairy Tales presents

Wonderland

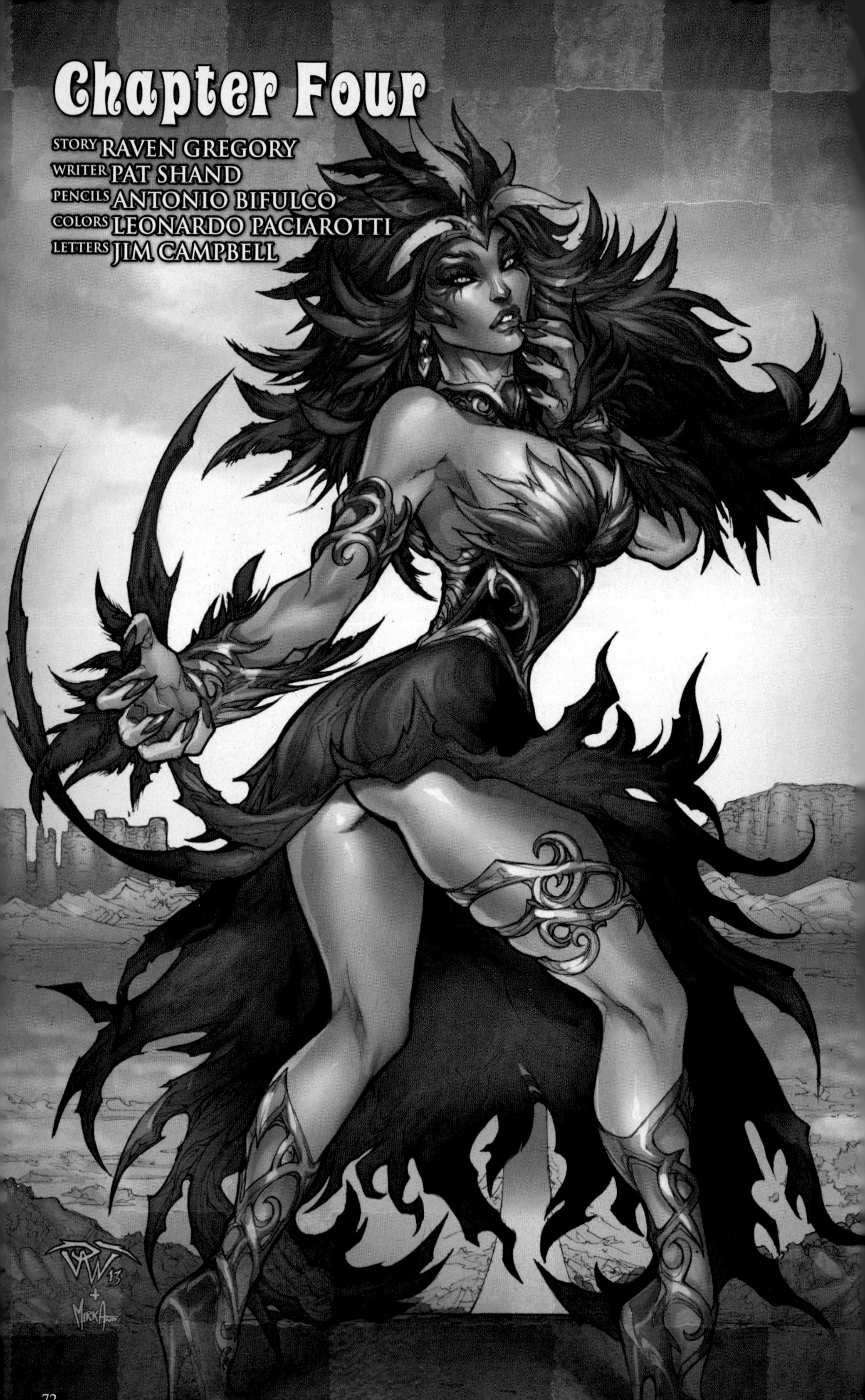
Chapter Four
STORY RAVEN GREGORY
WRITER PAT SHAND
PENCILS ANTONIO BIFULCO
COLORS LEONARDO PACIAROTTI
LETTERS JIM CAMPBELL

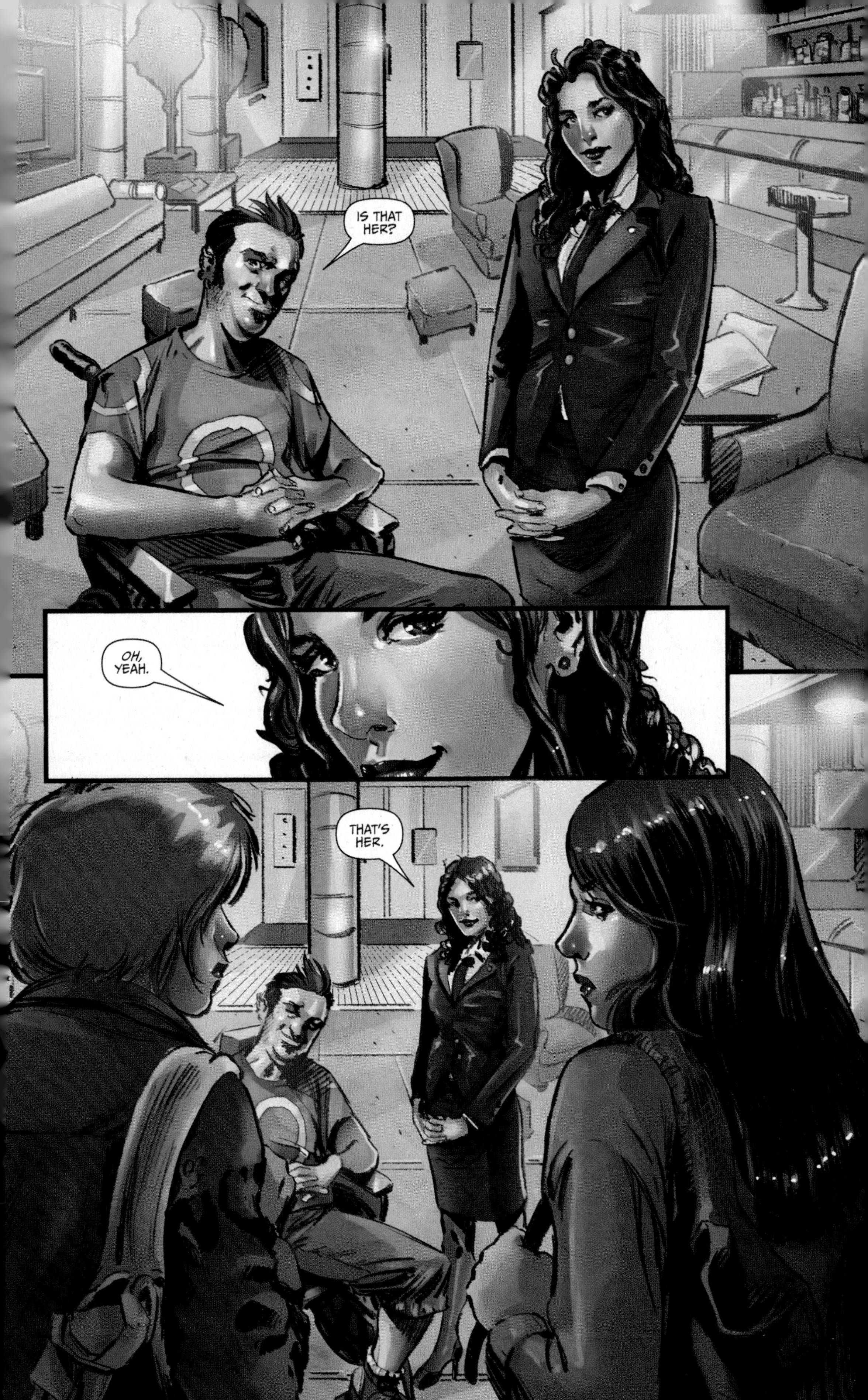
IS THAT HER?
OH, YEAH.
THAT'S HER.

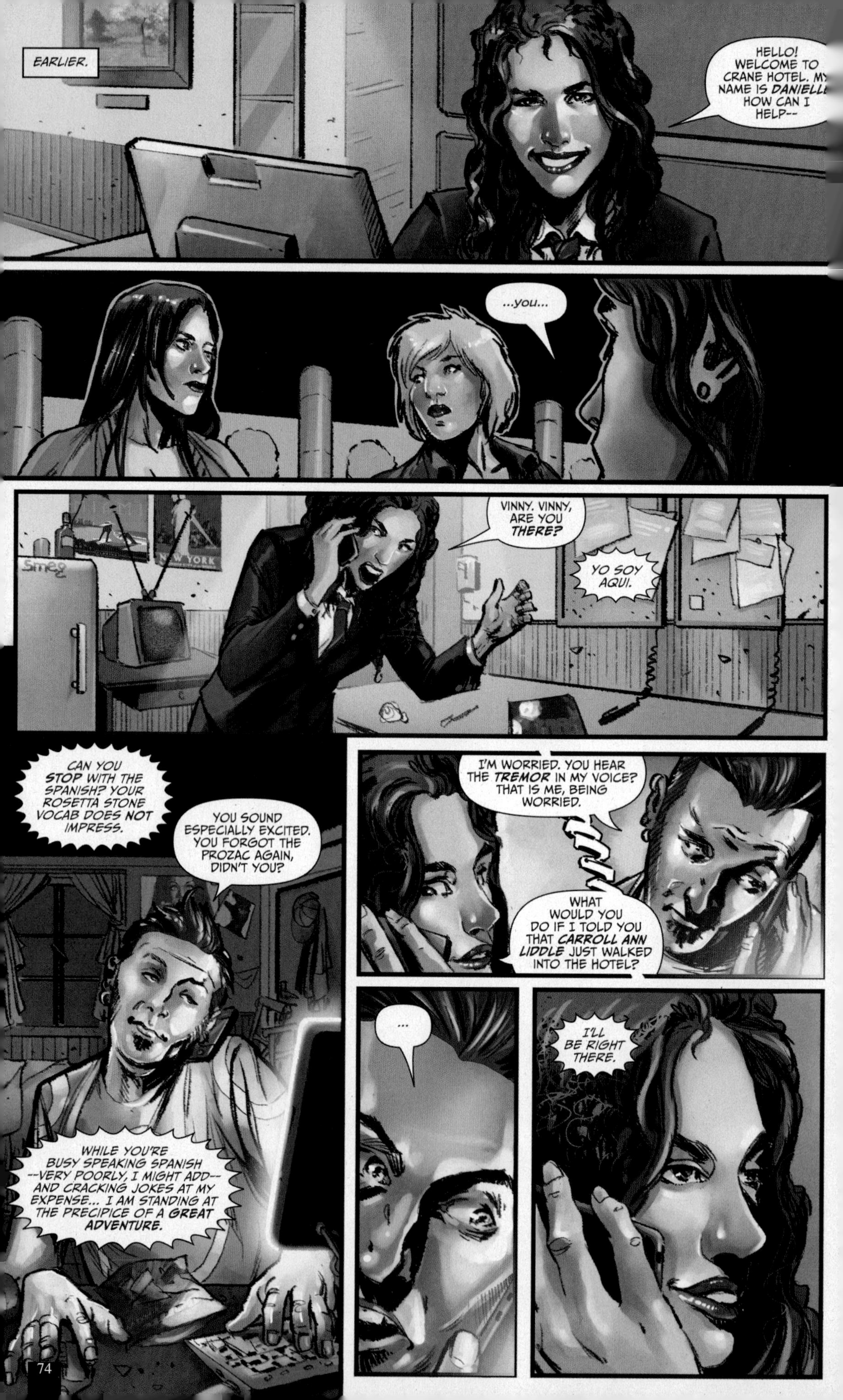
EARLIER.
HELLO! WELCOME TO CRANE HOTEL. MY NAME IS DANIELLE. HOW CAN I HELP--
...you...
VINNY. VINNY, ARE YOU THERE?
YO SOY AQUI.
CAN YOU STOP WITH THE SPANISH? YOUR ROSETTA STONE VOCAB DOES NOT IMPRESS.
YOU SOUND ESPECIALLY EXCITED. YOU FORGOT THE PROZAC AGAIN, DIDN'T YOU?
WHILE YOU'RE BUSY SPEAKING SPANISH --VERY POORLY, I MIGHT ADD-- AND CRACKING JOKES AT MY EXPENSE... I AM STANDING AT THE PRECIPICE OF A GREAT ADVENTURE.
I'M WORRIED. YOU HEAR THE TREMOR IN MY VOICE? THAT IS ME, BEING WORRIED.
WHAT WOULD YOU DO IF I TOLD YOU THAT CARROLL ANN LIDDLE JUST WALKED INTO THE HOTEL?
...
I'LL BE RIGHT THERE.

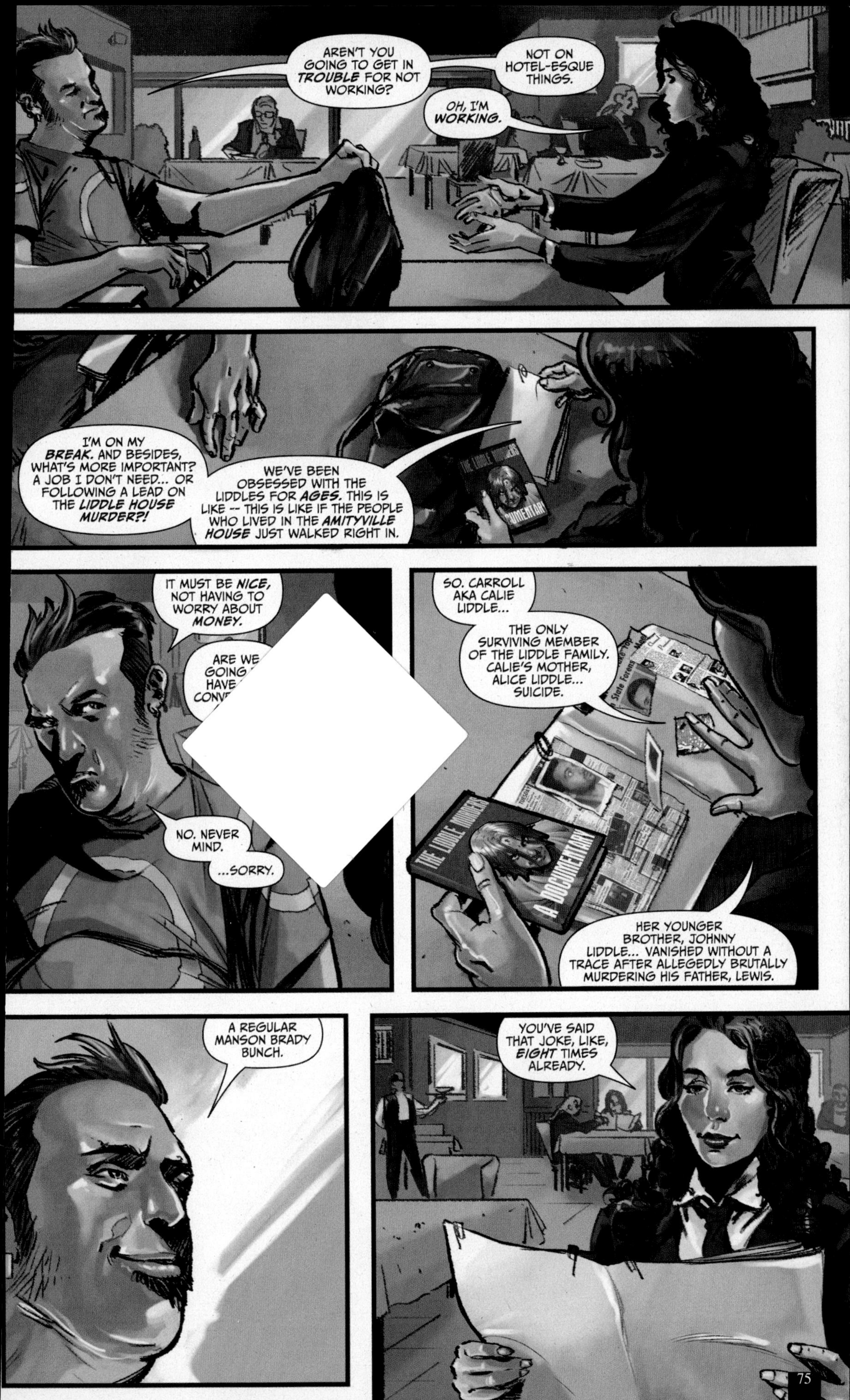

AREN'T YOU GOING TO GET IN TROUBLE FOR NOT WORKING?
NOT ON HOTEL-ESQUE THINGS.
OH, I'M WORKING.
I'M ON MY BREAK. AND BESIDES, WHAT'S MORE IMPORTANT? A JOB I DON'T NEED... OR FOLLOWING A LEAD ON THE LIDDLE HOUSE MURDER?!
WE'VE BEEN OBSESSED WITH THE LIDDLES FOR AGES. THIS IS LIKE -- THIS IS LIKE IF THE PEOPLE WHO LIVED IN THE AMITYVILLE HOUSE JUST WALKED RIGHT IN.
IT MUST BE NICE, NOT HAVING TO WORRY ABOUT MONEY.
ARE WE GOING
NO. NEVER MIND.
...SORRY.
SO. CARROLL AKA CALIE LIDDLE...
THE ONLY SURVIVING MEMBER OF THE LIDDLE FAMILY. CALIE'S MOTHER, ALICE LIDDLE... SUICIDE.
THE LIDDLE MURDERS
A DOCUMENTARY
HER YOUNGER BROTHER, JOHNNY LIDDLE... VANISHED WITHOUT A TRACE AFTER ALLEGEDLY BRUTALLY MURDERING HIS FATHER, LEWIS.
A REGULAR MANSON BRADY BUNCH.
YOU'VE SAID THAT JOKE, LIKE, EIGHT TIMES ALREADY.

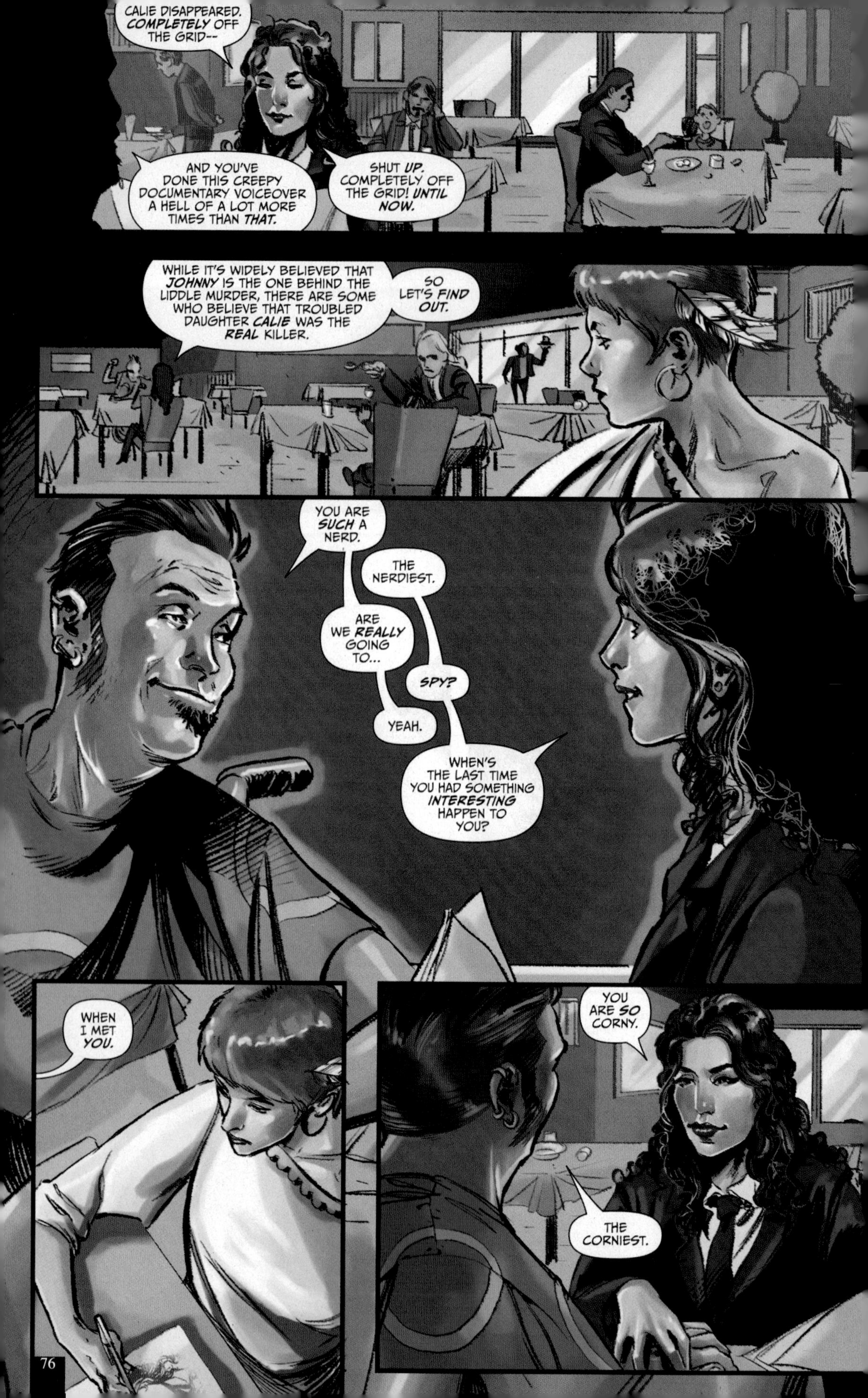

CALIE DISAPPEARED. COMPLETELY OFF THE GRID--
AND YOU'VE DONE THIS CREEPY DOCUMENTARY VOICEOVER A HELL OF A LOT MORE TIMES THAN THAT.
SHUT UP. COMPLETELY OFF THE GRID! UNTIL NOW.
WHILE IT'S WIDELY BELIEVED THAT JOHNNY IS THE ONE BEHIND THE LIDDLE MURDER, THERE ARE SOME WHO BELIEVE THAT TROUBLED DAUGHTER CALIE WAS THE REAL KILLER.
SO LET'S FIND OUT.
YOU ARE SUCH A NERD.
THE NERDIEST.
ARE WE REALLY GOING TO...
SPY?
YEAH.
WHEN'S THE LAST TIME YOU HAD SOMETHING INTERESTING HAPPEN TO YOU?
WHEN I MET YOU.
YOU ARE SO CORNY.
THE CORNIEST.

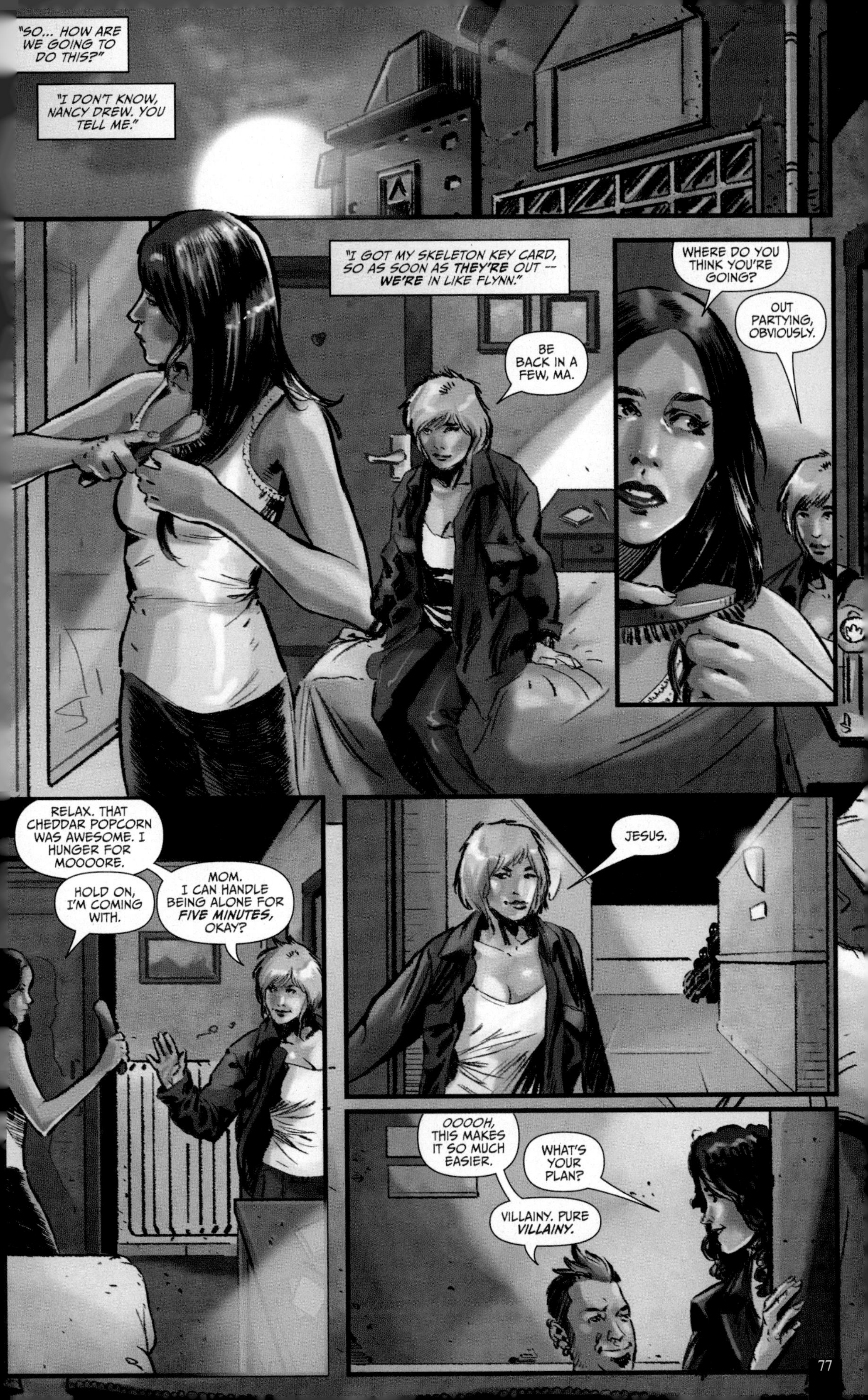

"SO... HOW ARE WE GOING TO DO THIS?"
"I DON'T KNOW, NANCY DREW. YOU TELL ME."
"I GOT MY SKELETON KEY CARD, SO AS SOON AS **THEY'RE** OUT -- **WE'RE** IN LIKE FLYNN."
BE BACK IN A FEW, MA.
WHERE DO YOU THINK YOU'RE GOING?
OUT PARTYING, OBVIOUSLY.
RELAX. THAT CHEDDAR POPCORN WAS AWESOME. I HUNGER FOR MOOOORE.
HOLD ON, I'M COMING WITH.
MOM. I CAN HANDLE BEING ALONE FOR ***FIVE MINUTES,*** OKAY?
JESUS.
OOOOH, THIS MAKES IT SO MUCH EASIER.
WHAT'S YOUR PLAN?
VILLAINY. PURE ***VILLAINY.***

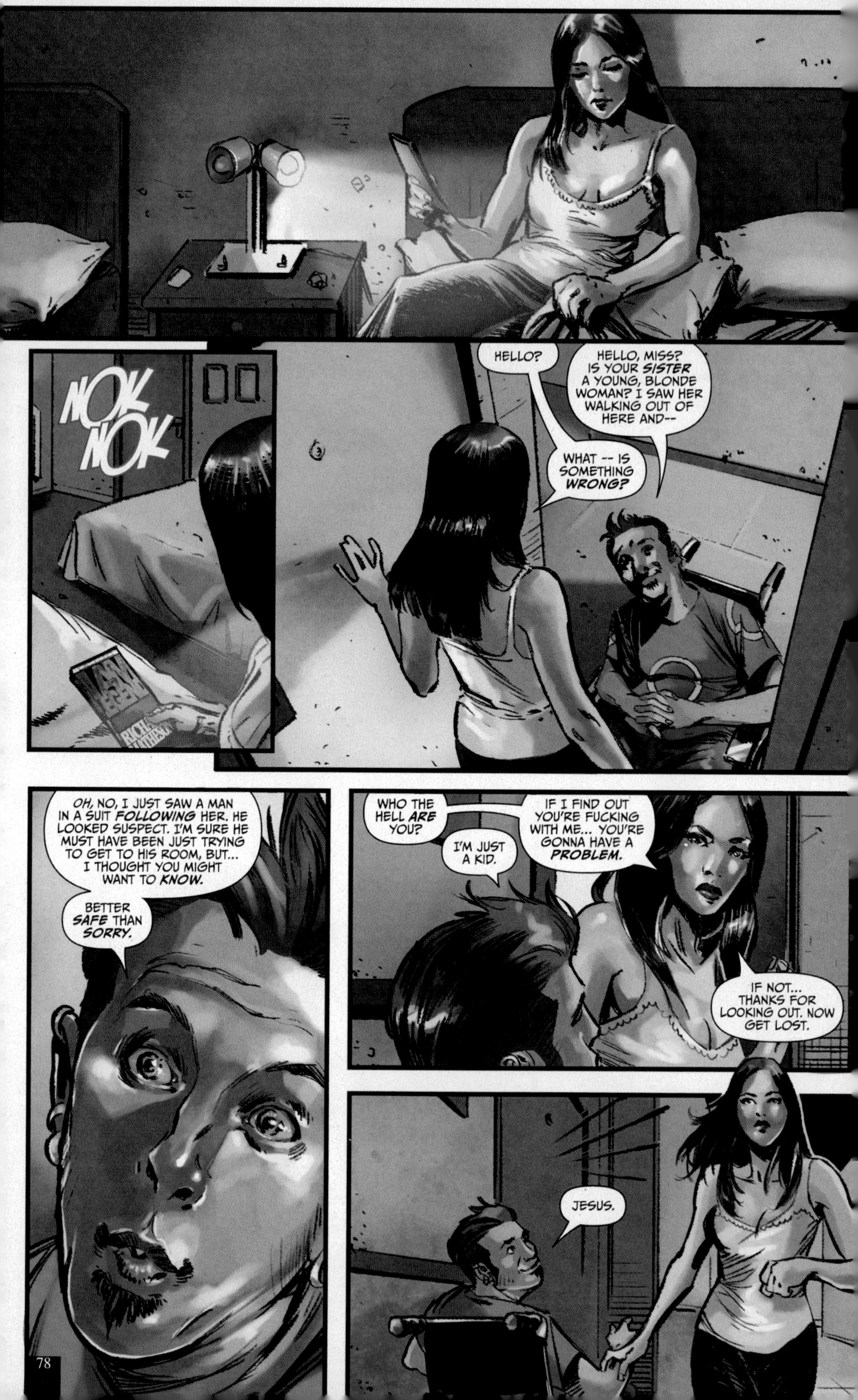
NOK NOK
HELLO?
HELLO, MISS? IS YOUR SISTER A YOUNG, BLONDE WOMAN? I SAW HER WALKING OUT OF HERE AND--
WHAT -- IS SOMETHING WRONG?
OH, NO, I JUST SAW A MAN IN A SUIT FOLLOWING HER. HE LOOKED SUSPECT. I'M SURE HE MUST HAVE BEEN JUST TRYING TO GET TO HIS ROOM, BUT... I THOUGHT YOU MIGHT WANT TO KNOW.
BETTER SAFE THAN SORRY.
WHO THE HELL ARE YOU?
I'M JUST A KID.
IF I FIND OUT YOU'RE FUCKING WITH ME... YOU'RE GONNA HAVE A PROBLEM.
IF NOT... THANKS FOR LOOKING OUT. NOW GET LOST.
JESUS.

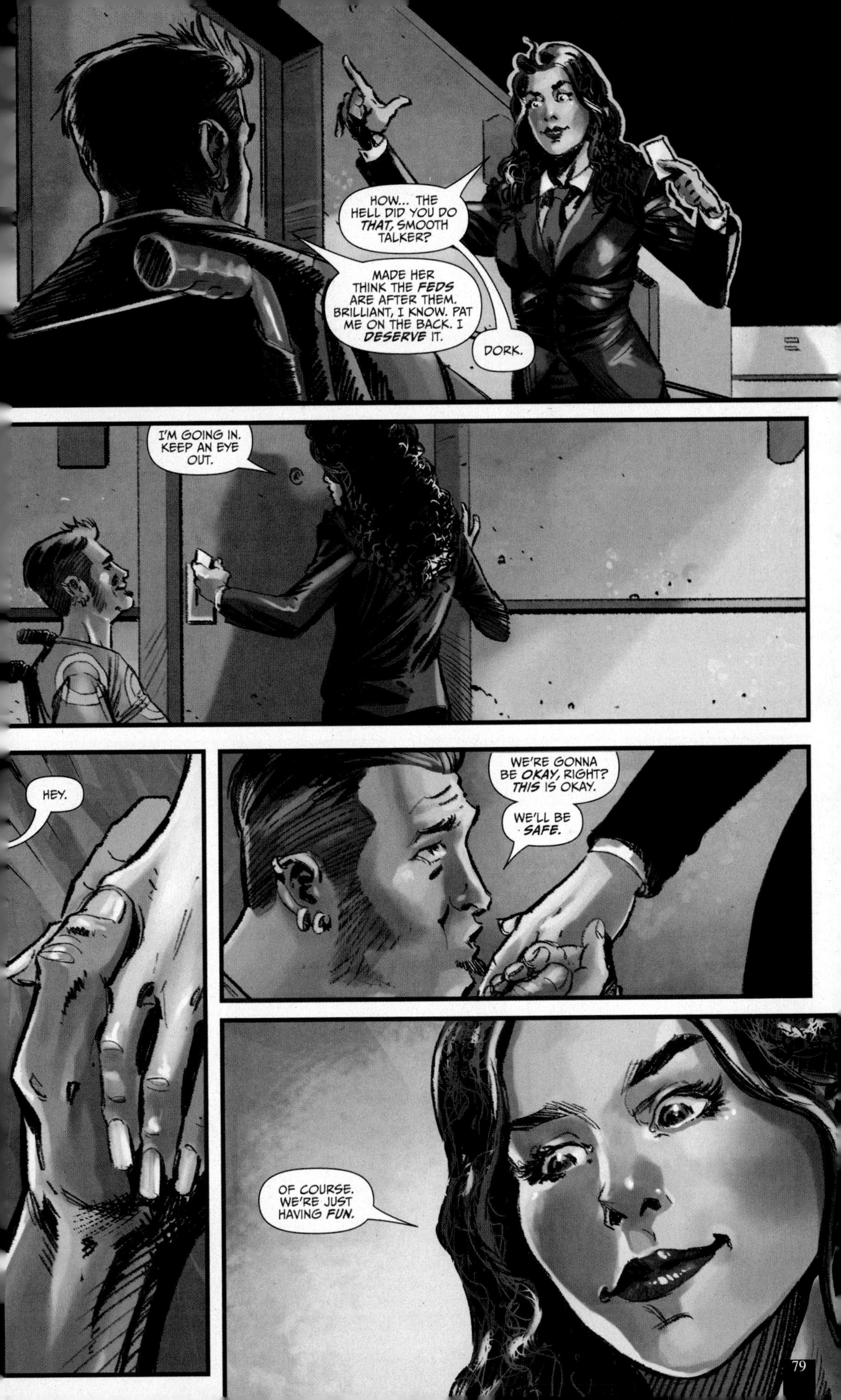
HOW... THE HELL DID YOU DO *THAT,* SMOOTH TALKER?
MADE HER THINK THE *FEDS* ARE AFTER THEM. BRILLIANT, I KNOW. PAT ME ON THE BACK. I *DESERVE* IT.
DORK.
I'M GOING IN. KEEP AN EYE OUT.
HEY.
WE'RE GONNA BE *OKAY,* RIGHT? *THIS* IS OKAY.
WE'LL BE *SAFE.*
OF COURSE. WE'RE JUST HAVING *FUN.*

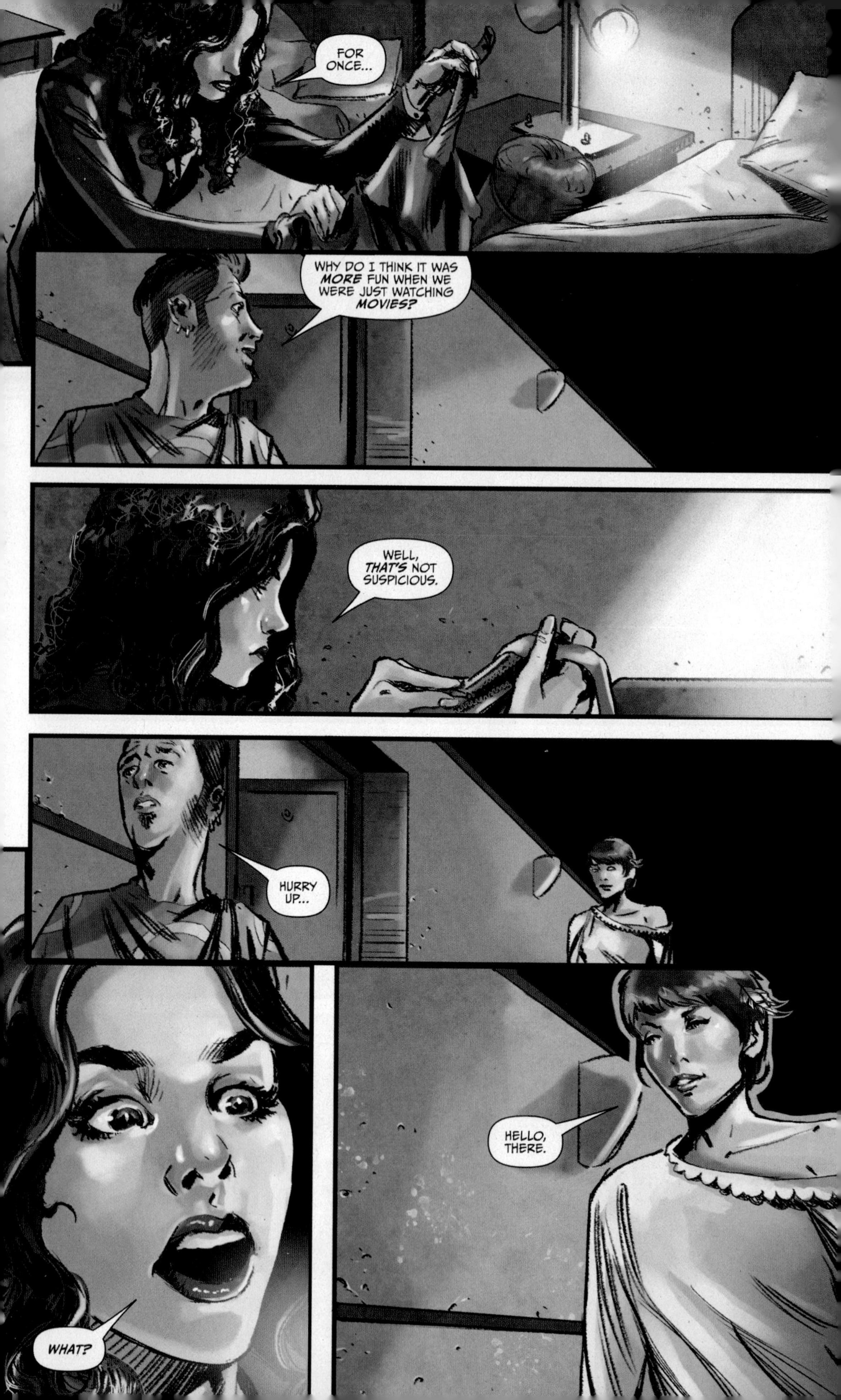
FOR ONCE...
WHY DO I THINK IT WAS *MORE* FUN WHEN WE WERE JUST WATCHING *MOVIES?*
WELL, *THAT'S* NOT SUSPICIOUS.
HURRY UP...
HELLO, THERE.
WHAT?

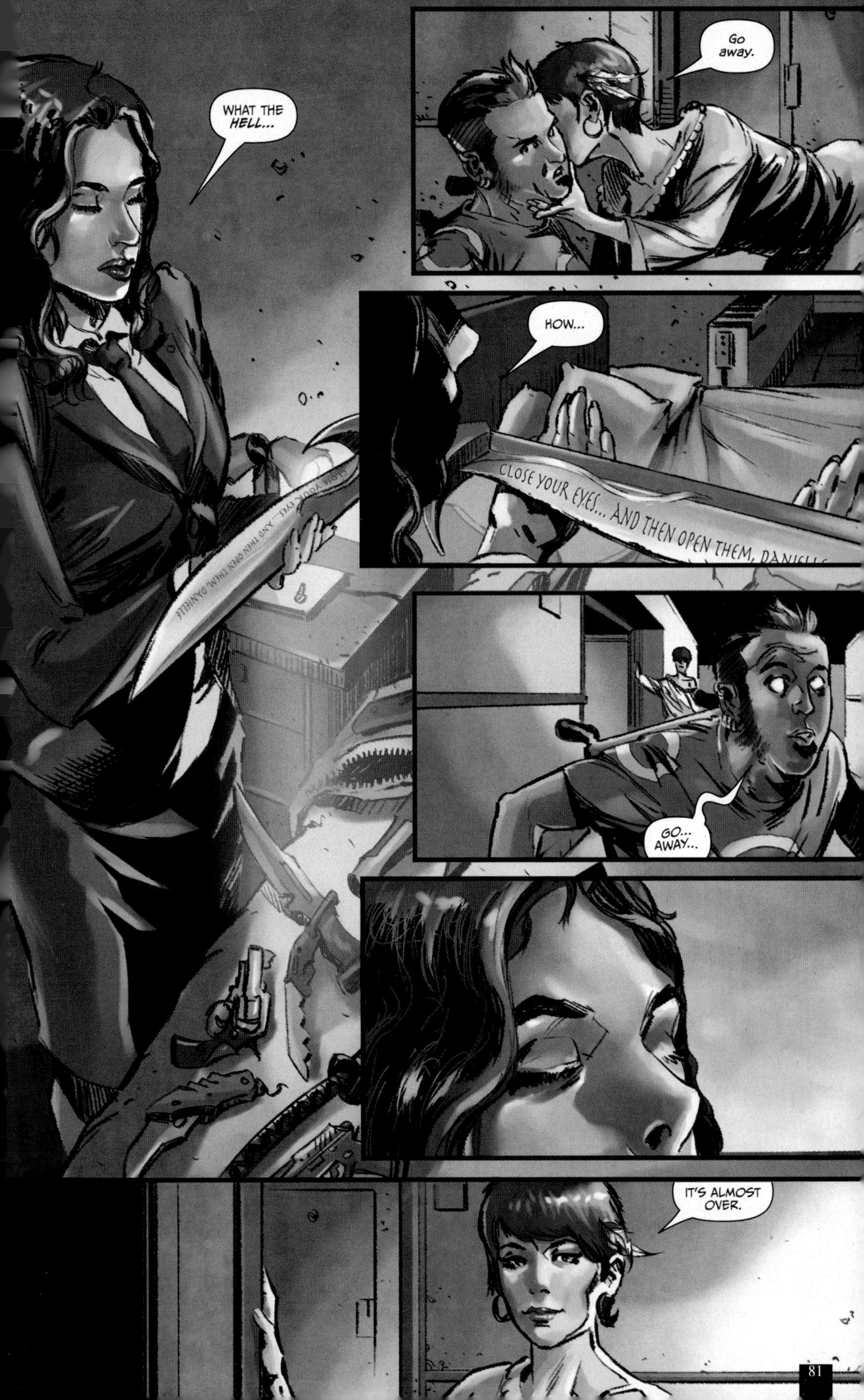
WHAT THE HELL...
CLOSE YOUR EYES... AND THEN OPEN THEM, DANIELLE
Go away.
HOW...
CLOSE YOUR EYES... AND THEN OPEN THEM, DANIELLE
GO... AWAY...
IT'S ALMOST OVER.

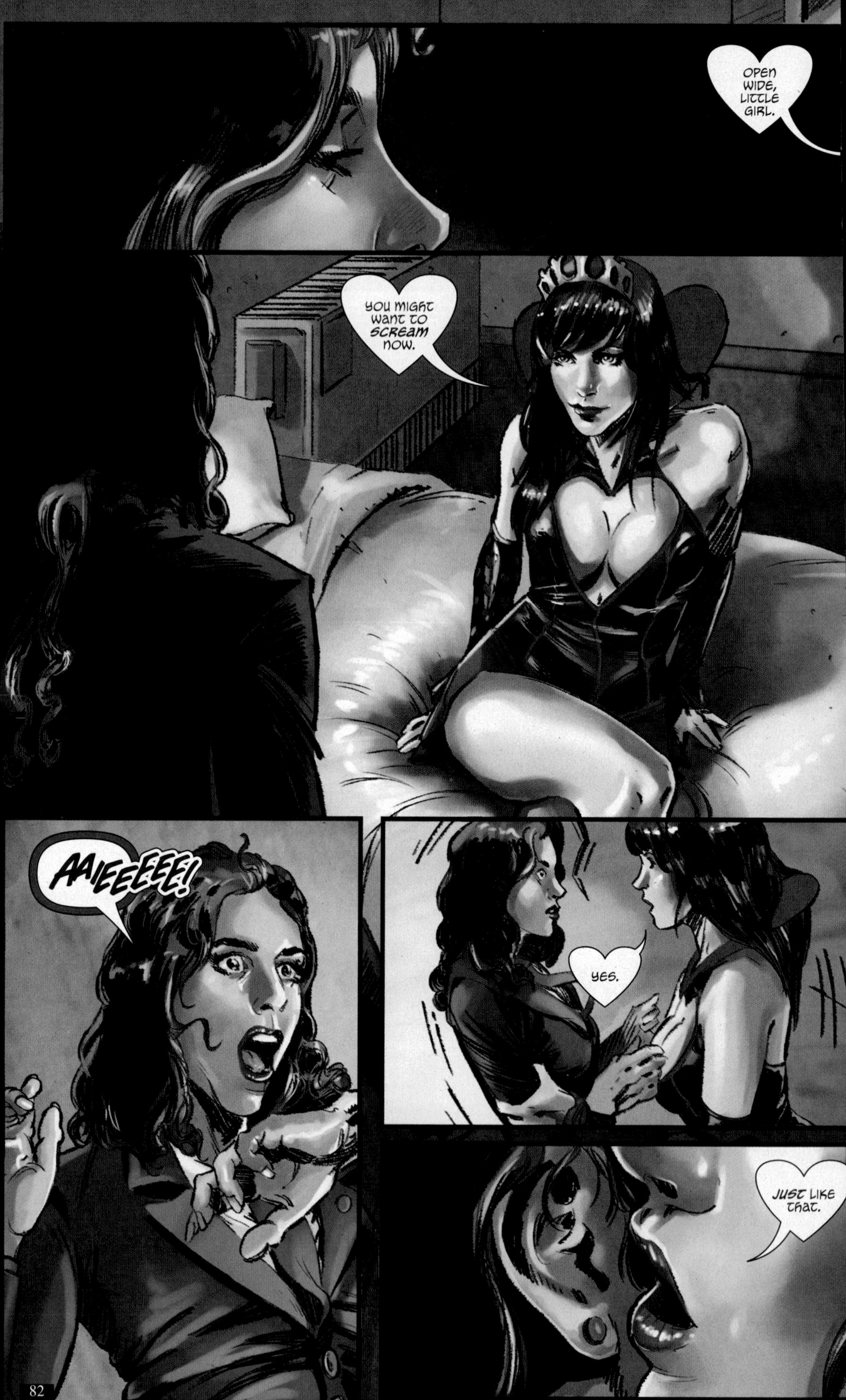
OPEN WIDE, LITTLE GIRL.
YOU MIGHT WANT TO SCREAM NOW.
AAIEEEEEE!
YES.
JUST LIKE THAT.

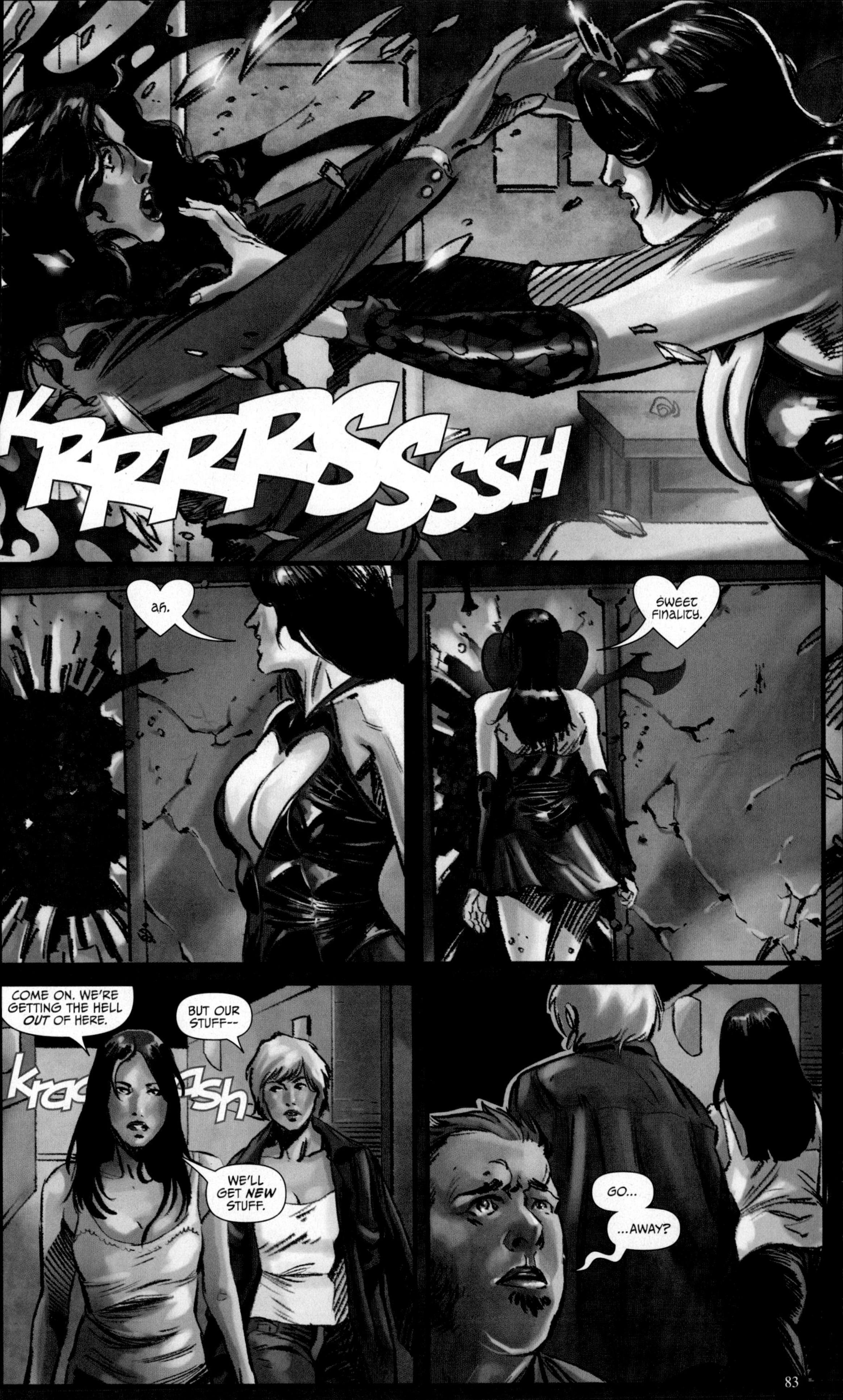
KRRRRSSSSSH
ah.
Sweet finality.
COME ON. WE'RE GETTING THE HELL OUT OF HERE.
BUT OUR STUFF--
WE'LL GET NEW STUFF.
GO...
...AWAY?

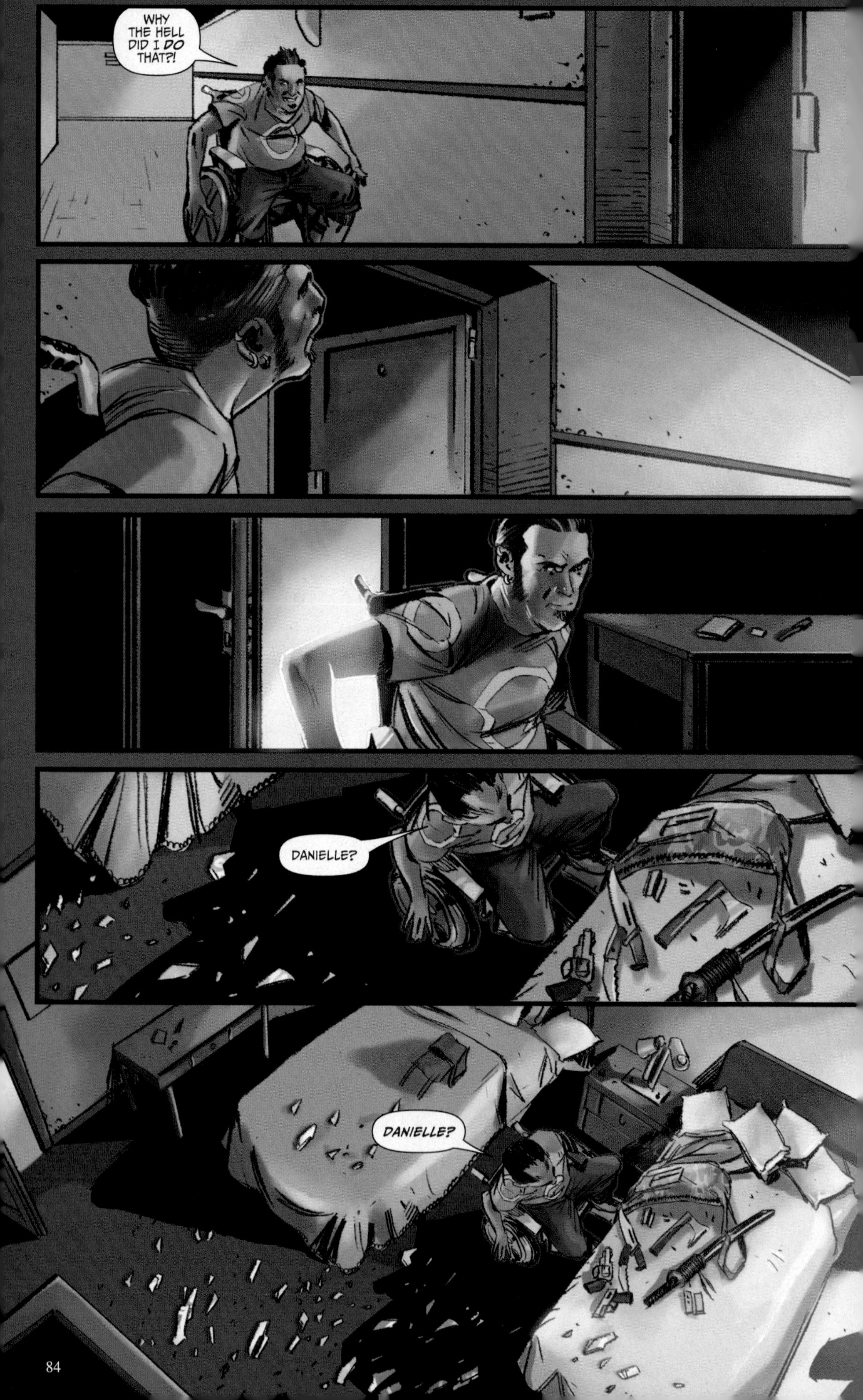
WHY THE HELL DID I DO THAT?!
DANIELLE?
DANIELLE?

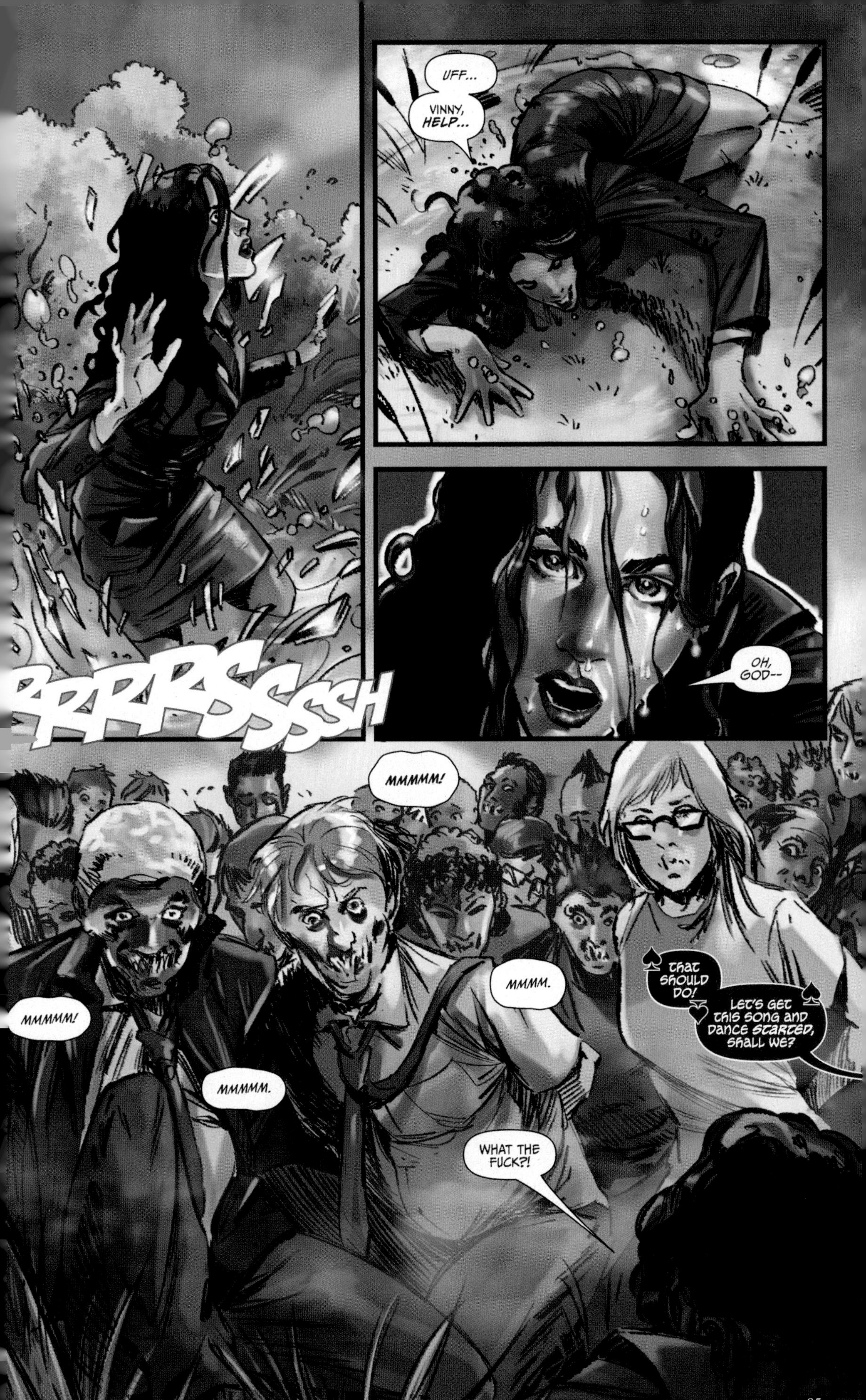
BRRRRSSSSH
UFF...
VINNY, HELP...
OH, GOD--
MMMMM!
MMMM.
THAT SHOULD DO!
LET'S GET THIS SONG AND DANCE STARTED, SHALL WE?
MMMMM!
MMMMM.
WHAT THE FUCK?!

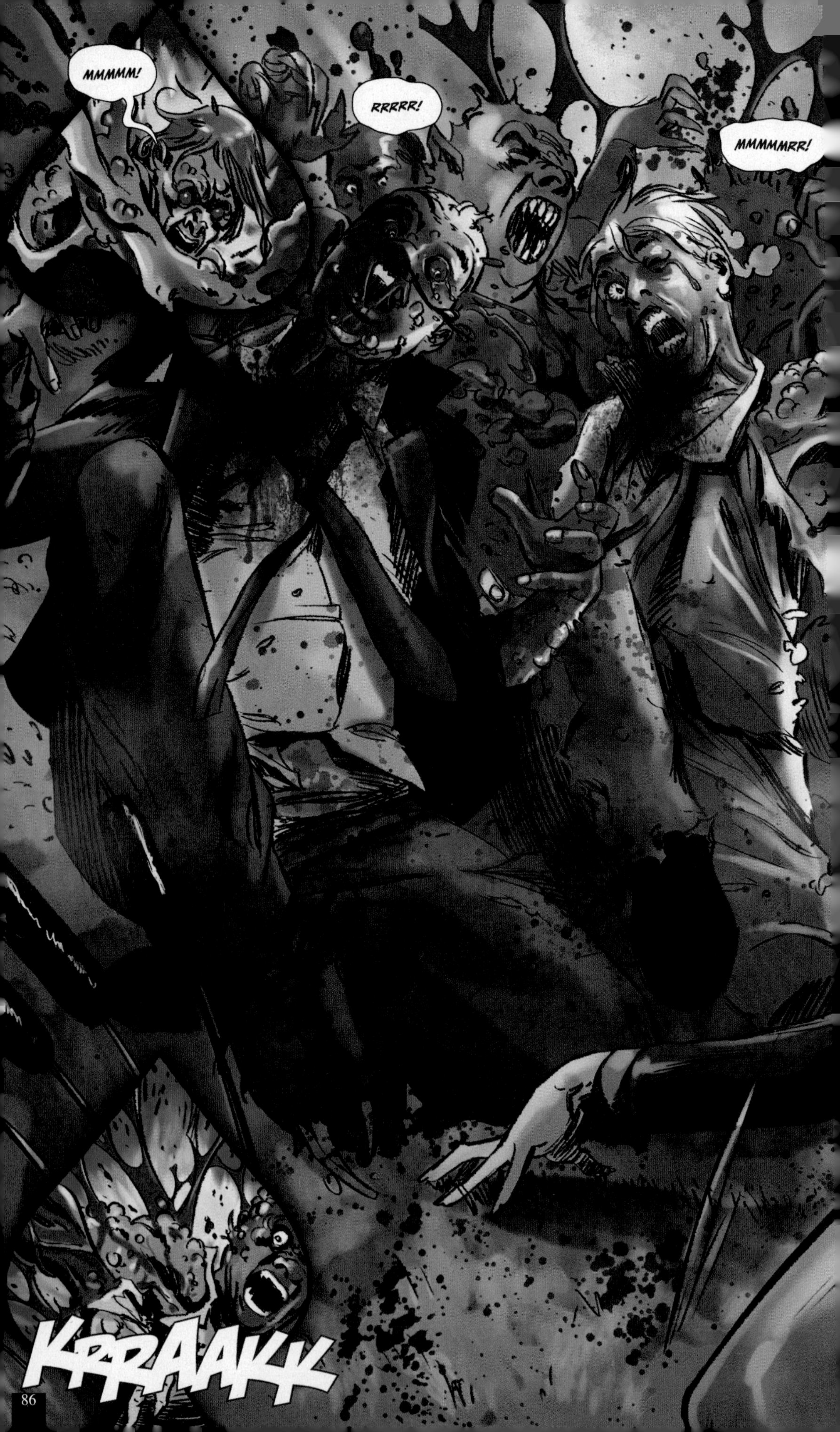
MMMMM!
RRRRR!
MMMMMRR!
KRAAKK

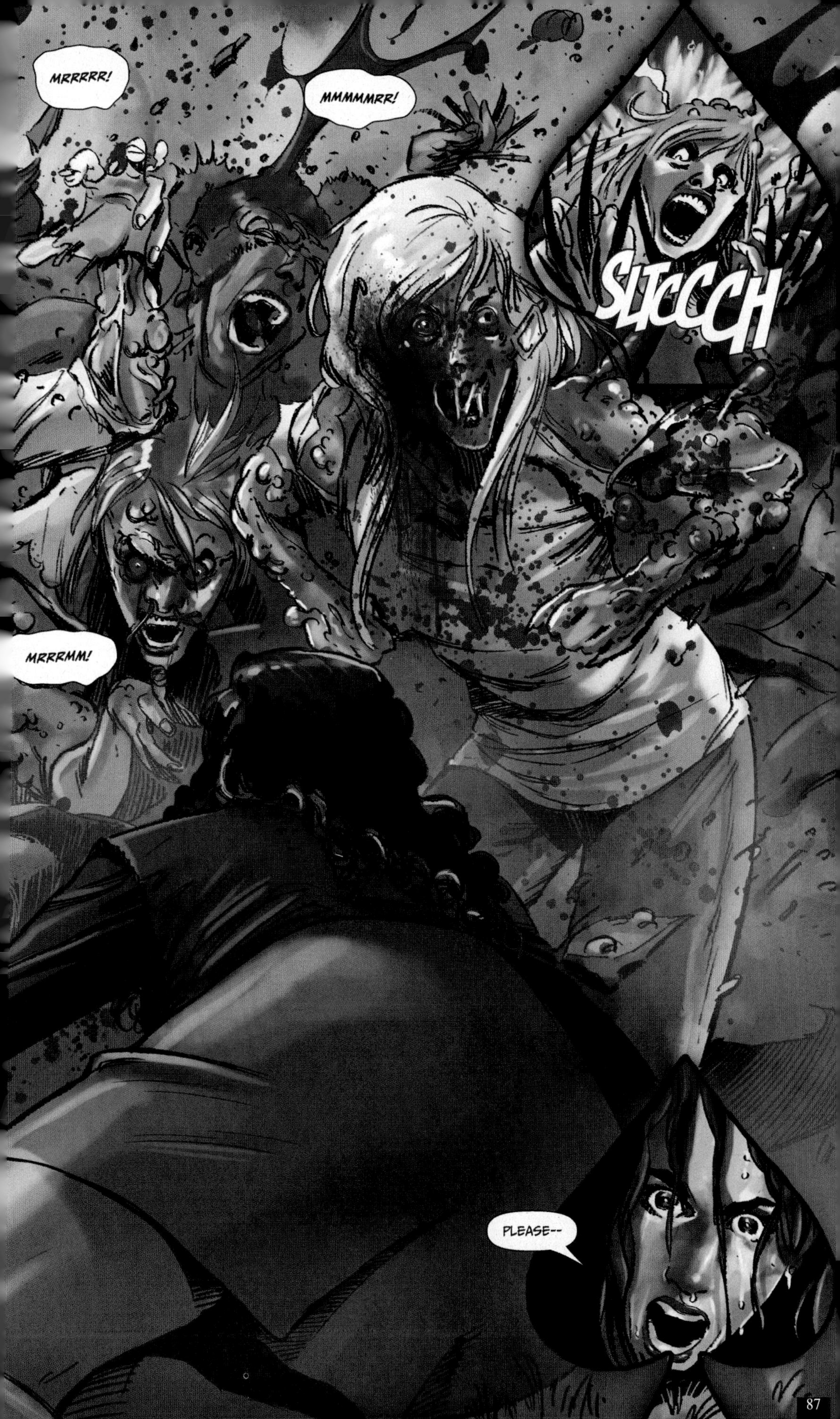
MRRRRR!
MMMMMRR!
SLICCCH
MRRRMM!
PLEASE--

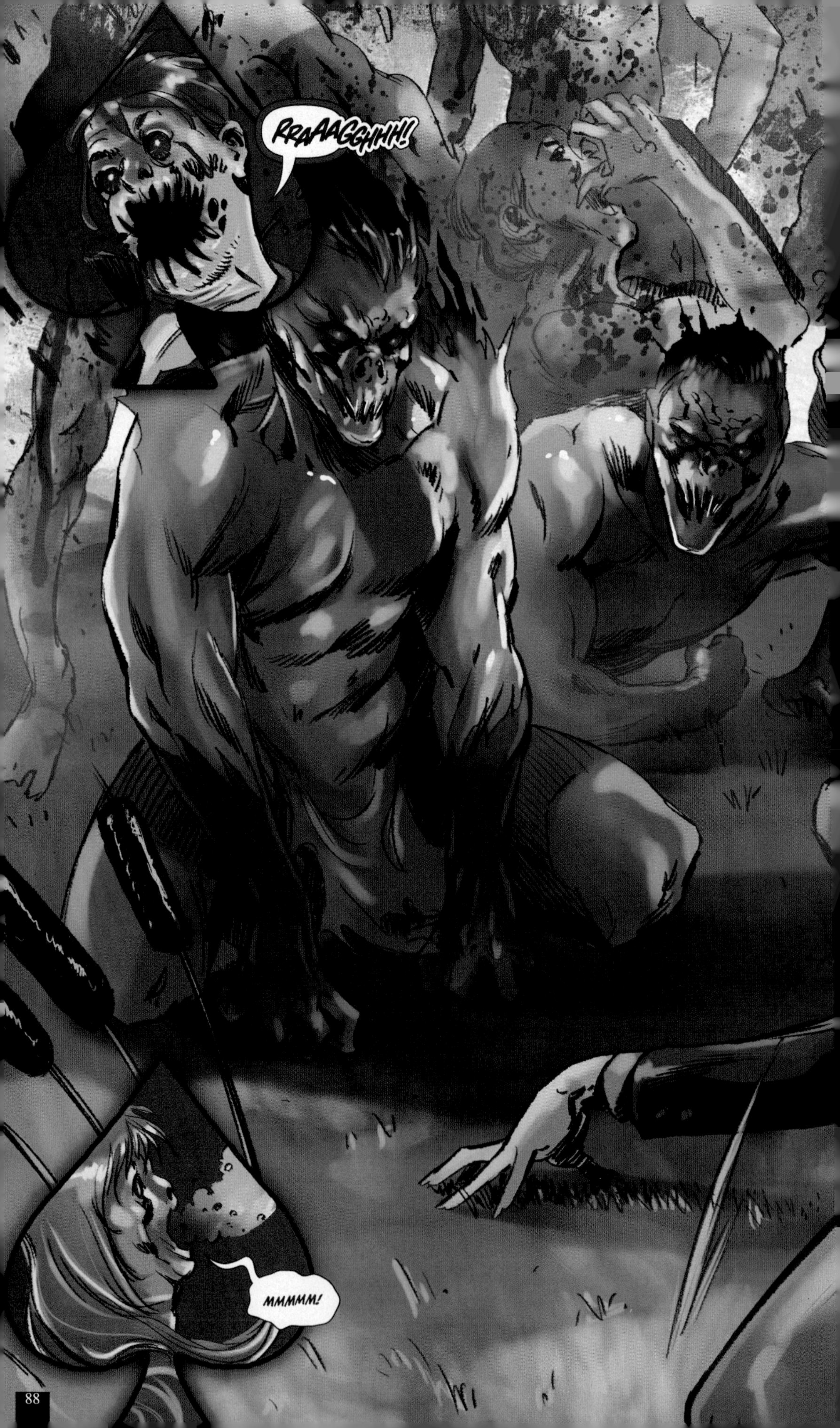
RRAAAGGHHH!
MMMMM!

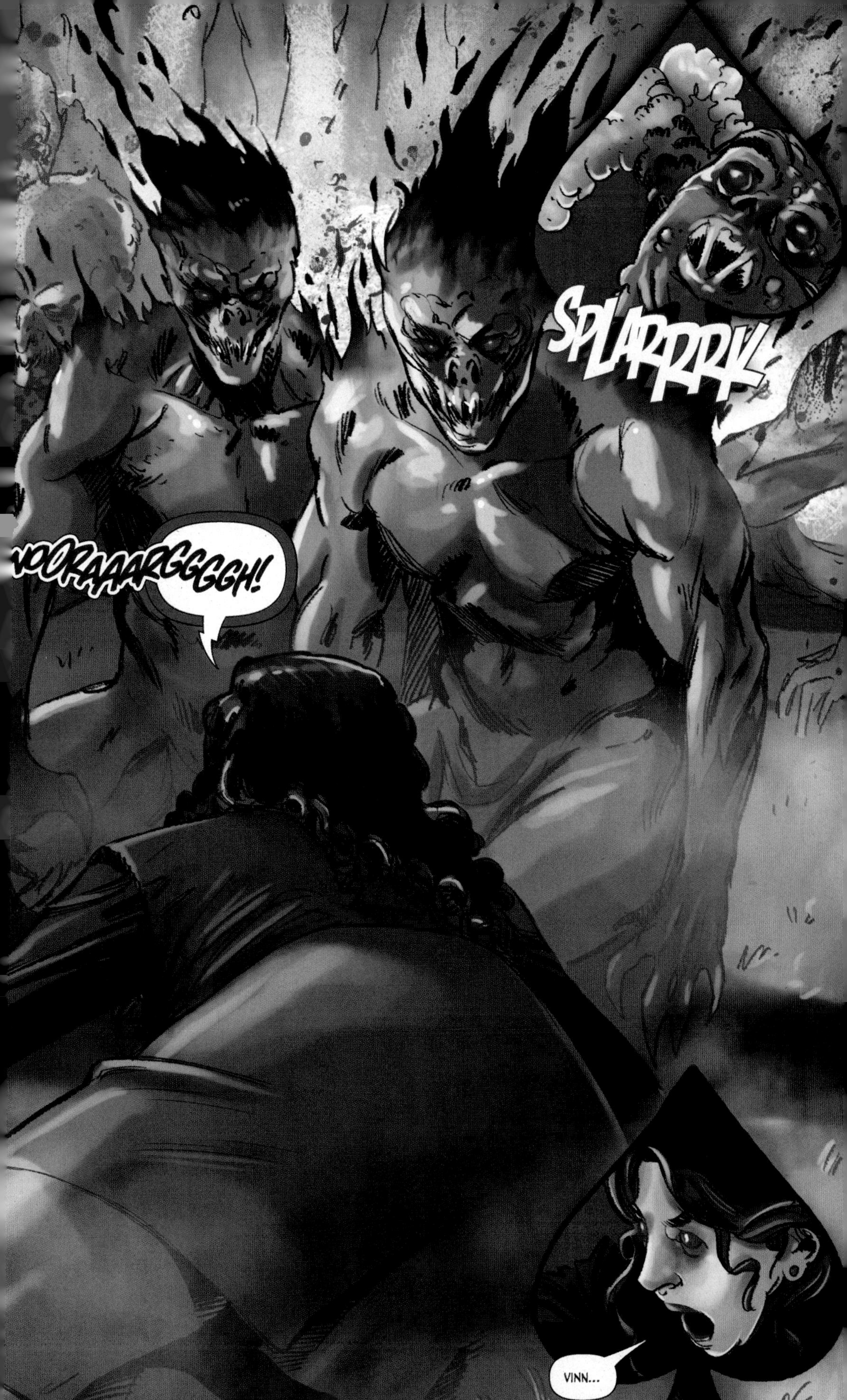
SPLARRRK!
WOORAAARGGGGH!
VINN...

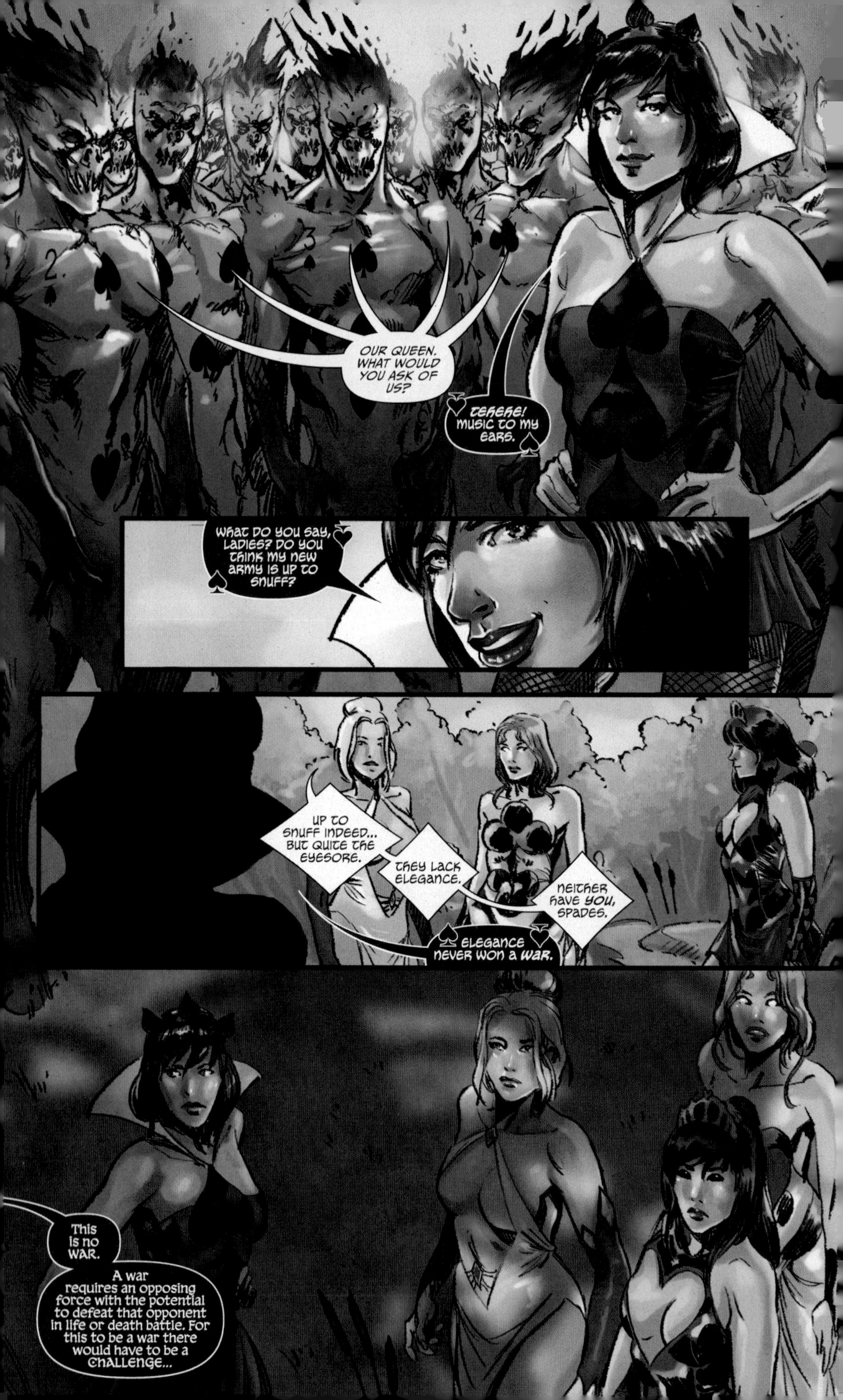
OUR QUEEN. WHAT WOULD YOU ASK OF US?
TEHEHE! MUSIC TO MY EARS.
WHAT DO YOU SAY, LADIES? DO YOU THINK MY NEW ARMY IS UP TO SNUFF?
UP TO SNUFF INDEED... BUT QUITE THE EYESORE.
THEY LACK ELEGANCE.
NEITHER HAVE YOU, SPADES.
ELEGANCE NEVER WON A WAR.
This is no WAR.
A war requires an opposing force with the potential to defeat that opponent in life or death battle. For this to be a war there would have to be a CHALLENGE...

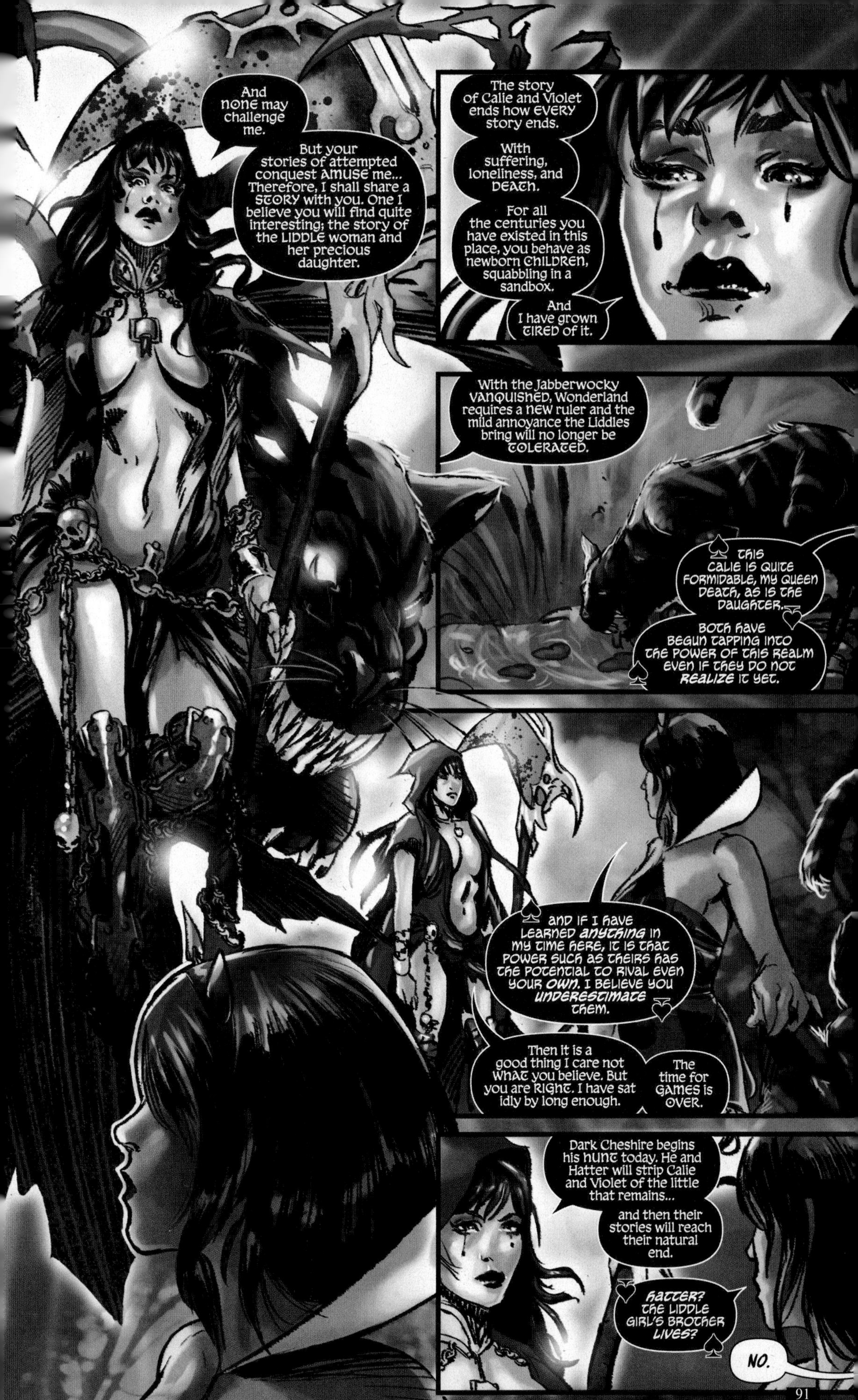

And NONE may challenge me.
But your stories of attempted conquest AMUSE me... Therefore, I shall share a STORY with you. One I believe you will find quite interesting; the story of the LIDDLE woman and her precious daughter.
The story of Calie and Violet ends how EVERY story ends.
With suffering, loneliness, and DEATH.
For all the centuries you have existed in this place, you behave as newborn CHILDREN, squabbling in a sandbox.
And I have grown TIRED of it.
With the Jabberwocky VANQUISHED, Wonderland requires a NEW ruler and the mild annoyance the Liddles bring will no longer be TOLERATED.
THIS CALIE IS QUITE FORMIDABLE, MY QUEEN DEATH, AS IS THE DAUGHTER.
BOTH HAVE BEGUN TAPPING INTO THE POWER OF THIS REALM EVEN IF THEY DO NOT REALIZE IT YET.
AND IF I HAVE LEARNED ANYTHING IN MY TIME HERE, IT IS THAT POWER SUCH AS THEIRS HAS THE POTENTIAL TO RIVAL EVEN YOUR OWN. I BELIEVE YOU UNDERESTIMATE THEM.
Then it is a good thing I care not WHAT you believe. But you are RIGHT. I have sat idly by long enough.
The time for GAMES is OVER.
Dark Cheshire begins his HUNT today. He and Hatter will strip Calie and Violet of the little that remains...
and then their stories will reach their natural end.
HATTER? THE LIDDLE GIRL'S BROTHER LIVES?
NO.

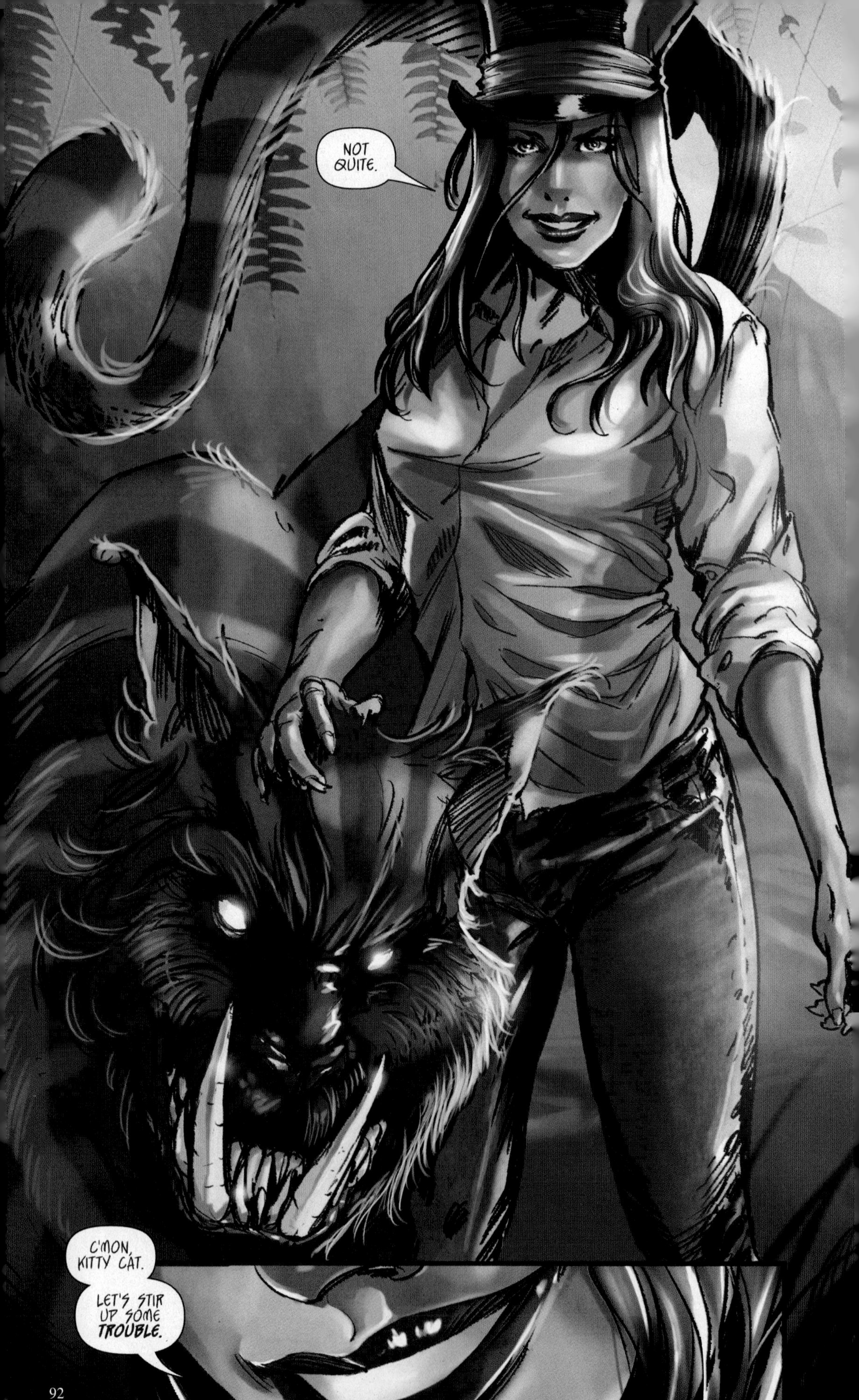

NOT QUITE.
C'MON, KITTY CAT.
LET'S STIR UP SOME **TROUBLE**.

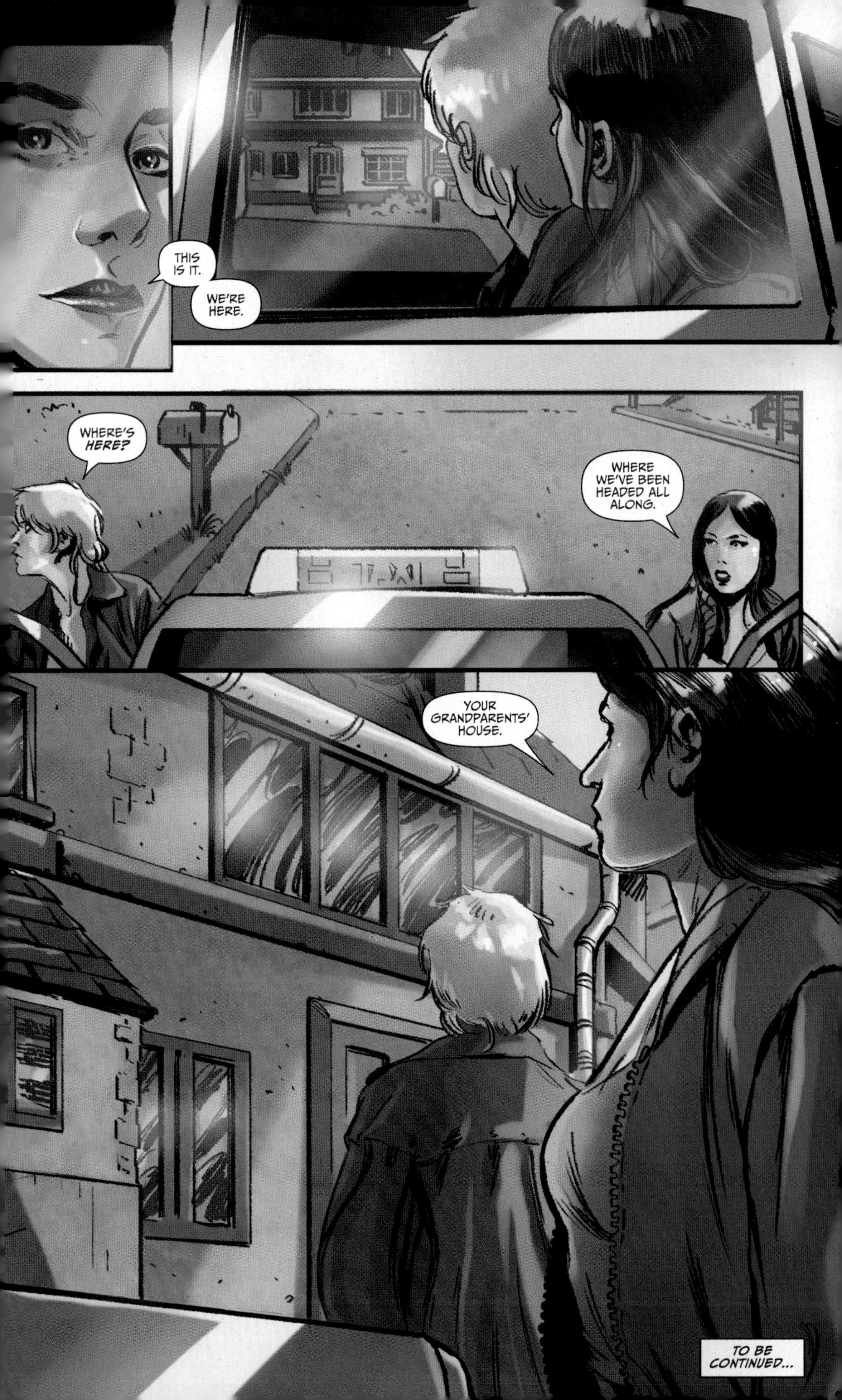
THIS IS IT.
WE'RE HERE.
WHERE'S *HERE?*
WHERE WE'VE BEEN HEADED ALL ALONG.
YOUR GRANDPARENTS' HOUSE.
TO BE CONTINUED...

Chapter Five

WRITER RAVEN GREGORY
PENCILS JG MIRANDA
COLORS LEONARDO PACIAROTTI
LETTERS JIM CAMPBELL

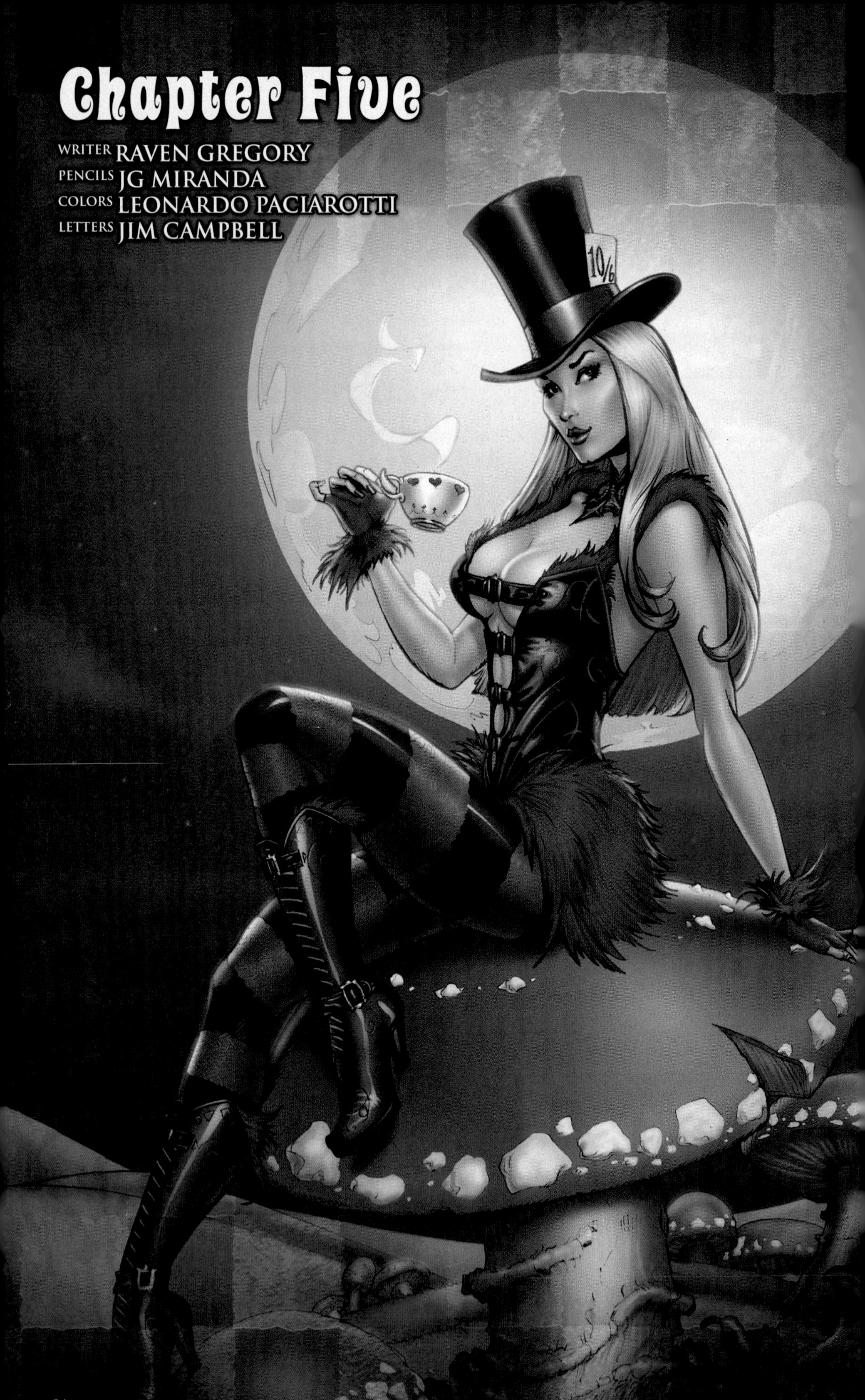
10/6

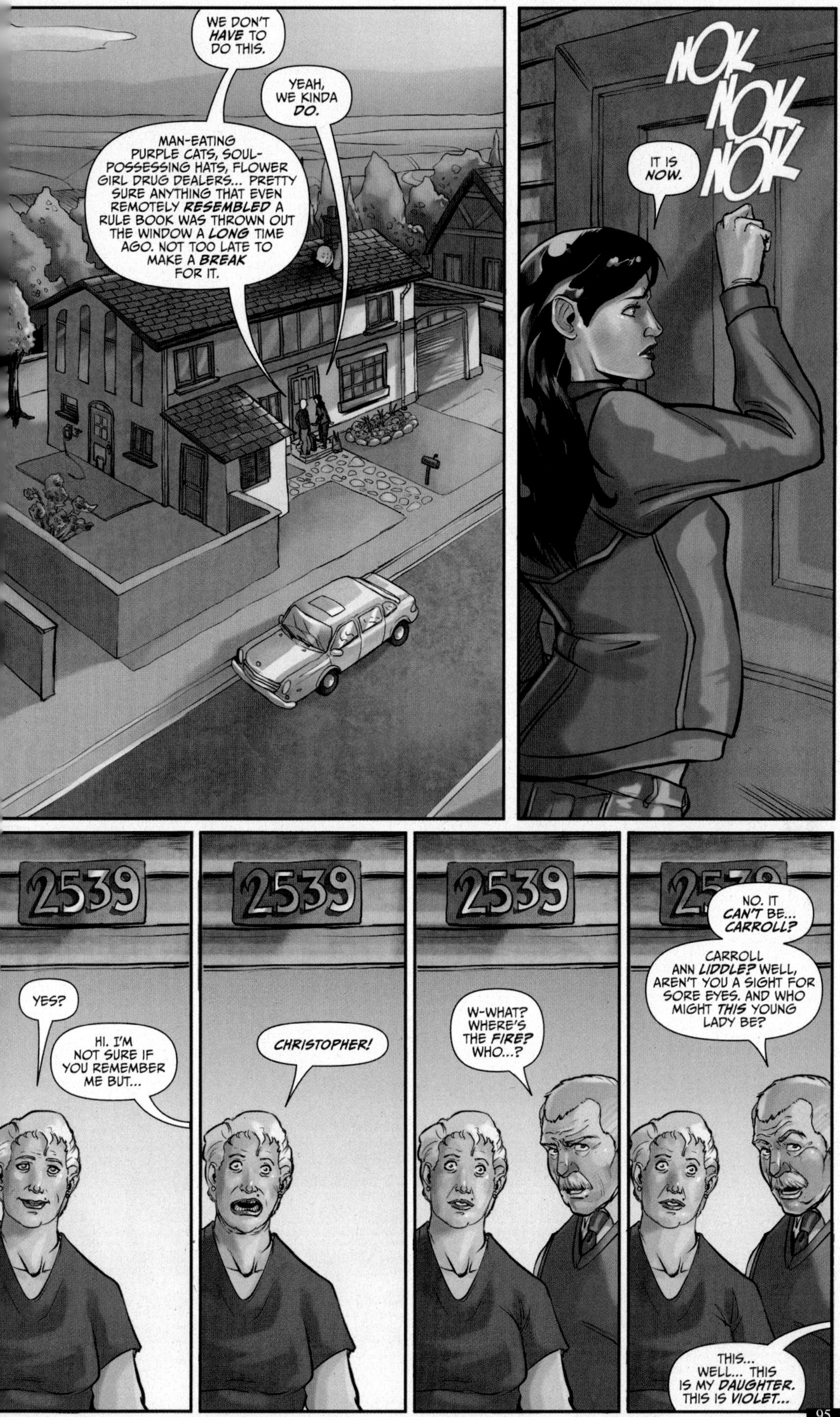
WE DON'T HAVE TO DO THIS.
YEAH, WE KINDA DO.
MAN-EATING PURPLE CATS, SOUL-POSSESSING HATS, FLOWER GIRL DRUG DEALERS... PRETTY SURE ANYTHING THAT EVEN REMOTELY RESEMBLED A RULE BOOK WAS THROWN OUT THE WINDOW A LONG TIME AGO. NOT TOO LATE TO MAKE A BREAK FOR IT.
NOK NOK NOK
IT IS NOW.
2539
YES?
HI. I'M NOT SURE IF YOU REMEMBER ME BUT...
2539
CHRISTOPHER!
2539
W-WHAT? WHERE'S THE FIRE? WHO...?
NO. IT CAN'T BE... CARROLL?
CARROLL ANN LIDDLE? WELL, AREN'T YOU A SIGHT FOR SORE EYES. AND WHO MIGHT THIS YOUNG LADY BE?
THIS... WELL... THIS IS MY DAUGHTER. THIS IS VIOLET...

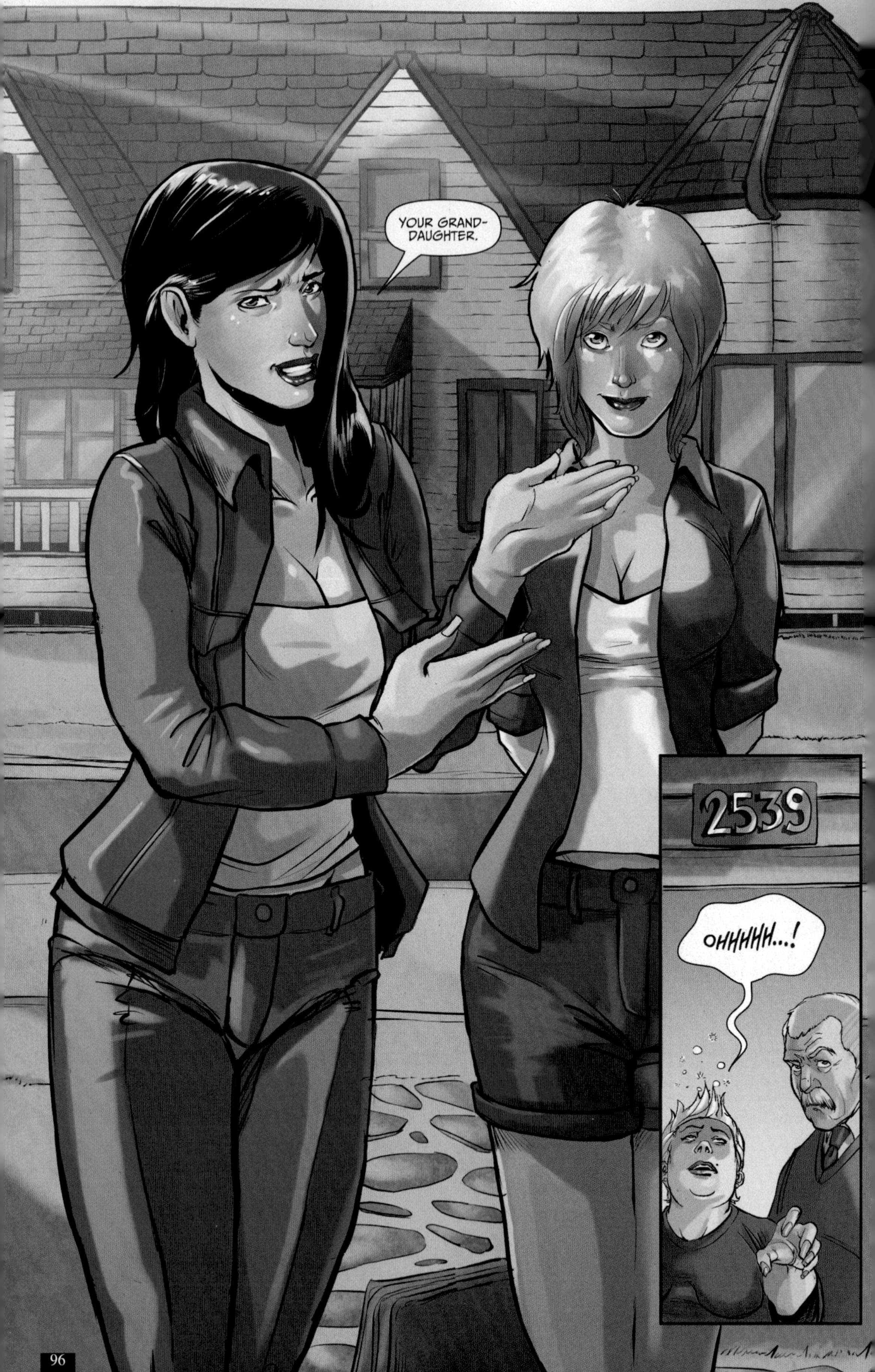
YOUR GRAND-DAUGHTER.
2539
OHHHHH...!

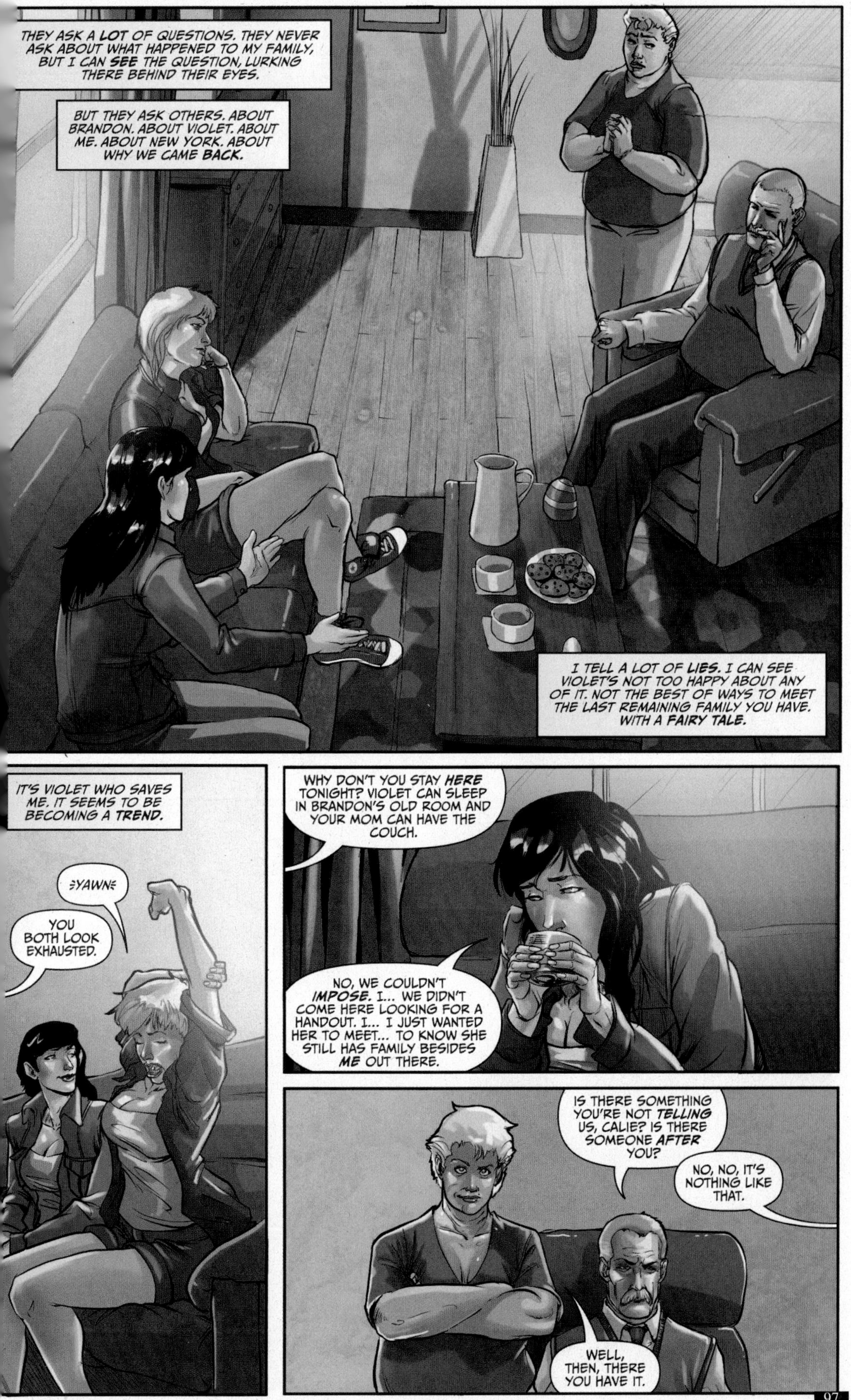

THEY ASK A LOT OF QUESTIONS. THEY NEVER ASK ABOUT WHAT HAPPENED TO MY FAMILY, BUT I CAN SEE THE QUESTION, LURKING THERE BEHIND THEIR EYES.
BUT THEY ASK OTHERS. ABOUT BRANDON. ABOUT VIOLET. ABOUT ME. ABOUT NEW YORK. ABOUT WHY WE CAME BACK.
I TELL A LOT OF LIES. I CAN SEE VIOLET'S NOT TOO HAPPY ABOUT ANY OF IT. NOT THE BEST OF WAYS TO MEET THE LAST REMAINING FAMILY YOU HAVE. WITH A FAIRY TALE.
IT'S VIOLET WHO SAVES ME. IT SEEMS TO BE BECOMING A TREND.
YAWN
YOU BOTH LOOK EXHAUSTED.
WHY DON'T YOU STAY HERE TONIGHT? VIOLET CAN SLEEP IN BRANDON'S OLD ROOM AND YOUR MOM CAN HAVE THE COUCH.
NO, WE COULDN'T IMPOSE. I... WE DIDN'T COME HERE LOOKING FOR A HANDOUT. I... I JUST WANTED HER TO MEET... TO KNOW SHE STILL HAS FAMILY BESIDES ME OUT THERE.
IS THERE SOMETHING YOU'RE NOT TELLING US, CALIE? IS THERE SOMEONE AFTER YOU?
NO, NO, IT'S NOTHING LIKE THAT.
WELL, THEN, THERE YOU HAVE IT.

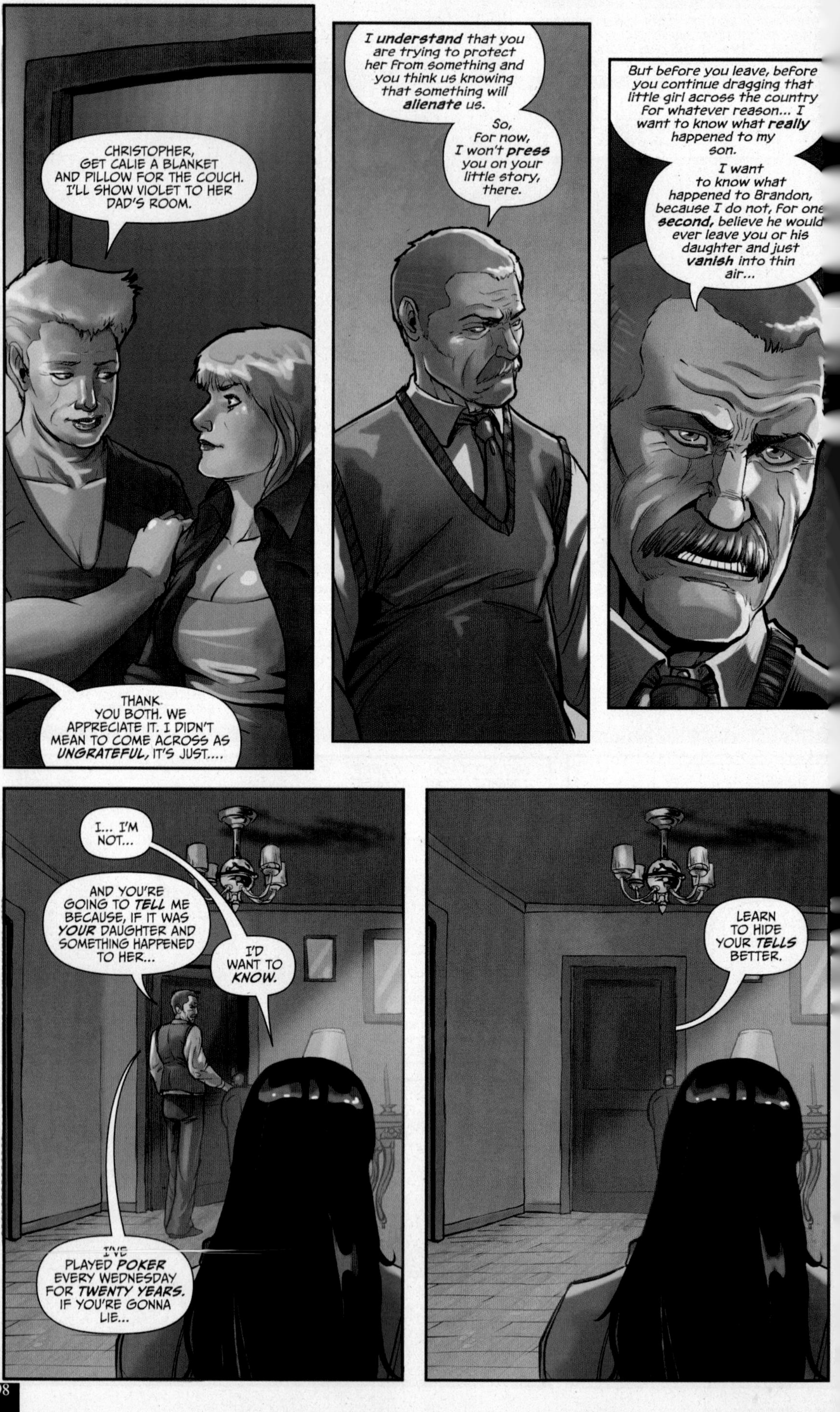
CHRISTOPHER, GET CALIE A BLANKET AND PILLOW FOR THE COUCH. I'LL SHOW VIOLET TO HER DAD'S ROOM.
THANK YOU BOTH. WE APPRECIATE IT. I DIDN'T MEAN TO COME ACROSS AS UNGRATEFUL, IT'S JUST....
I understand that you are trying to protect her from something and you think us knowing that something will alienate us.
So, for now, I won't press you on your little story, there.
But before you leave, before you continue dragging that little girl across the country for whatever reason... I want to know what really happened to my son.
I want to know what happened to Brandon, because I do not, for one second, believe he would ever leave you or his daughter and just vanish into thin air...
I... I'M NOT...
AND YOU'RE GOING TO TELL ME BECAUSE, IF IT WAS YOUR DAUGHTER AND SOMETHING HAPPENED TO HER...
I'D WANT TO KNOW.
I'VE PLAYED POKER EVERY WEDNESDAY FOR TWENTY YEARS. IF YOU'RE GONNA LIE...
LEARN TO HIDE YOUR TELLS BETTER.

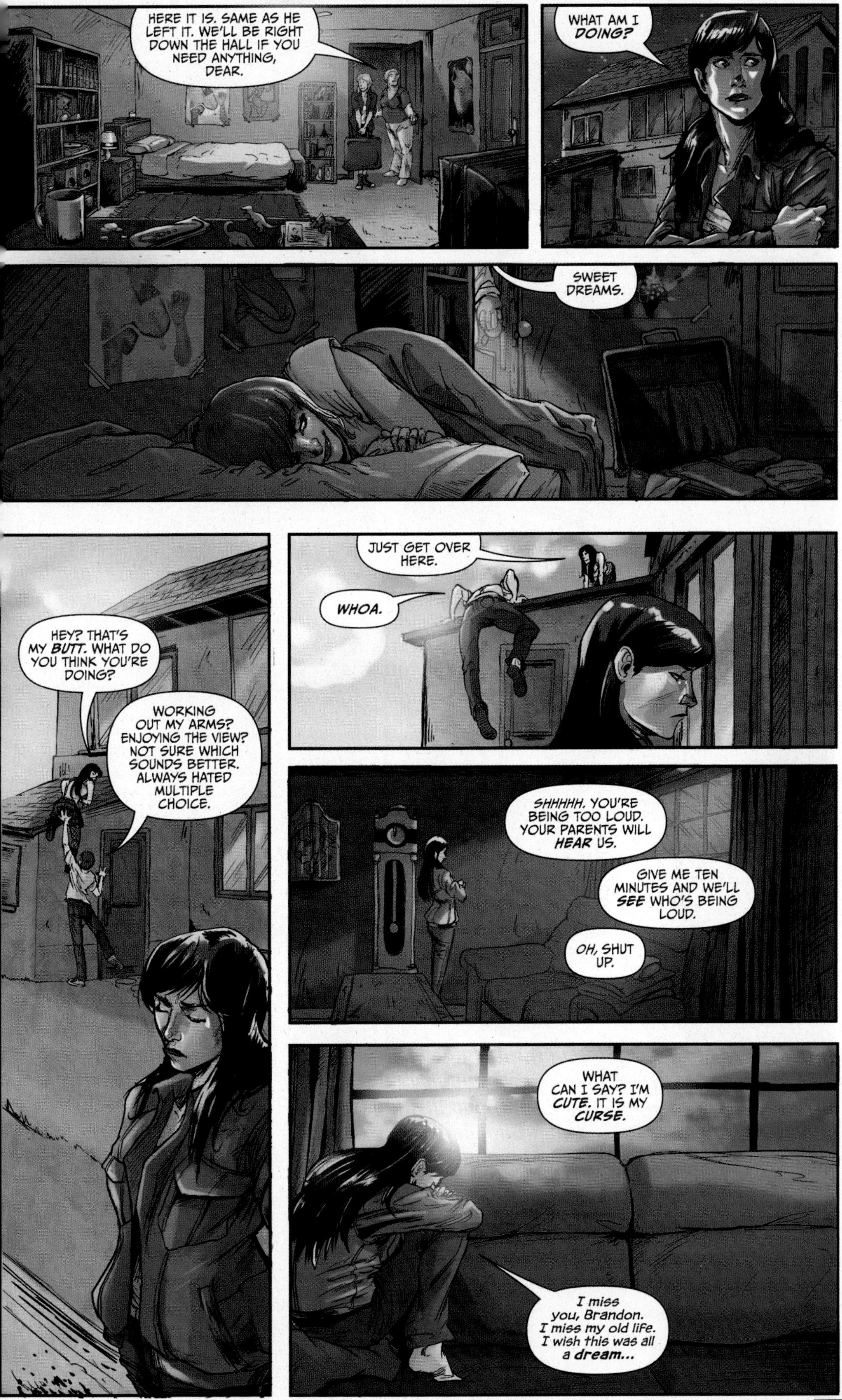
HERE IT IS. SAME AS HE LEFT IT. WE'LL BE RIGHT DOWN THE HALL IF YOU NEED ANYTHING, DEAR.
WHAT AM I DOING?
SWEET DREAMS.
HEY? THAT'S MY BUTT. WHAT DO YOU THINK YOU'RE DOING?
WORKING OUT MY ARMS? ENJOYING THE VIEW? NOT SURE WHICH SOUNDS BETTER. ALWAYS HATED MULTIPLE CHOICE.
JUST GET OVER HERE.
WHOA.
SHHHHH. YOU'RE BEING TOO LOUD. YOUR PARENTS WILL HEAR US.
GIVE ME TEN MINUTES AND WE'LL SEE WHO'S BEING LOUD.
OH, SHUT UP.
WHAT CAN I SAY? I'M CUTE. IT IS MY CURSE.
I miss you, Brandon. I miss my old life. I wish this was all a dream...

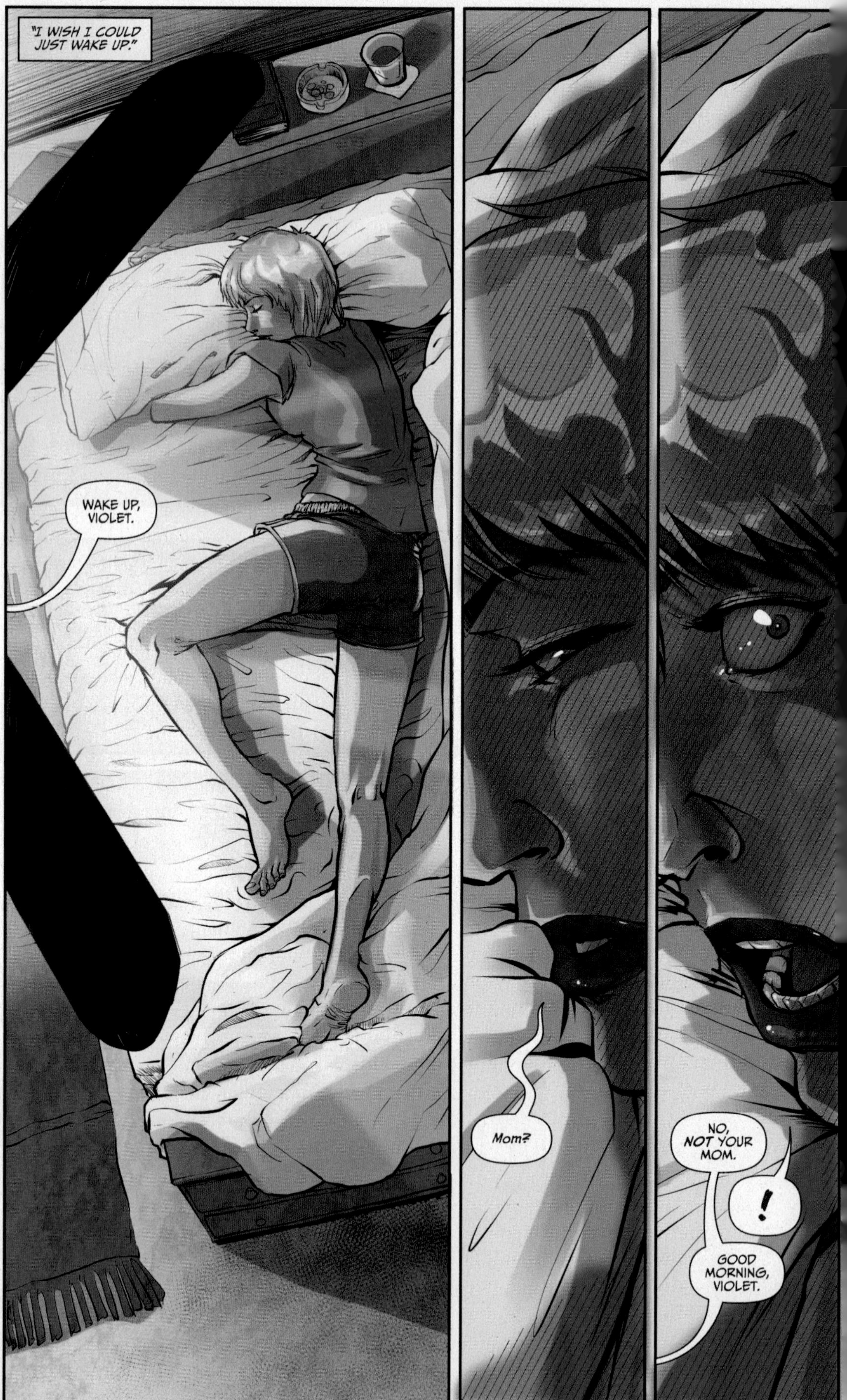
"I WISH I COULD JUST WAKE UP."
WAKE UP, VIOLET.
Mom?
NO, NOT YOUR MOM.
!
GOOD MORNING, VIOLET.

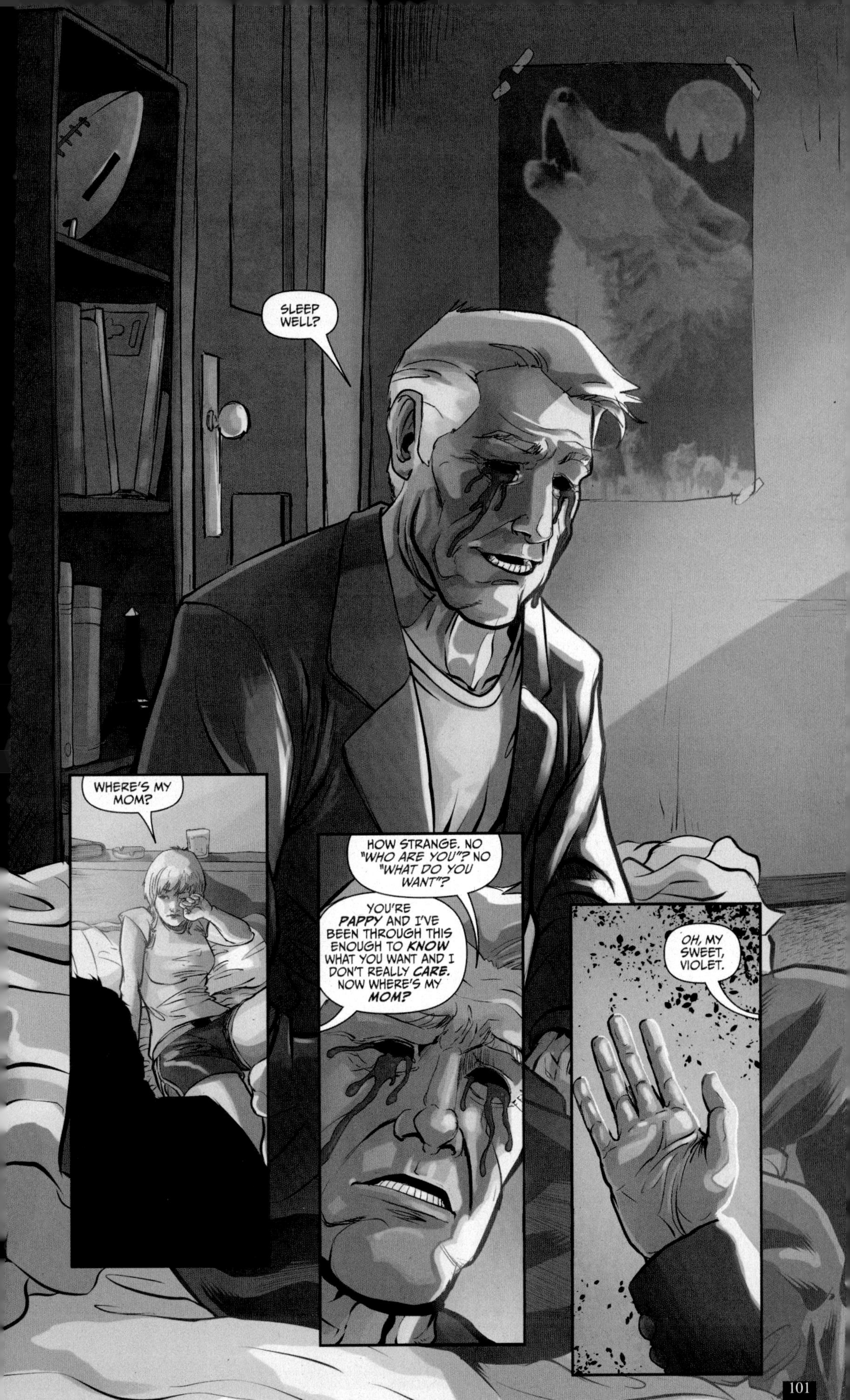
SLEEP WELL?
WHERE'S MY MOM?
HOW STRANGE. NO "WHO ARE YOU"? NO "WHAT DO YOU WANT"?
YOU'RE PAPPY AND I'VE BEEN THROUGH THIS ENOUGH TO KNOW WHAT YOU WANT AND I DON'T REALLY CARE. NOW WHERE'S MY MOM?
OH, MY SWEET, VIOLET.

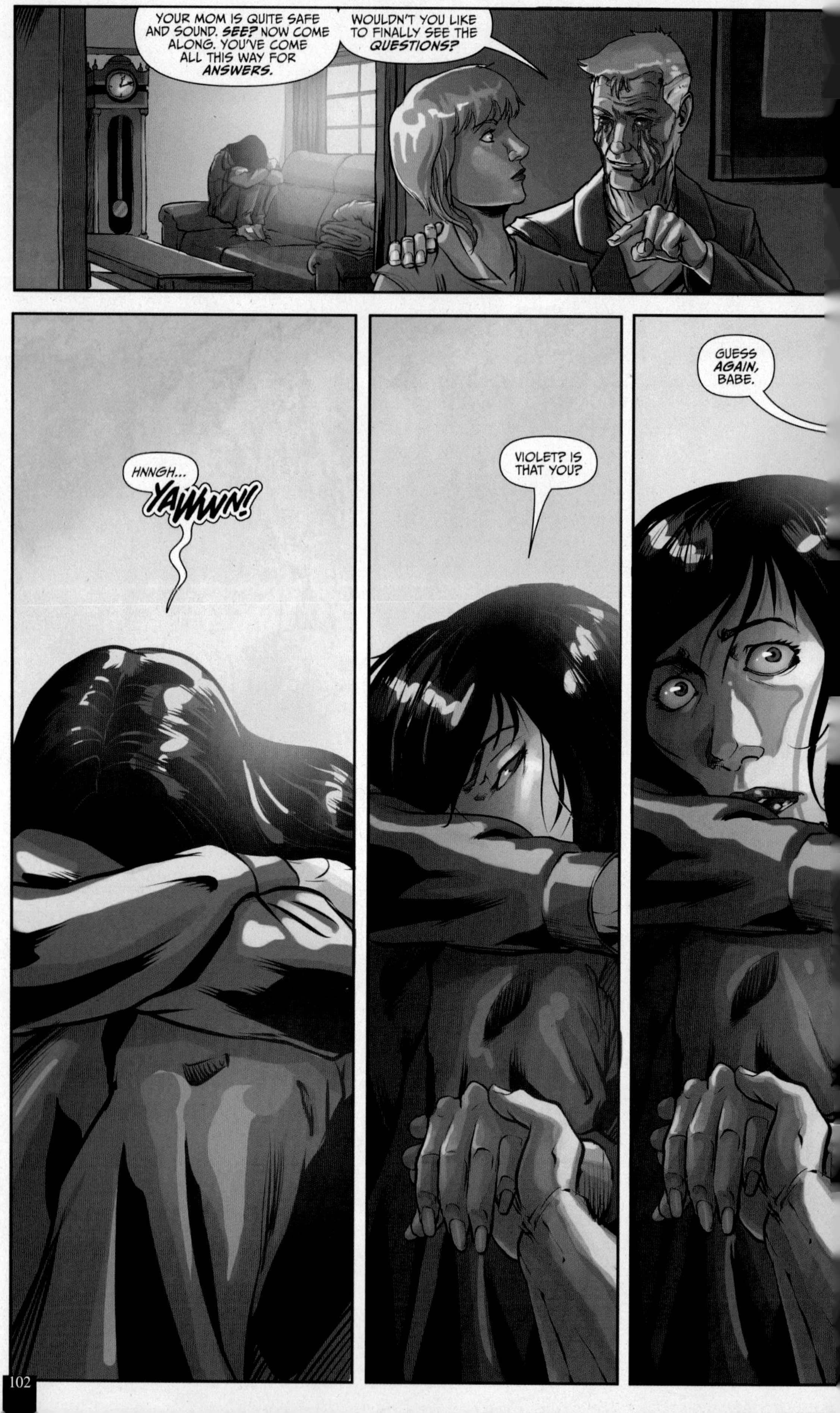
YOUR MOM IS QUITE SAFE AND SOUND. SEE? NOW COME ALONG. YOU'VE COME ALL THIS WAY FOR ANSWERS.
WOULDN'T YOU LIKE TO FINALLY SEE THE QUESTIONS?
HNNGH...
YAWWN!
VIOLET? IS THAT YOU?
GUESS AGAIN, BABE.

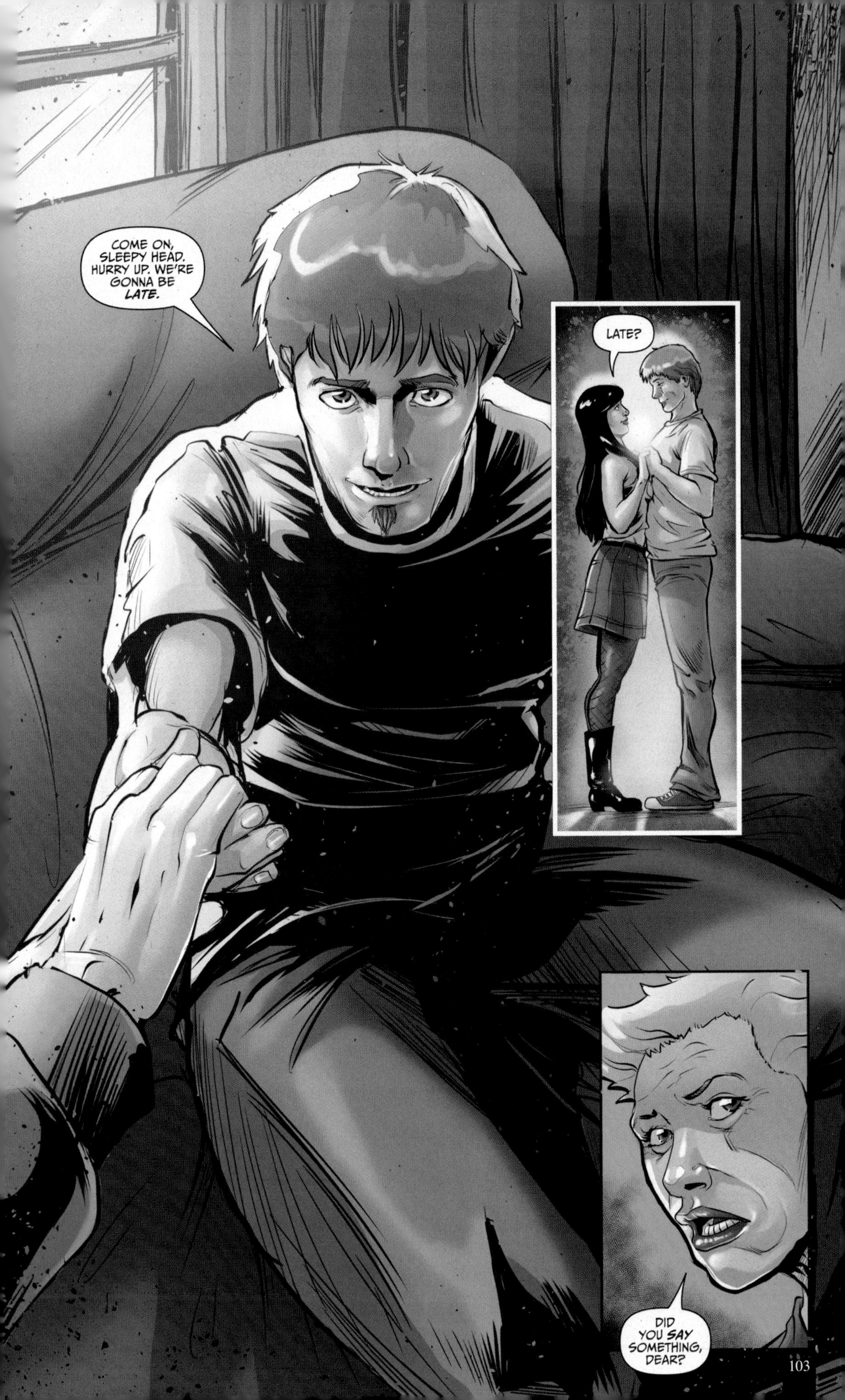
COME ON, SLEEPY HEAD. HURRY UP. WE'RE GONNA BE LATE.
LATE?
DID YOU SAY SOMETHING, DEAR?

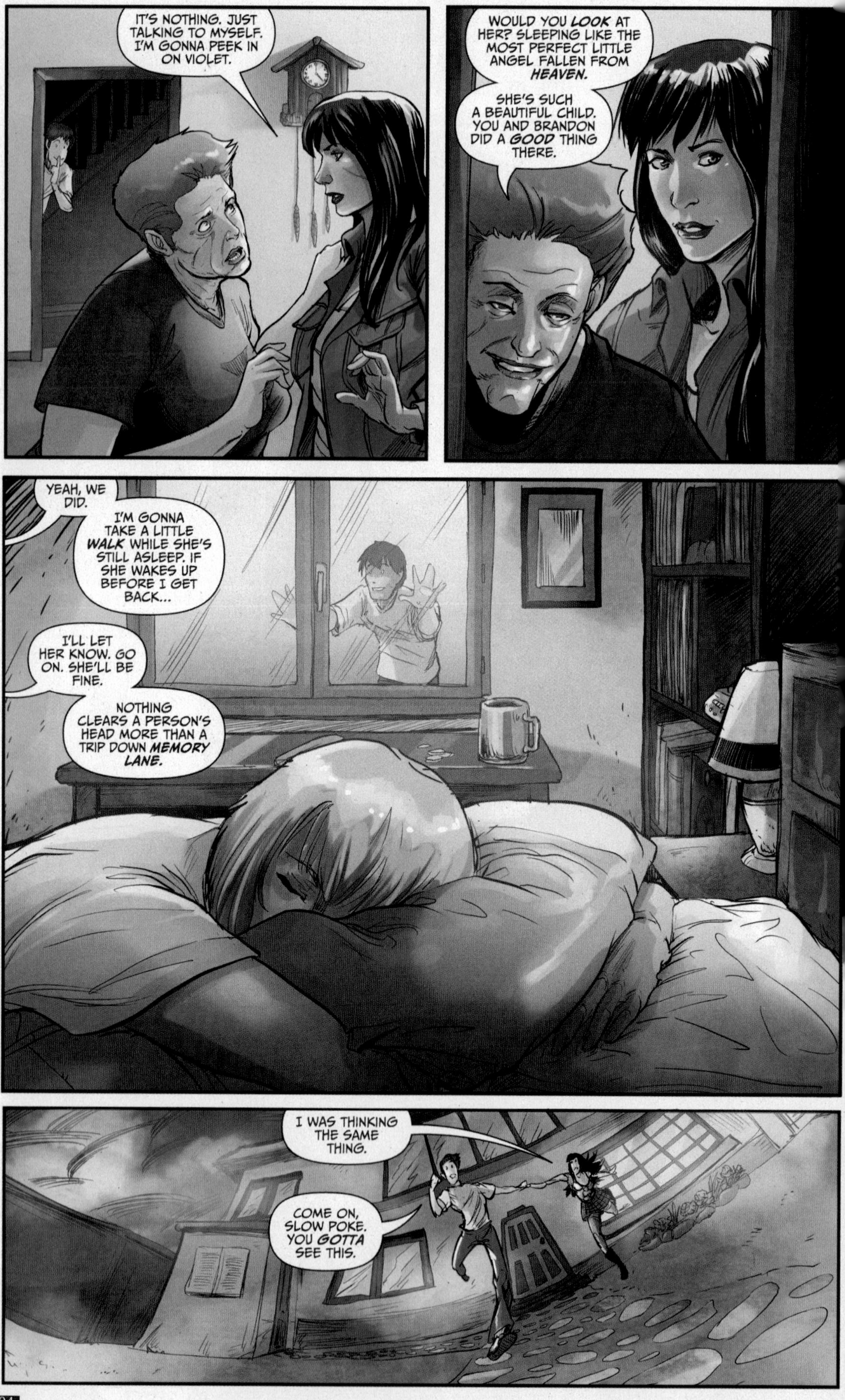
IT'S NOTHING. JUST TALKING TO MYSELF. I'M GONNA PEEK IN ON VIOLET.
WOULD YOU LOOK AT HER? SLEEPING LIKE THE MOST PERFECT LITTLE ANGEL FALLEN FROM HEAVEN.
SHE'S SUCH A BEAUTIFUL CHILD. YOU AND BRANDON DID A GOOD THING THERE.
YEAH, WE DID.
I'M GONNA TAKE A LITTLE WALK WHILE SHE'S STILL ASLEEP. IF SHE WAKES UP BEFORE I GET BACK...
I'LL LET HER KNOW. GO ON. SHE'LL BE FINE.
NOTHING CLEARS A PERSON'S HEAD MORE THAN A TRIP DOWN MEMORY LANE.
I WAS THINKING THE SAME THING.
COME ON, SLOW POKE. YOU GOTTA SEE THIS.

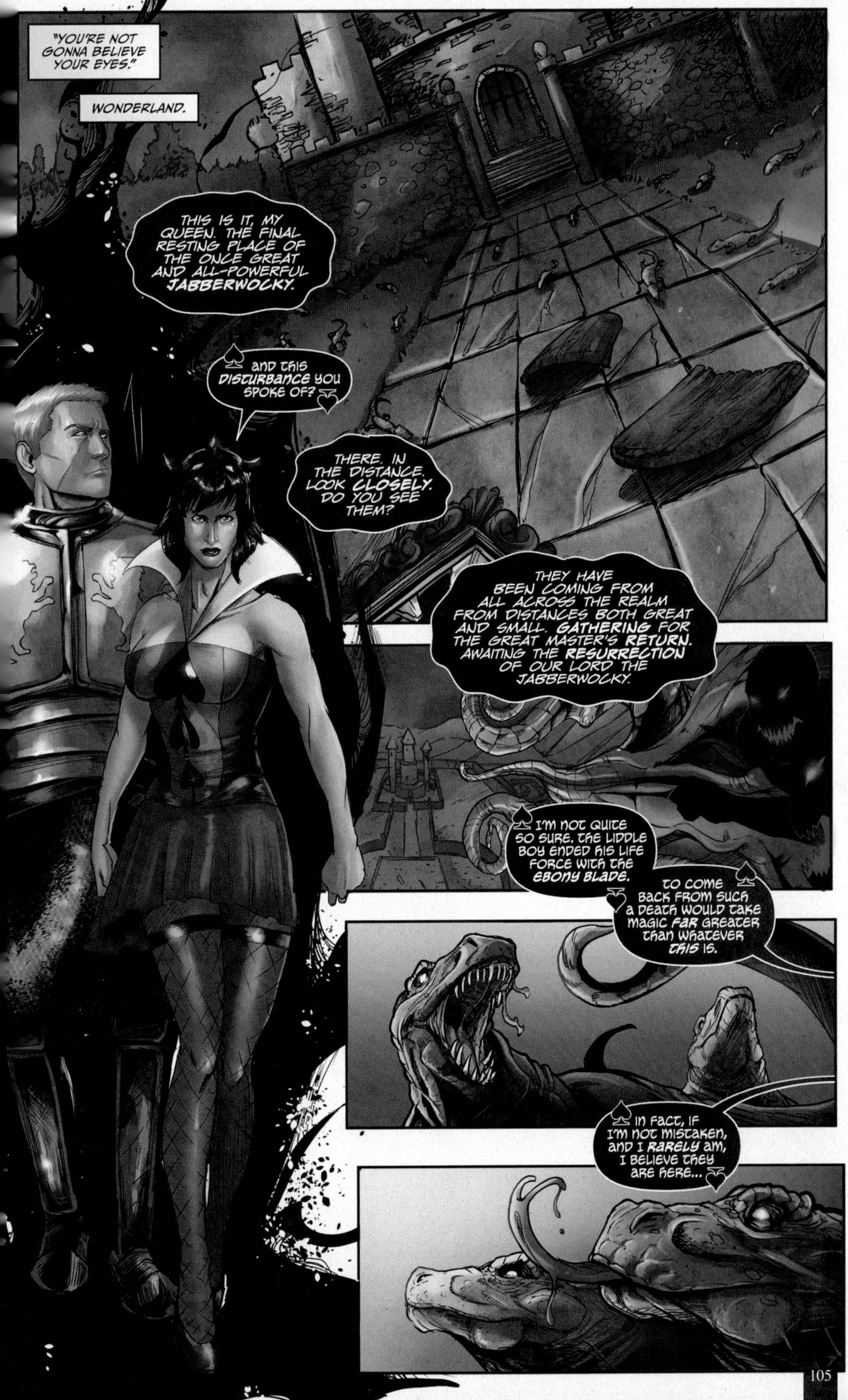

"YOU'RE NOT GONNA BELIEVE YOUR EYES."
WONDERLAND.
THIS IS IT, MY QUEEN. THE FINAL RESTING PLACE OF THE ONCE GREAT AND ALL-POWERFUL JABBERWOCKY.
AND THIS DISTURBANCE YOU SPOKE OF?
THERE. IN THE DISTANCE. LOOK CLOSELY. DO YOU SEE THEM?
THEY HAVE BEEN COMING FROM ALL ACROSS THE REALM FROM DISTANCES BOTH GREAT AND SMALL. GATHERING FOR THE GREAT MASTER'S RETURN. AWAITING THE RESURRECTION OF OUR LORD THE JABBERWOCKY.
I'M NOT QUITE SO SURE. THE LIDDLE BOY ENDED HIS LIFE FORCE WITH THE EBONY BLADE.
TO COME BACK FROM SUCH A DEATH WOULD TAKE MAGIC FAR GREATER THAN WHATEVER THIS IS.
IN FACT, IF I'M NOT MISTAKEN, AND I RARELY AM, I BELIEVE THEY ARE HERE...

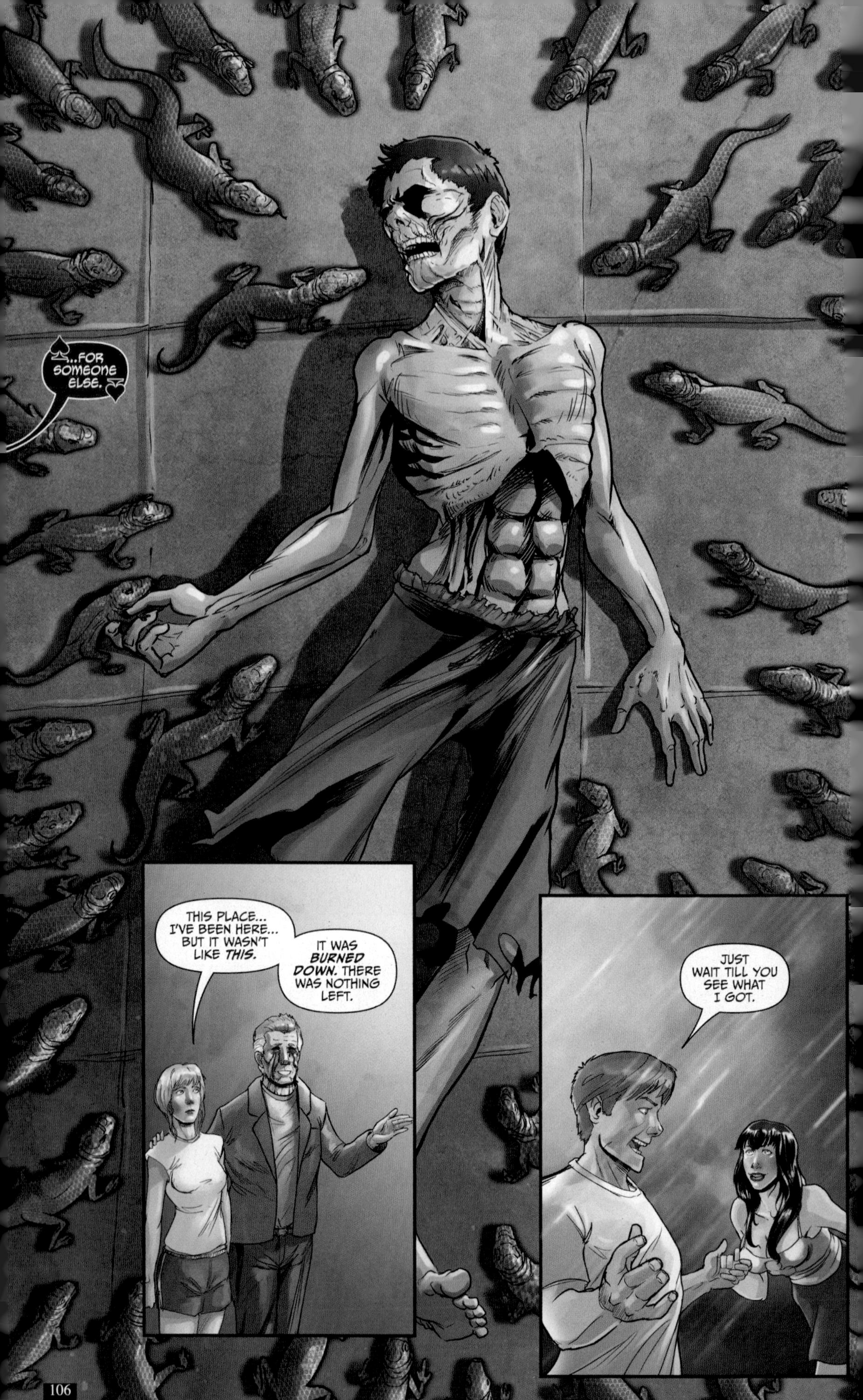
...FOR SOMEONE ELSE.
THIS PLACE... I'VE BEEN HERE... BUT IT WASN'T LIKE THIS.
IT WAS BURNED DOWN. THERE WAS NOTHING LEFT.
JUST WAIT TILL YOU SEE WHAT I GOT.

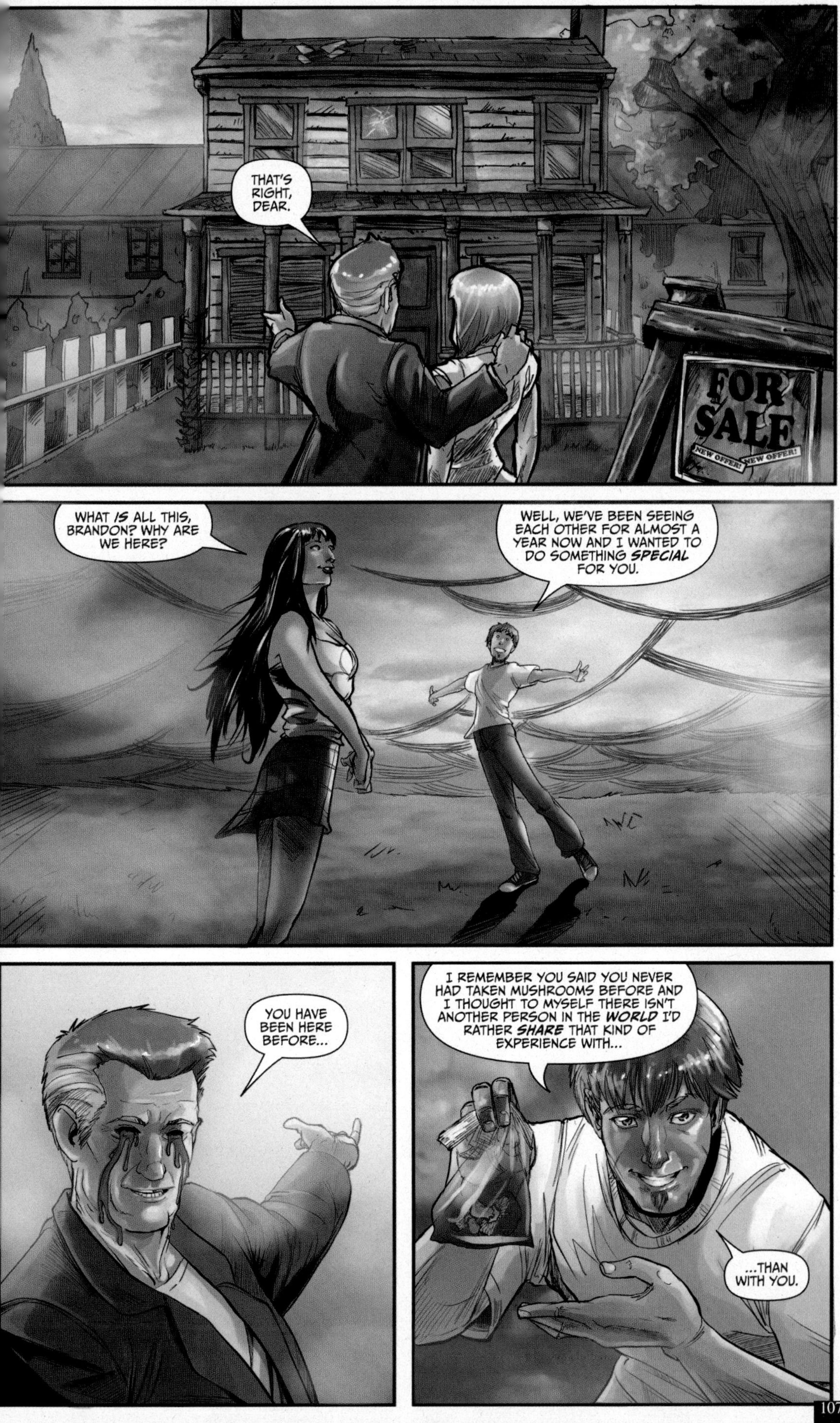
THAT'S RIGHT, DEAR.
FOR SALE
NEW OFFER! NEW OFFER!
WHAT *IS* ALL THIS, BRANDON? WHY ARE WE HERE?
WELL, WE'VE BEEN SEEING EACH OTHER FOR ALMOST A YEAR NOW AND I WANTED TO DO SOMETHING *SPECIAL* FOR YOU.
YOU HAVE BEEN HERE BEFORE...
I REMEMBER YOU SAID YOU NEVER HAD TAKEN MUSHROOMS BEFORE AND I THOUGHT TO MYSELF THERE ISN'T ANOTHER PERSON IN THE *WORLD* I'D RATHER *SHARE* THAT KIND OF EXPERIENCE WITH...
...THAN WITH YOU.

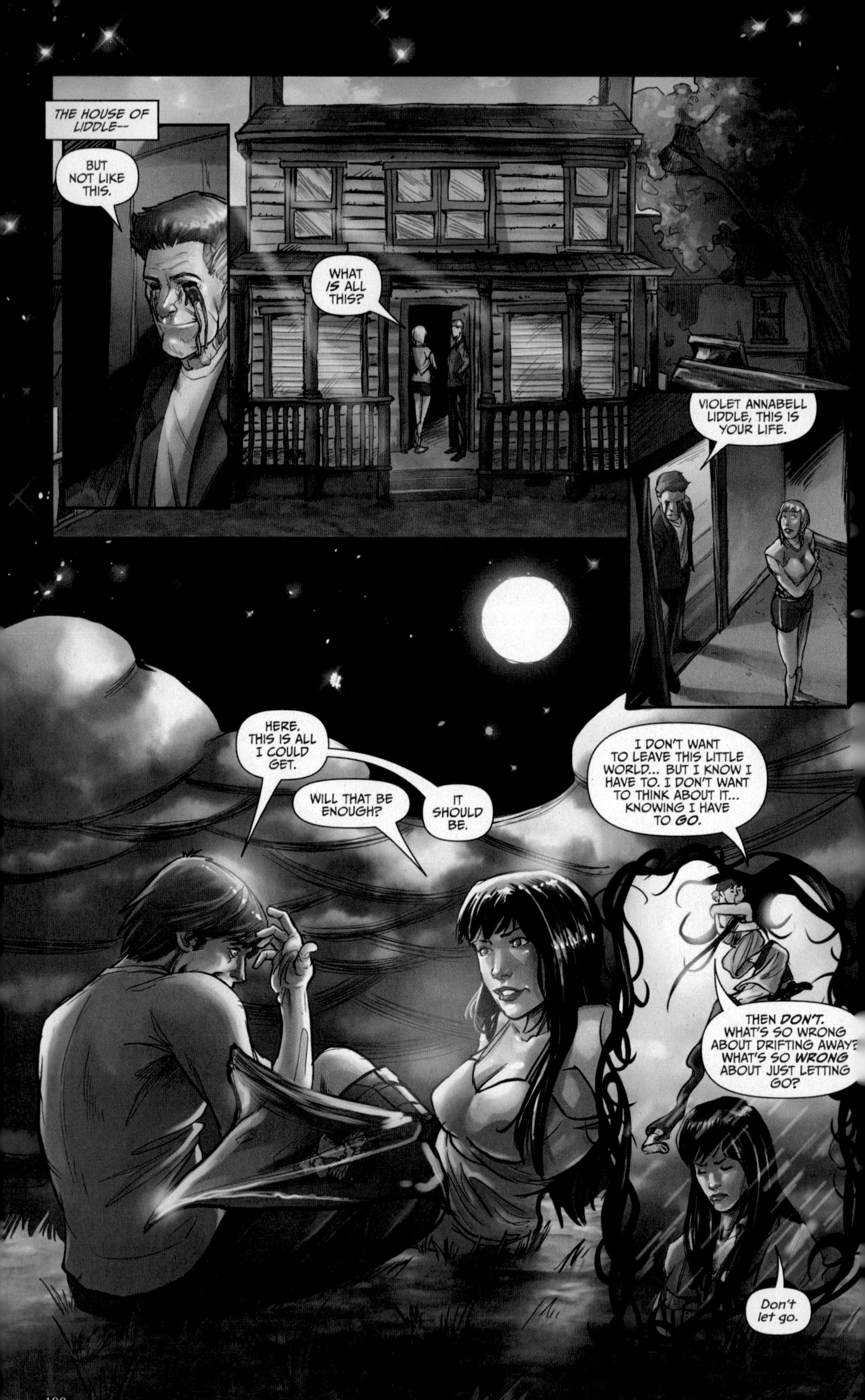

THE HOUSE OF LIDDLE--
BUT NOT LIKE THIS.
WHAT IS ALL THIS?
VIOLET ANNABELL LIDDLE, THIS IS YOUR LIFE.
HERE. THIS IS ALL I COULD GET.
WILL THAT BE ENOUGH?
IT SHOULD BE.
I DON'T WANT TO LEAVE THIS LITTLE WORLD... BUT I KNOW I HAVE TO. I DON'T WANT TO THINK ABOUT IT... KNOWING I HAVE TO GO.
THEN DON'T. WHAT'S SO WRONG ABOUT DRIFTING AWAY? WHAT'S SO WRONG ABOUT JUST LETTING GO?
Don't let go.

WELL, NOT REALLY *YOUR* LIFE. MORE THE LIFE OF YOUR MOTHER.

ACTUALLY, NOT REALLY *HER* LIFE, EITHER.

MORE HE VARIOUS *DEATHS* OF YOUR MOTHER'S LIFE.

LEWIS?

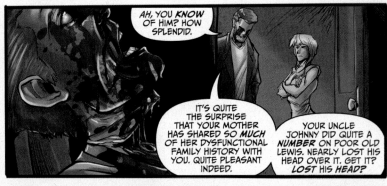

AH, YOU *KNOW* OF HIM? HOW SPLENDID.

IT'S QUITE THE SURPRISE THAT YOUR MOTHER HAS SHARED SO *MUCH* OF HER DYSFUNCTIONAL FAMILY HISTORY WITH YOU. QUITE PLEASANT INDEED.

YOUR UNCLE JOHNNY DID QUITE A *NUMBER* ON POOR OLD LEWIS. NEARLY LOST HIS HEAD OVER IT. GET IT? *LOST* HIS *HEAD?*

SO, DO YOU HANG OUT AT THE RACKET BALL COURTS OFTEN?

SOMETIMES. NOT REALLY A LUNCH ROOM KIND OF GUY. YOU?

BEEN AN OUTCAST ALL MY LIFE.

AND HOW'S *THAT* WORKING OUT FOR YOU?

BUT NOT BEFORE FINDING HIS FATHER'S *WHORE*. SNAPPED HER NECK WITH HIS *BARE HANDS.* SPEAKING OF WHICH.

HEY, ALICE, HOW'S IT HANGING?

CAN WE JUST GET *ON* WITH WHATEVER THIS IS?

WHAT? TOO *SOON?*

NOT TO WORRY, LITTLE VIOLET. AS BAD AS THINGS WERE...

THAT'S IT, ISN'T IT? IT'S NOT *WHAT I AM* DOING... IT'S THE *WHY.*

BETTER NOW.

109

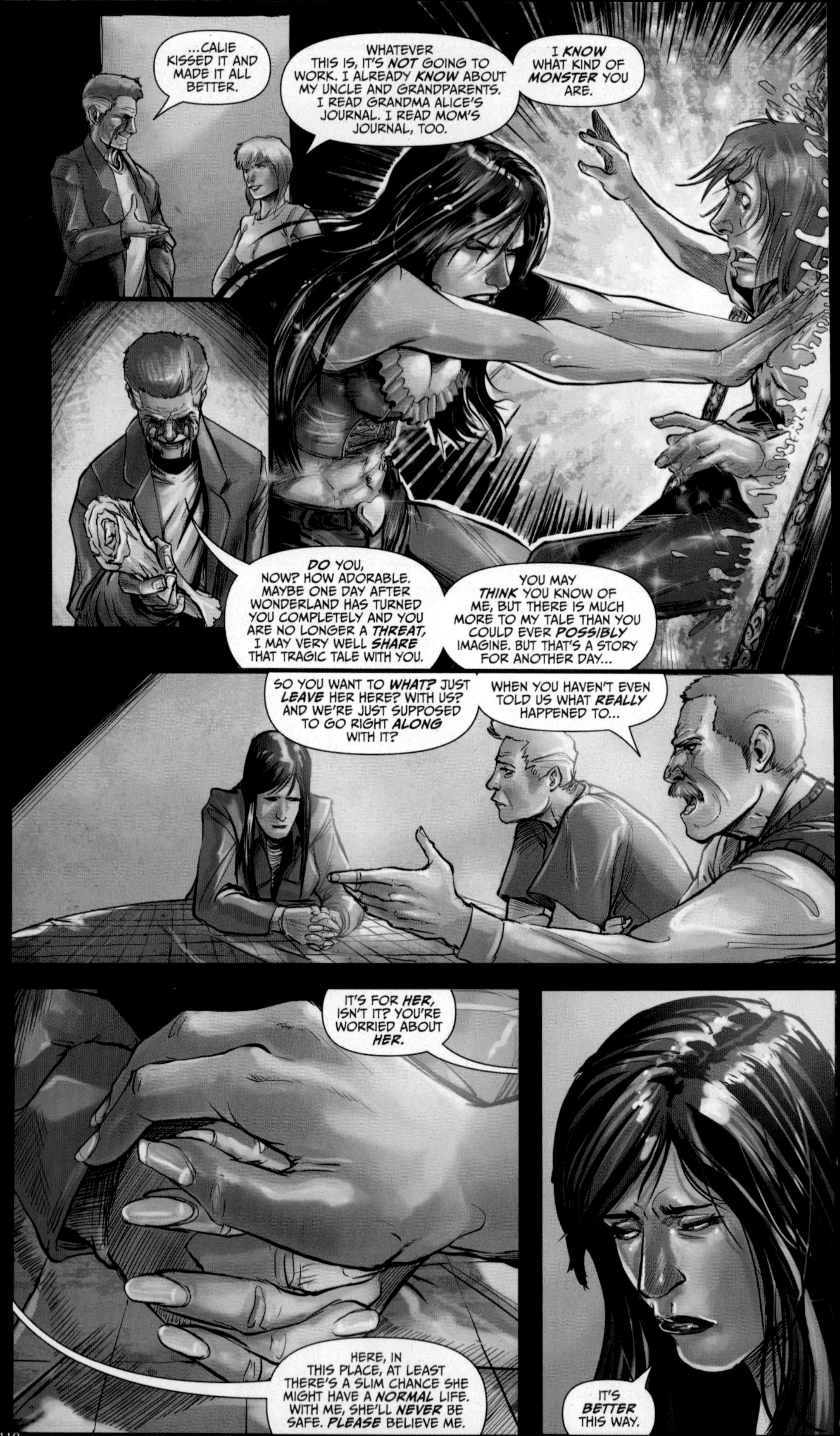
...CALIE KISSED IT AND MADE IT ALL BETTER.
WHATEVER THIS IS, IT'S NOT GOING TO WORK. I ALREADY KNOW ABOUT MY UNCLE AND GRANDPARENTS. I READ GRANDMA ALICE'S JOURNAL. I READ MOM'S JOURNAL, TOO.
I KNOW WHAT KIND OF MONSTER YOU ARE.
DO YOU, NOW? HOW ADORABLE. MAYBE ONE DAY AFTER WONDERLAND HAS TURNED YOU COMPLETELY AND YOU ARE NO LONGER A THREAT, I MAY VERY WELL SHARE THAT TRAGIC TALE WITH YOU.
YOU MAY THINK YOU KNOW OF ME, BUT THERE IS MUCH MORE TO MY TALE THAN YOU COULD EVER POSSIBLY IMAGINE. BUT THAT'S A STORY FOR ANOTHER DAY...
SO YOU WANT TO WHAT? JUST LEAVE HER HERE? WITH US? AND WE'RE JUST SUPPOSED TO GO RIGHT ALONG WITH IT?
WHEN YOU HAVEN'T EVEN TOLD US WHAT REALLY HAPPENED TO...
IT'S FOR HER, ISN'T IT? YOU'RE WORRIED ABOUT HER.
HERE, IN THIS PLACE, AT LEAST THERE'S A SLIM CHANCE SHE MIGHT HAVE A NORMAL LIFE. WITH ME, SHE'LL NEVER BE SAFE. PLEASE BELIEVE ME.
IT'S BETTER THIS WAY.

LET'S GET BACK TO *YOUR* STORY OF...

THE HAPPY *FLAPPING* AND *BUZZING* OF WHERE IT ALL BEGAN.

NOOOO! EW! EW! EW!

VIOLET, THAT YOU?

UH, YEAH. I *THINK*. MOM?!

SHE WENT OUT FOR A BIT. SAID SHE'LL BE RIGHT BACK. COME ON IN HERE. WE'RE IN THE LIVING ROOM.

GIRL IS *SILENT* LIKE THE WIND. NEVER EVEN HEARD YOU GET UP FROM BED. THOUGHT YOU WERE STILL *ASLEEP*.

COME HERE, HONEY. THOUGHT YOU MIGHT LIKE TO SEE THIS. IT'S YOUR DAD'S OLD *PHOTO ALBUM*.

YOUR MOM SAID YOU NEVER HAD THE CHANCE TO *MEET*. WHILE IT MIGHT NOT BE THE REAL THING, I THINK THIS INTRODUCTION HAS BEEN *LONG* OVERDUE.

SO, WHERE'D *YOU* GO, VIOLET?

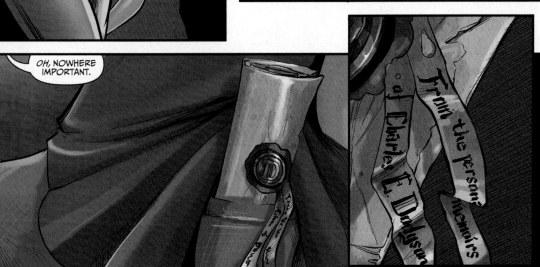

OH, NOWHERE IMPORTANT.

From the personal memoirs of Charles L. Dodgson

=SIGH=

YOU DESERVE A NORMAL LIFE.

YOU DESERVE A CHANCE AT *HAPPINESS.*

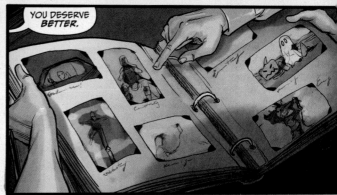

YOU DESERVE *BETTER.*

I SEE THAT NOW.

I JUST HOPE THAT SOMEDAY YOU'LL *FORGIVE* ME. THAT SOMEDAY YOU'LL *UNDERSTAND.*

UNDERSTAND WHAT?

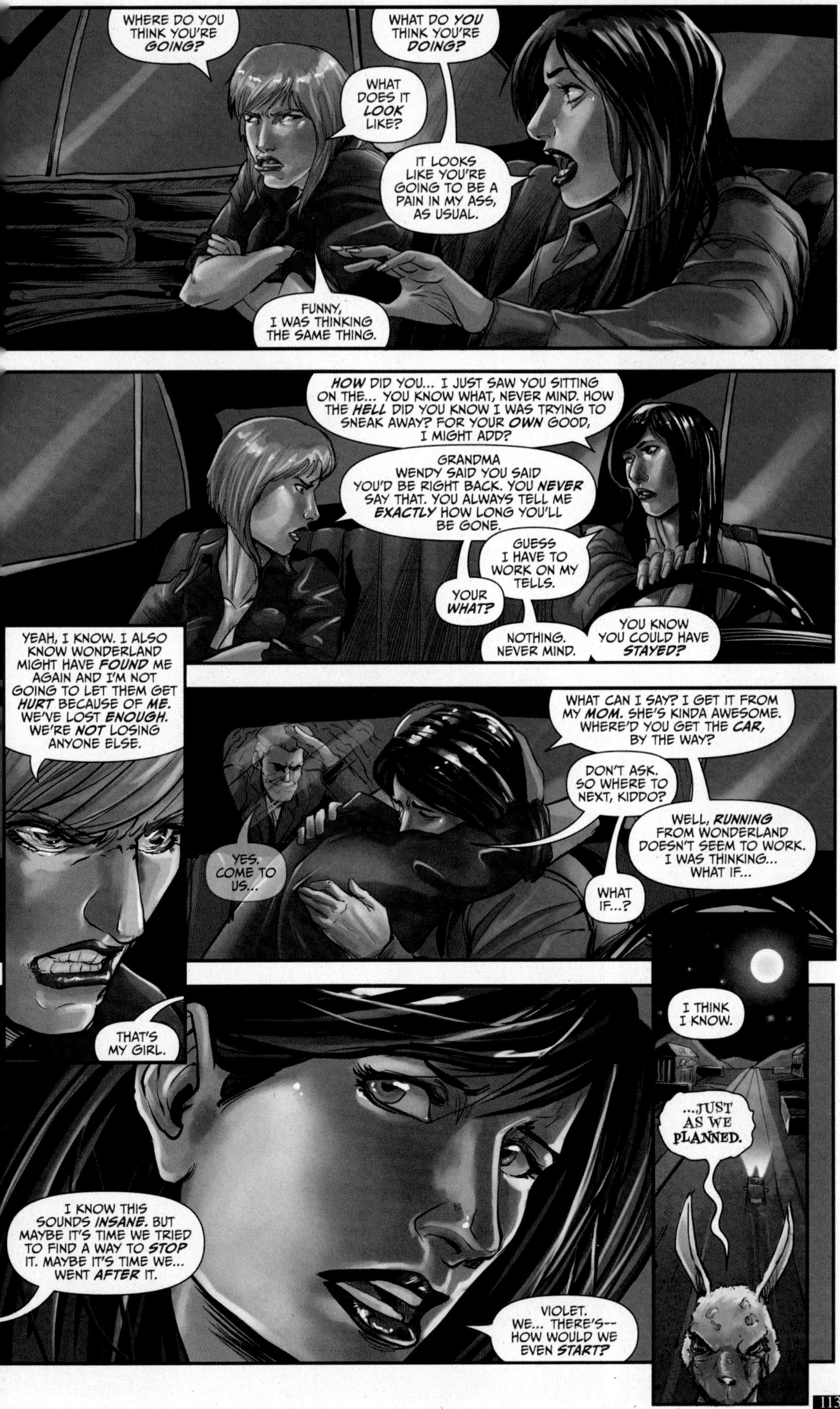
WHERE DO YOU THINK YOU'RE GOING?
WHAT DO YOU THINK YOU'RE DOING?
WHAT DOES IT LOOK LIKE?
IT LOOKS LIKE YOU'RE GOING TO BE A PAIN IN MY ASS, AS USUAL.
FUNNY, I WAS THINKING THE SAME THING.
HOW DID YOU... I JUST SAW YOU SITTING ON THE... YOU KNOW WHAT, NEVER MIND. HOW THE HELL DID YOU KNOW I WAS TRYING TO SNEAK AWAY? FOR YOUR OWN GOOD, I MIGHT ADD?
GRANDMA WENDY SAID YOU SAID YOU'D BE RIGHT BACK. YOU NEVER SAY THAT. YOU ALWAYS TELL ME EXACTLY HOW LONG YOU'LL BE GONE.
GUESS I HAVE TO WORK ON MY TELLS.
YOUR WHAT?
NOTHING. NEVER MIND.
YOU KNOW YOU COULD HAVE STAYED?
YEAH, I KNOW. I ALSO KNOW WONDERLAND MIGHT HAVE FOUND ME AGAIN AND I'M NOT GOING TO LET THEM GET HURT BECAUSE OF ME. WE'VE LOST ENOUGH. WE'RE NOT LOSING ANYONE ELSE.
WHAT CAN I SAY? I GET IT FROM MY MOM. SHE'S KINDA AWESOME. WHERE'D YOU GET THE CAR, BY THE WAY?
DON'T ASK. SO WHERE TO NEXT, KIDDO?
YES. COME TO US...
WELL, RUNNING FROM WONDERLAND DOESN'T SEEM TO WORK. I WAS THINKING... WHAT IF...
WHAT IF...?
THAT'S MY GIRL.
I KNOW THIS SOUNDS INSANE. BUT MAYBE IT'S TIME WE TRIED TO FIND A WAY TO STOP IT. MAYBE IT'S TIME WE... WENT AFTER IT.
VIOLET. WE... THERE'S-- HOW WOULD WE EVEN START?
I THINK I KNOW.
...JUST AS WE PLANNED.

CAN WE BE SEEN?

NO, MY QUEEN. WE HAVE DRAWN THE SURROUNDING DARKNESS TO US. THEY WILL NOT DETECT OUR PRESENCE.

GOOD...

"BECAUSE *WHATEVER* THIS IS..."

"IT'S HAPPENING NOW."

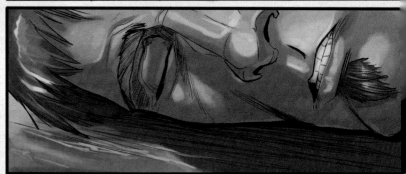

UNNGH...

W-WHERE AM I? W-WHAT H-H-HAPPENED...

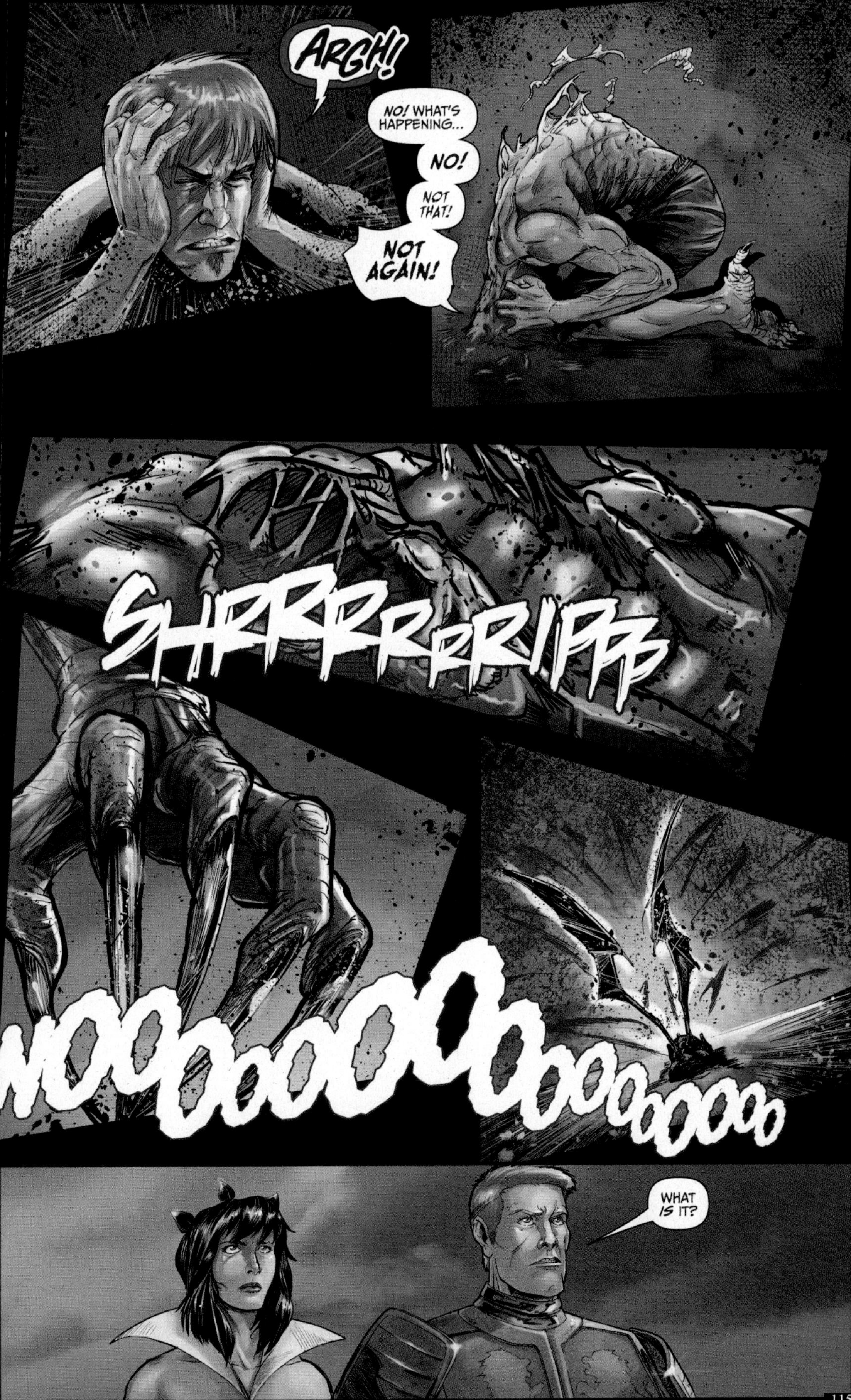
ARGH!
NO! WHAT'S HAPPENING...
NO!
NOT THAT!
NOT AGAIN!
SHRRRRRRIPPP
NOOOOOOOOOOOOOOOOOOO
WHAT IS IT?

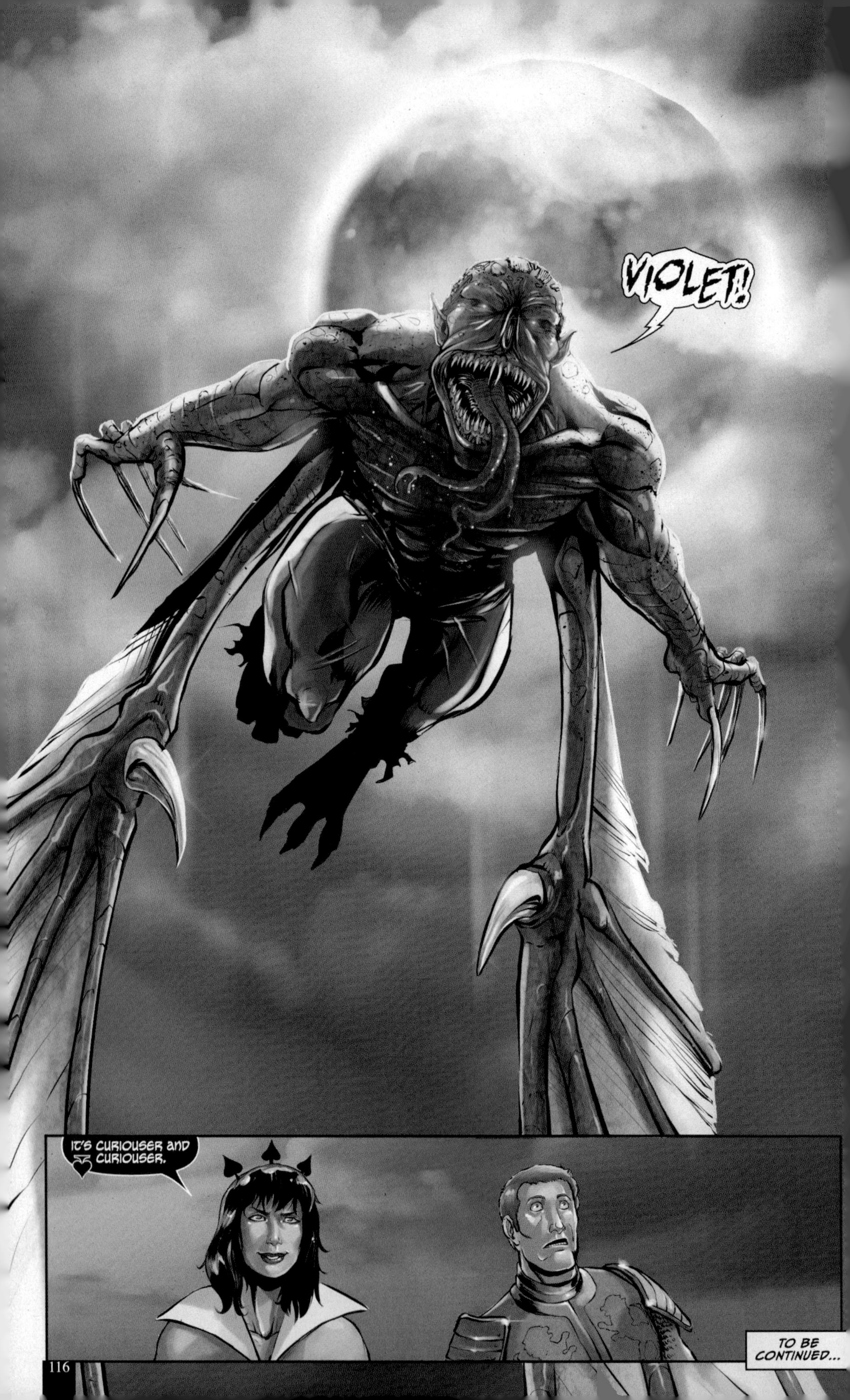
VIOLET!
IT'S CURIOUSER AND CURIOUSER.
TO BE CONTINUED...

Grimm Fairy Tales
presents

Wonderland

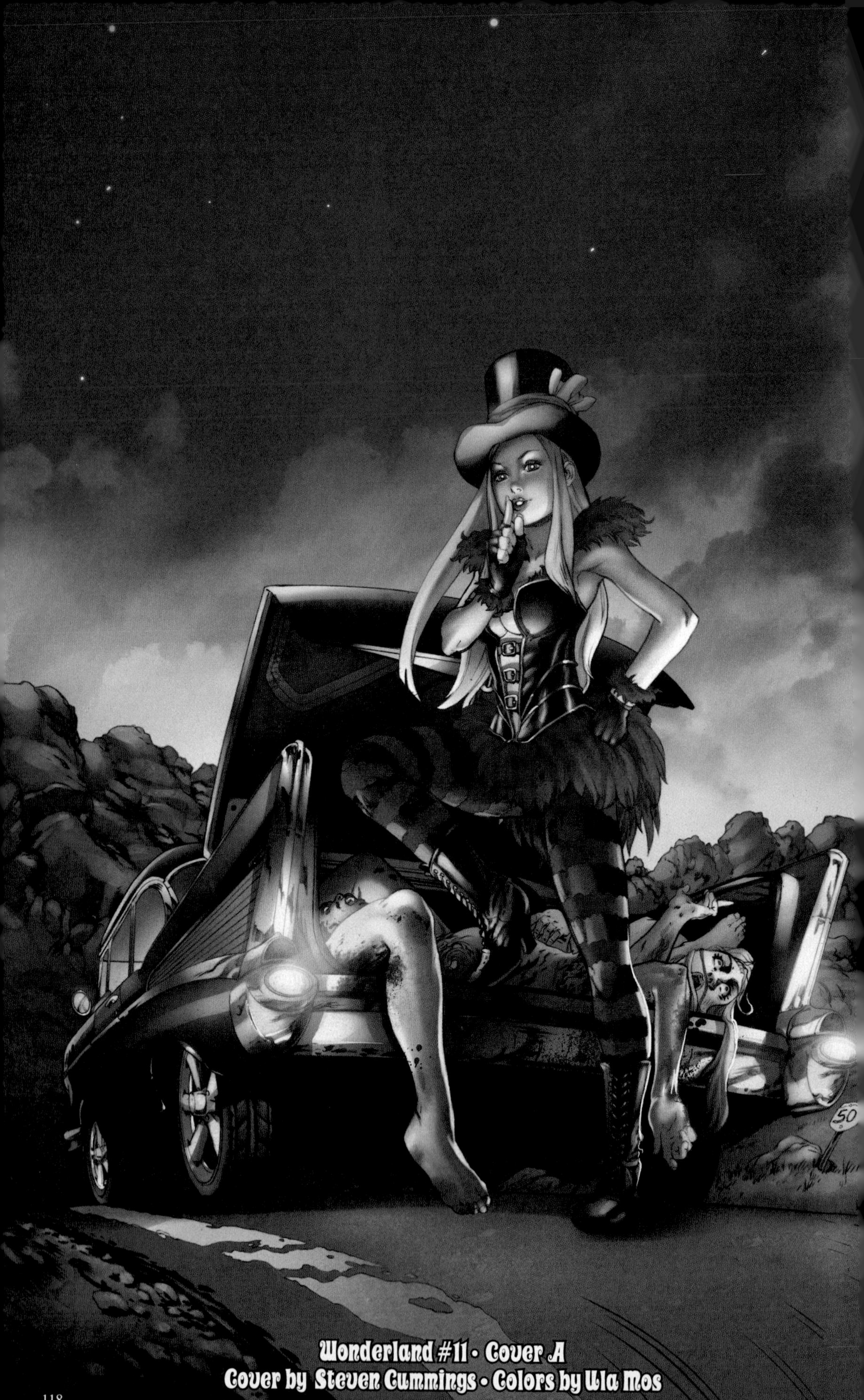
50

Wonderland #11 • Cover A
Cover by Steven Cummings • Colors by Ula Mos

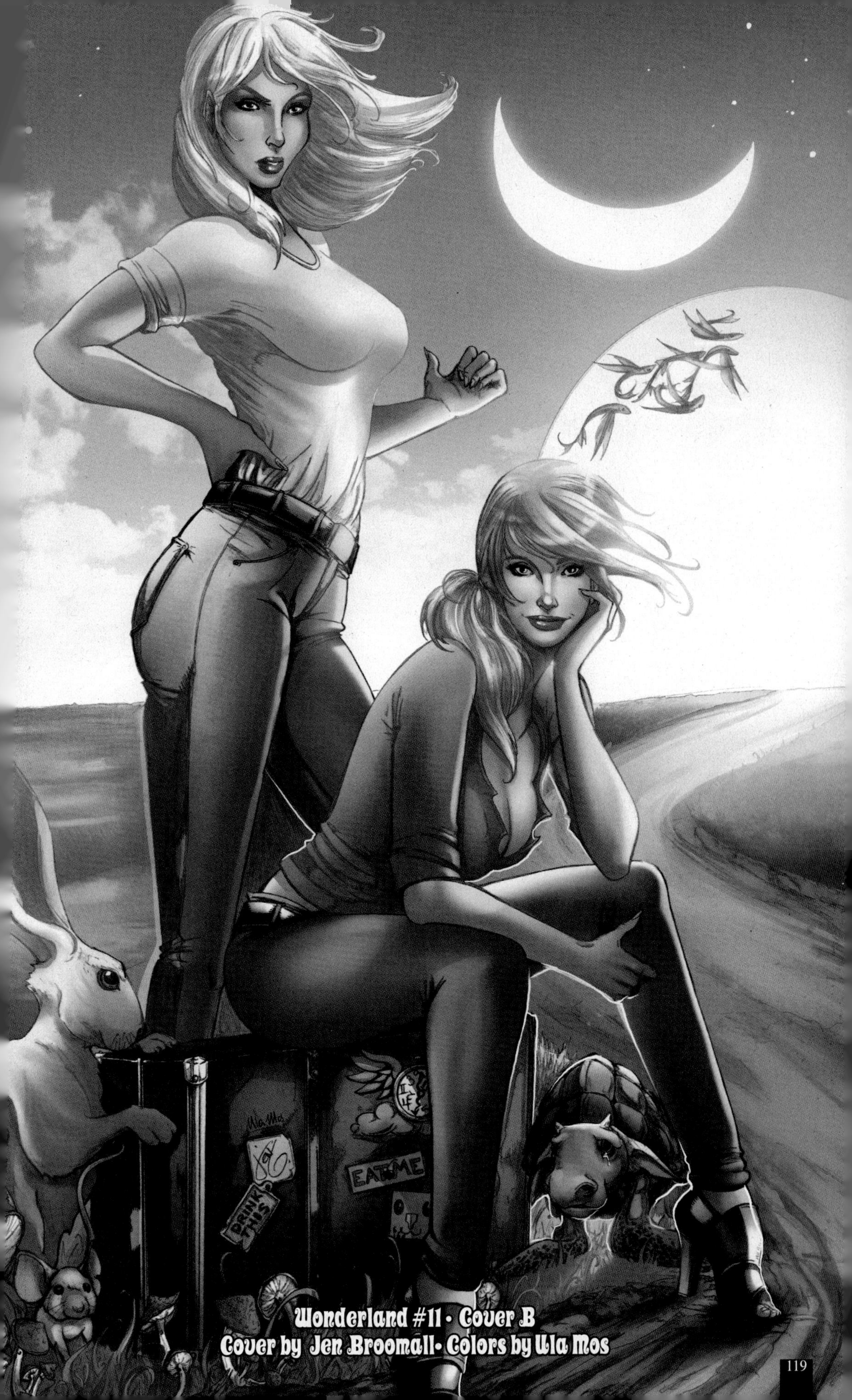
EAT ME
DRINK THIS

Wonderland #11 • Cover B
Cover by Jen Broomall• Colors by Ula Mos

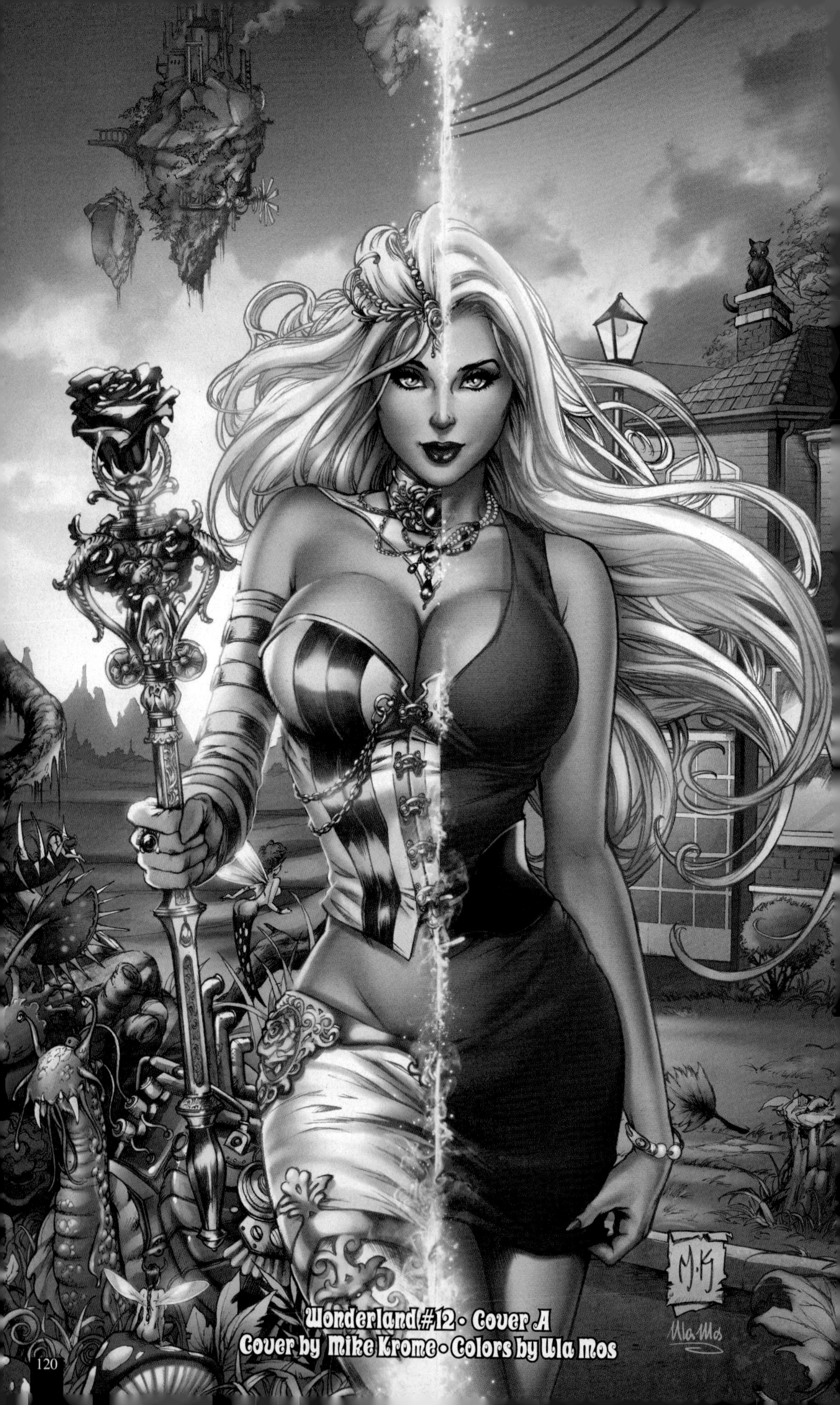

Wonderland #12 • Cover A
Cover by Mike Krome • Colors by Ula Mos

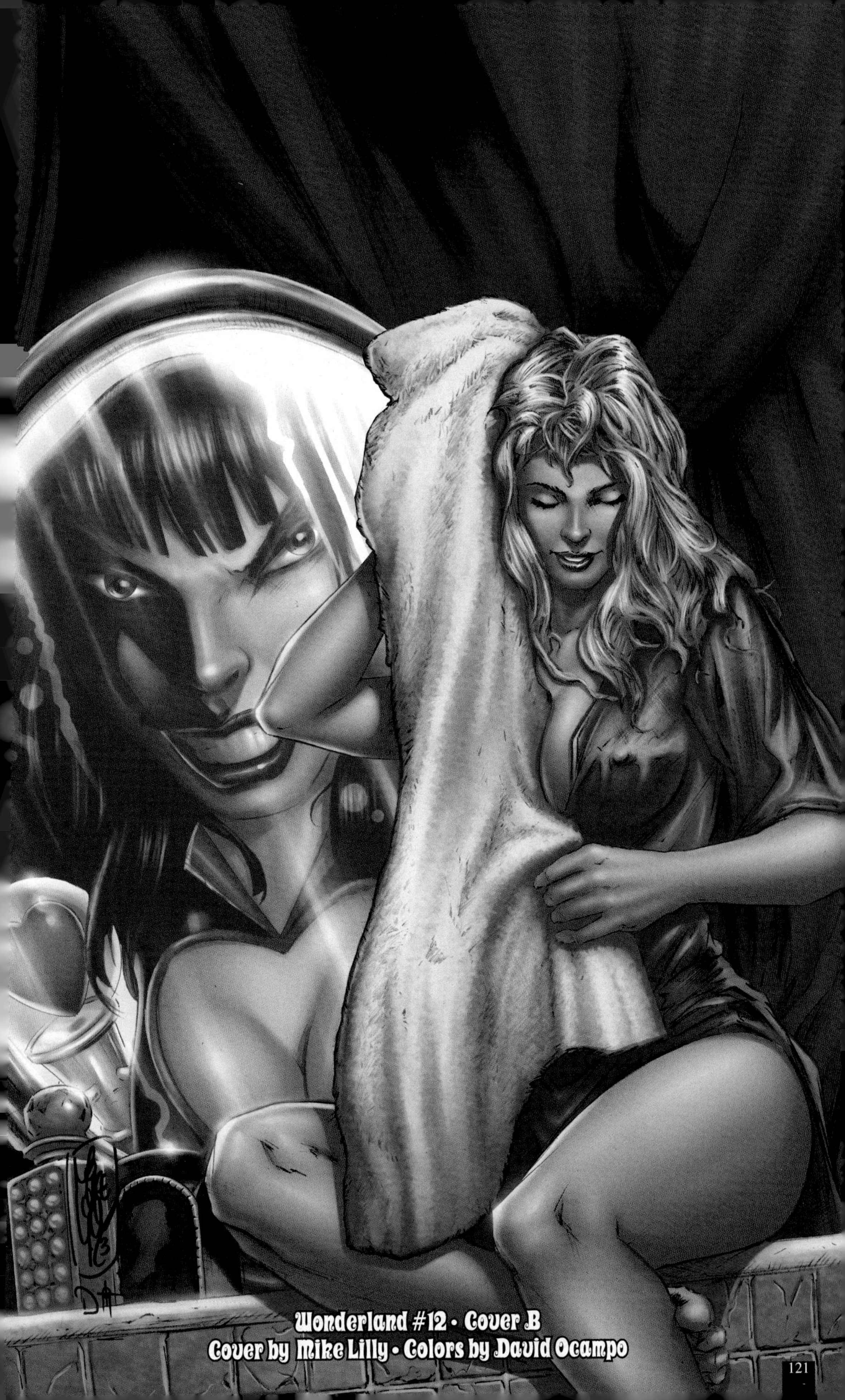

Wonderland #12 • Cover B
Cover by Mike Lilly • Colors by David Ocampo

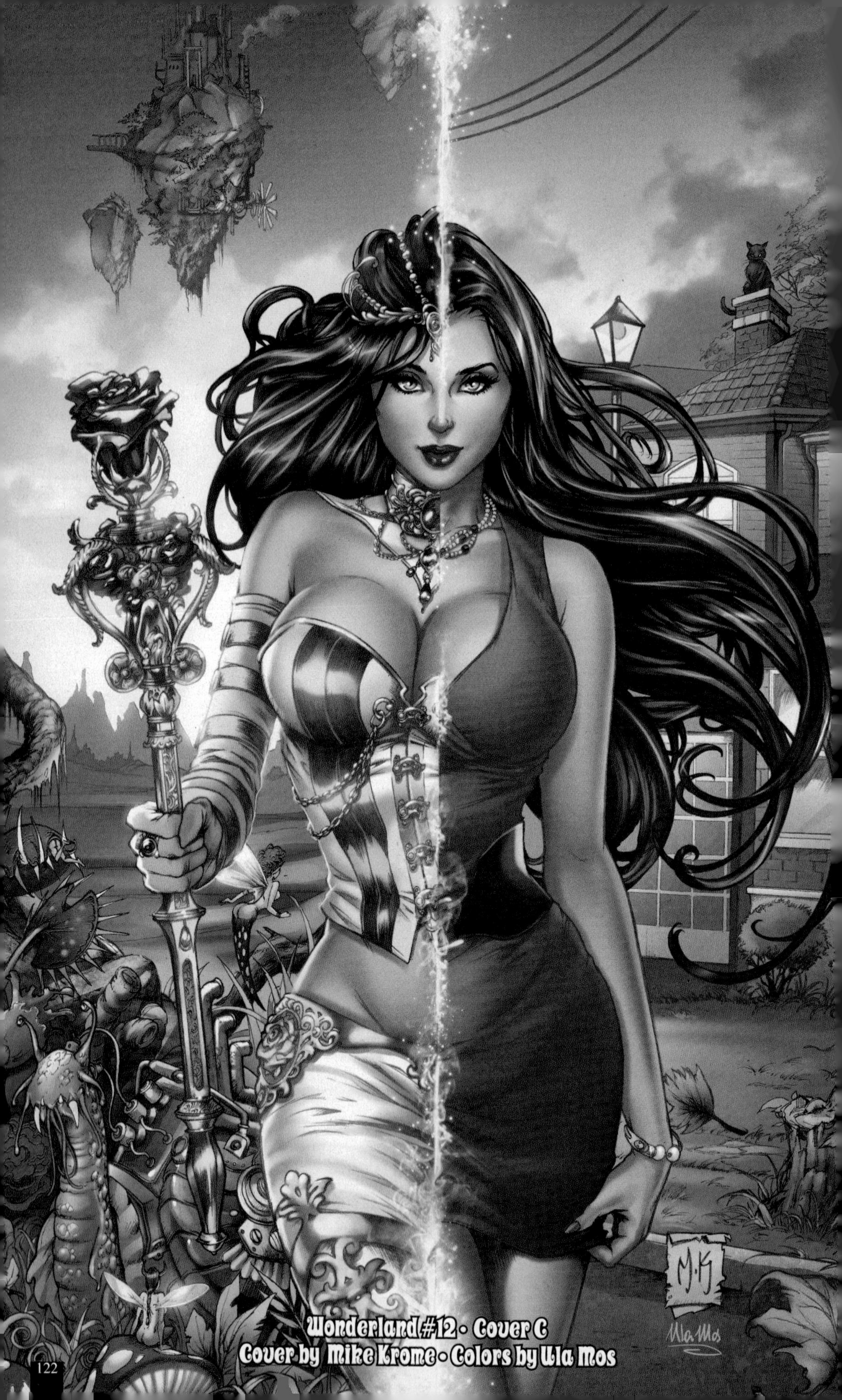

Wonderland #12 • Cover C
Cover by Mike Krome • Colors by Ula Mos

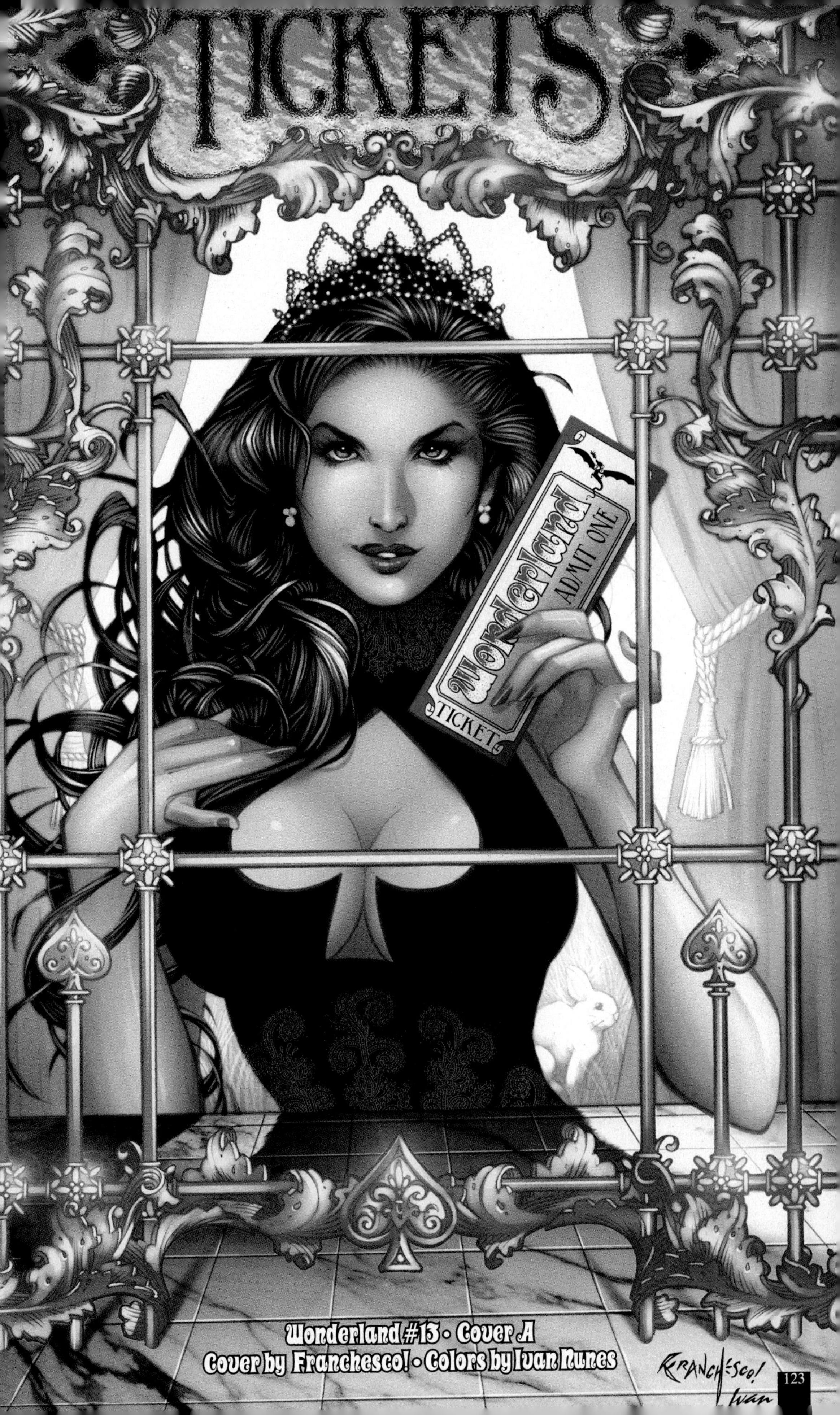
TICKETS
Wonderland
ADMIT ONE
TICKET
FRANCHESCO!
Ivan

Wonderland #13 • Cover A
Cover by Franchesco! • Colors by Ivan Nunes

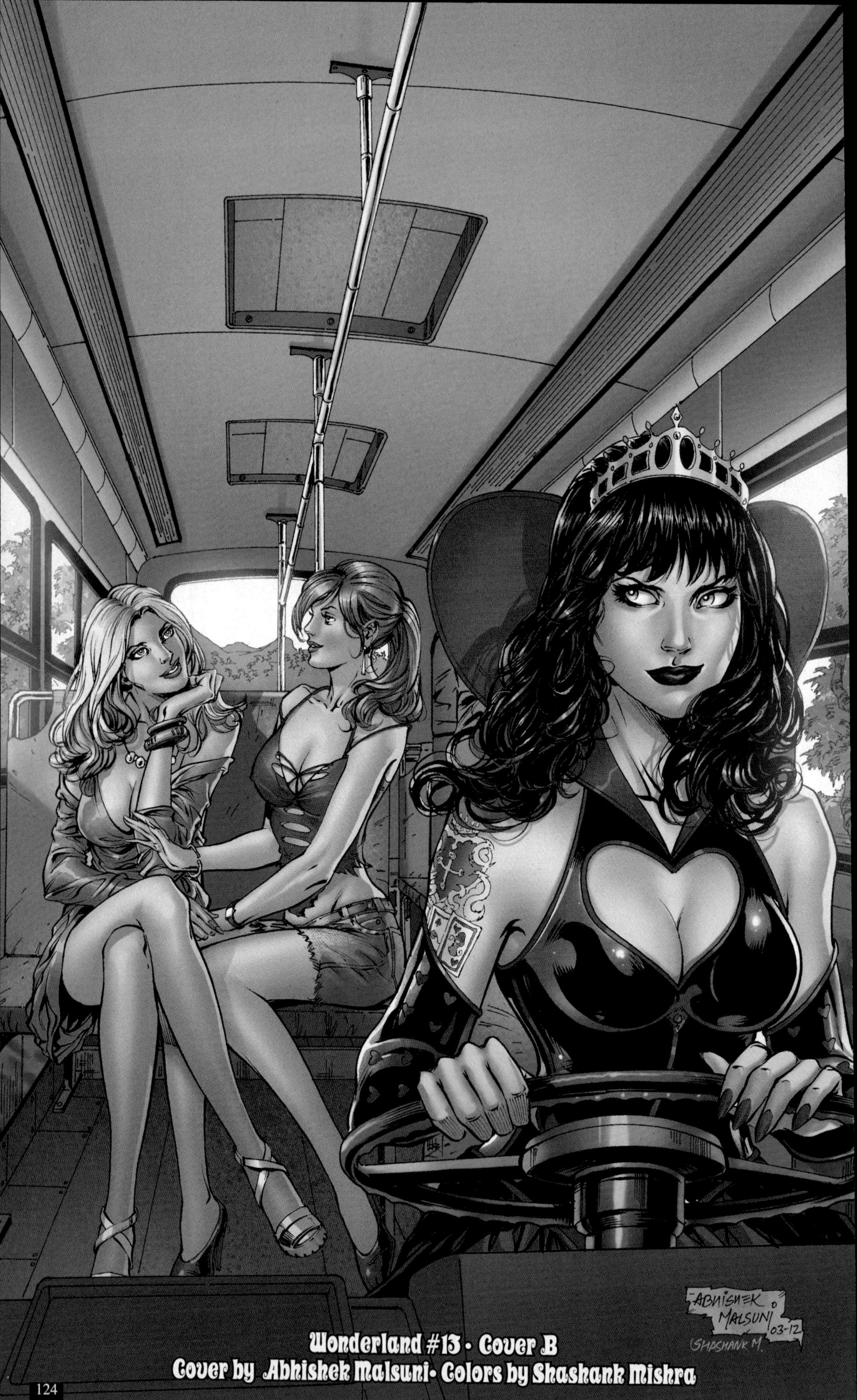
ABHISHEK MALSUNI 03-12
SHASHANK M.

Wonderland #13 • Cover B
Cover by Abhishek Malsuni• Colors by Shashank Mishra

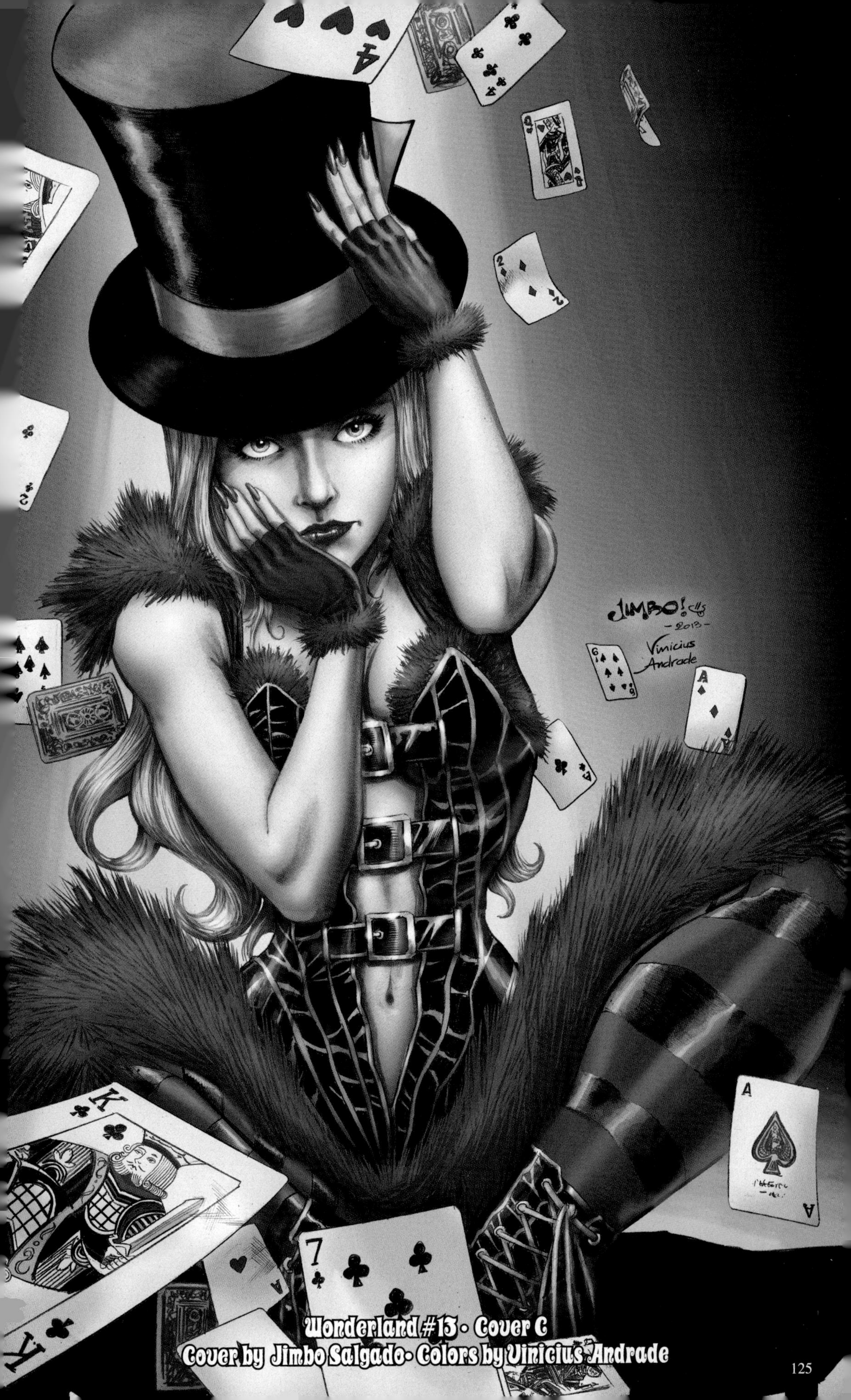
JIMBO!
2013
Vinicius Andrade

Wonderland #13 • Cover C
Cover by Jimbo Salgado• Colors by Vinicius Andrade

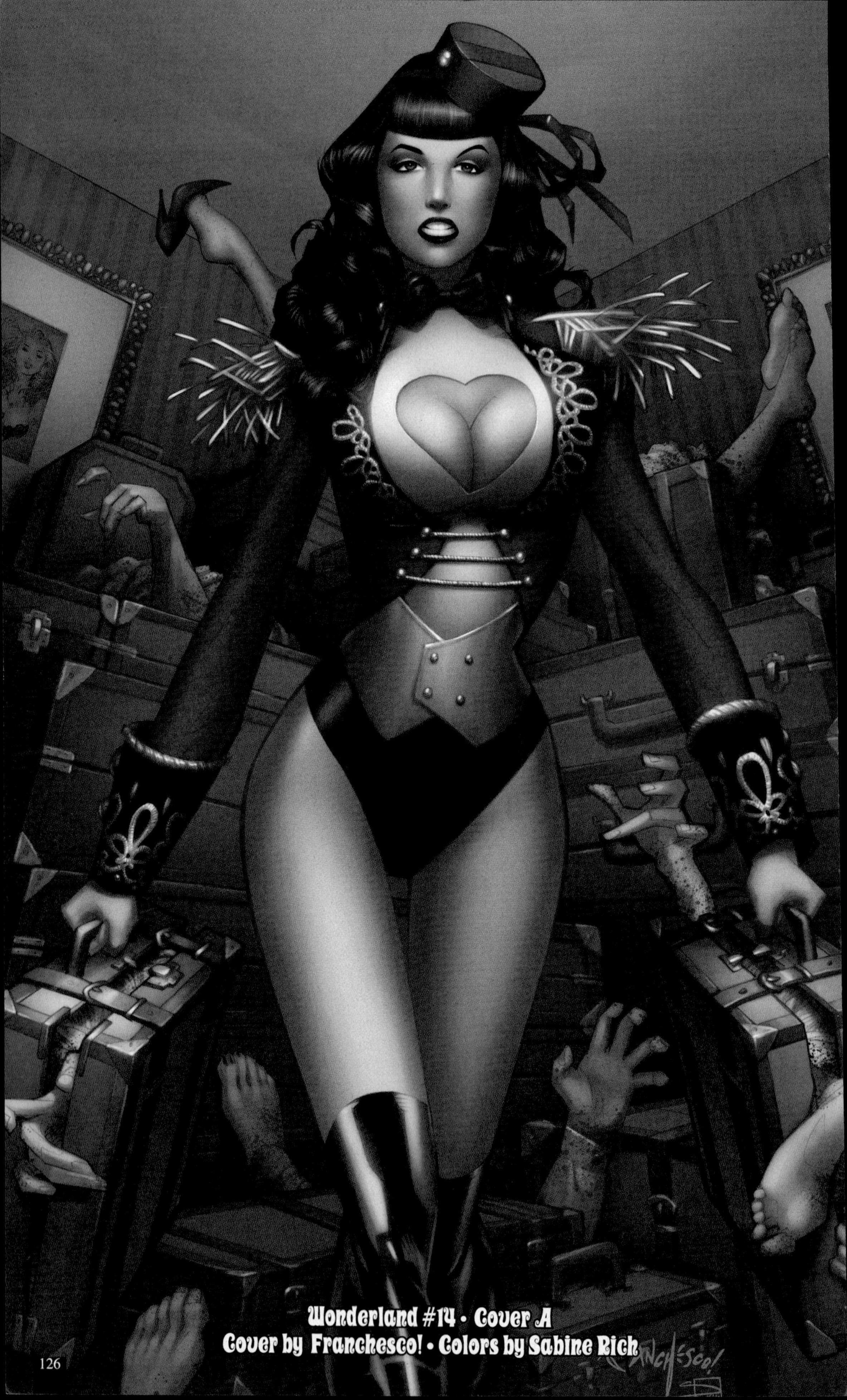

Wonderland #14 • Cover A
Cover by Franchesco! • Colors by Sabine Rich

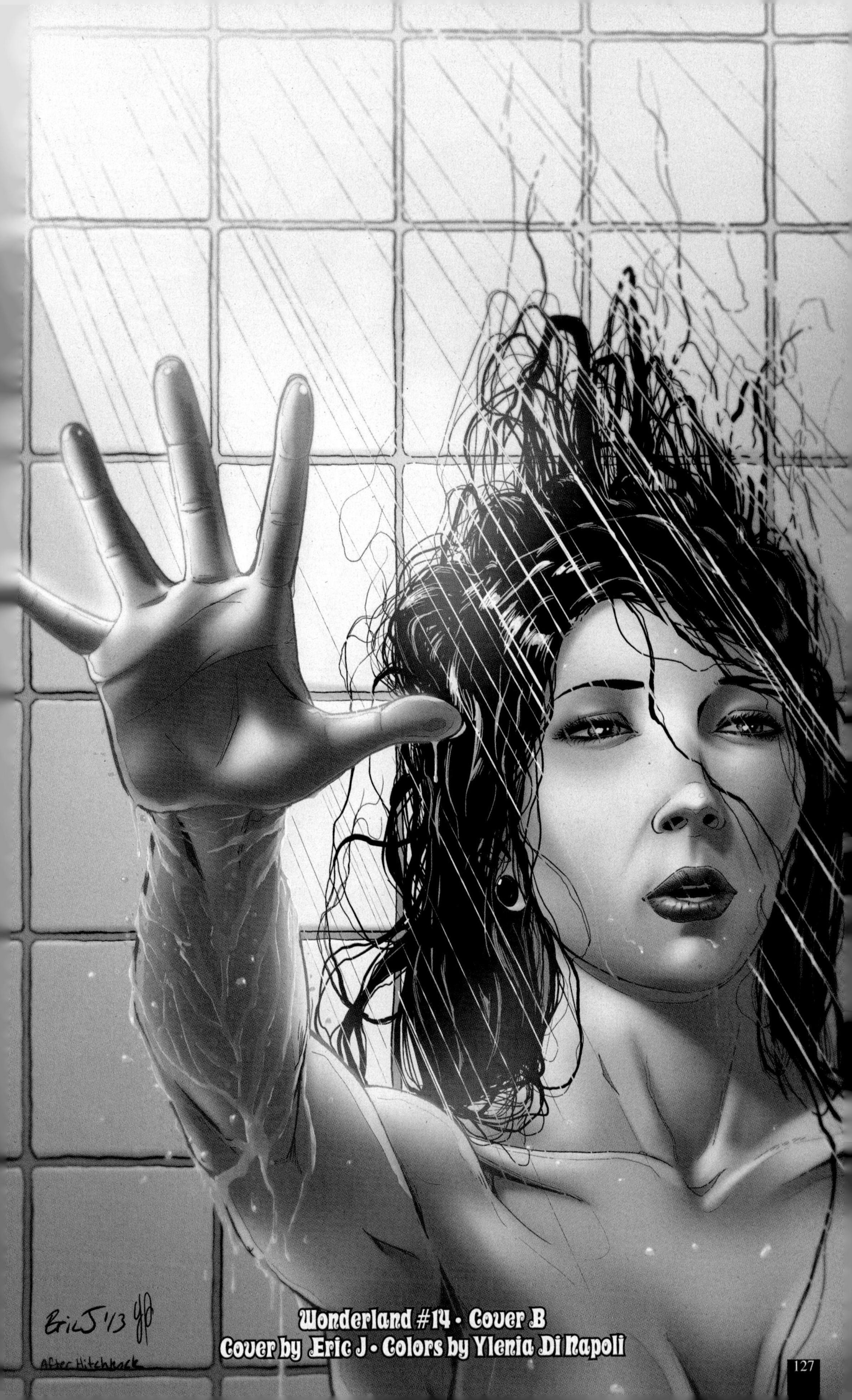
Eric J '13
After Hitchcock

Wonderland #14 • Cover B
Cover by Eric J • Colors by Ylenia Di Napoli

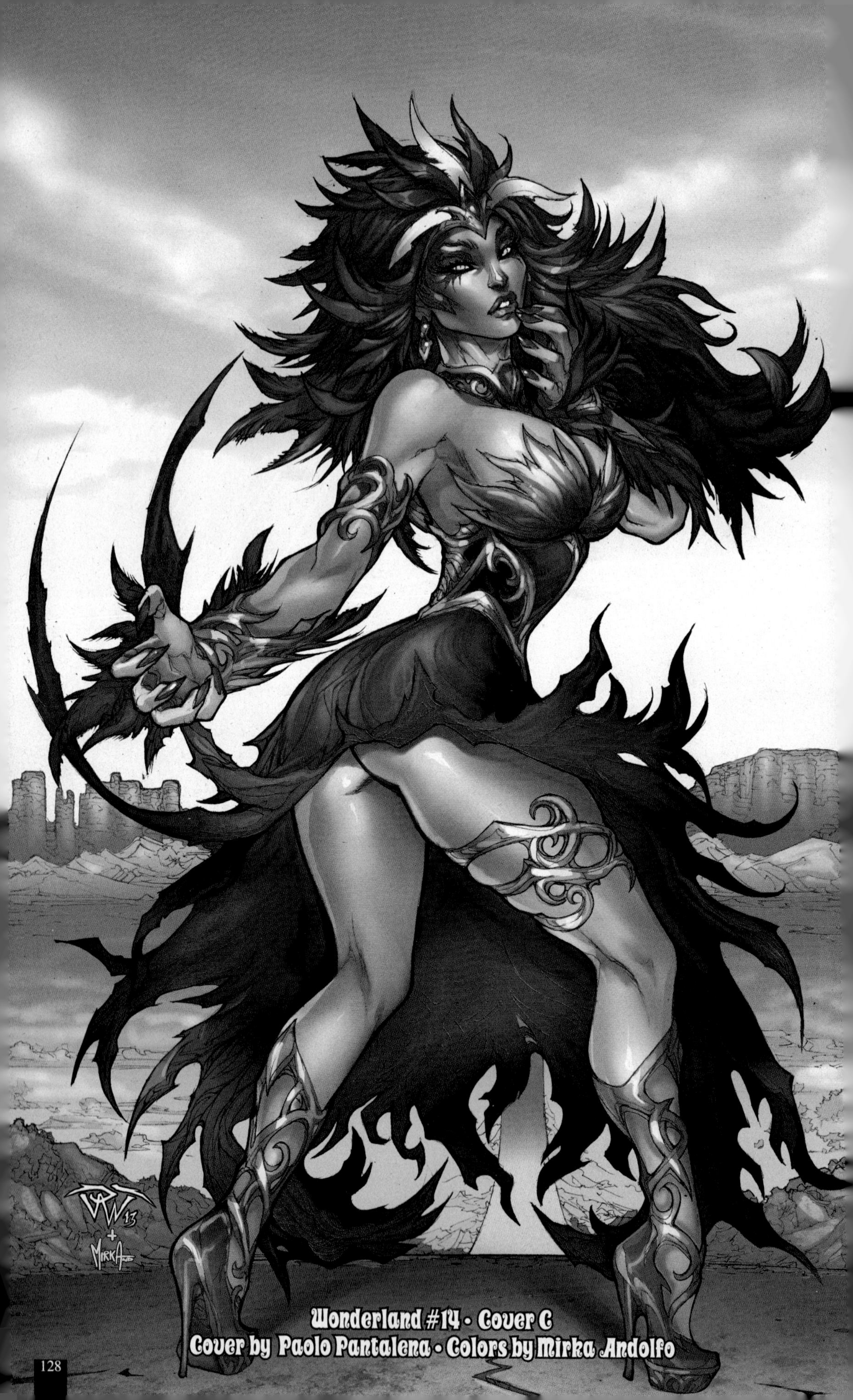

Wonderland #14 • Cover C
Cover by Paolo Pantalena • Colors by Mirka Andolfo

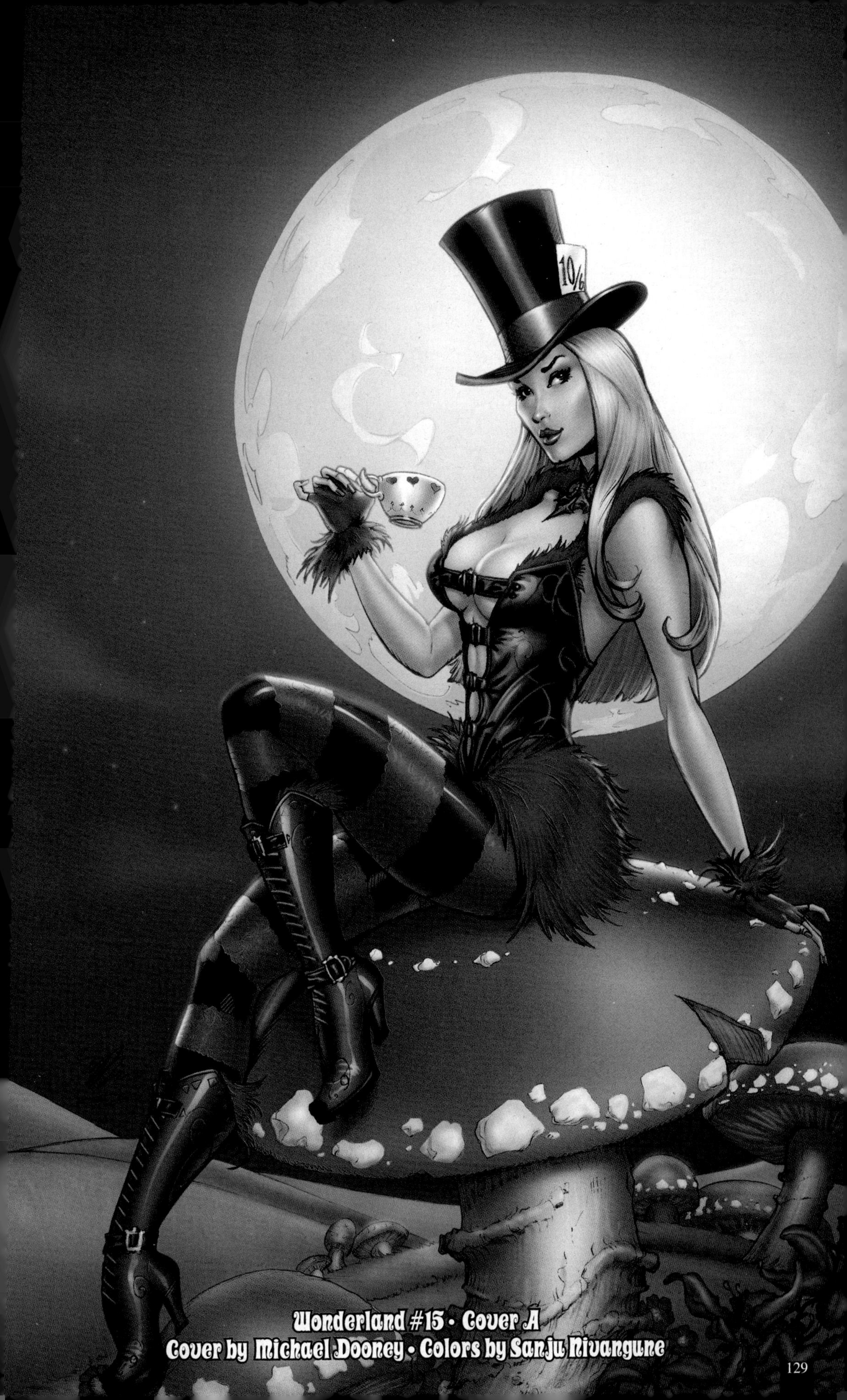
10/6

Wonderland #15 • Cover A
Cover by Michael Dooney • Colors by Sanju Nivangune

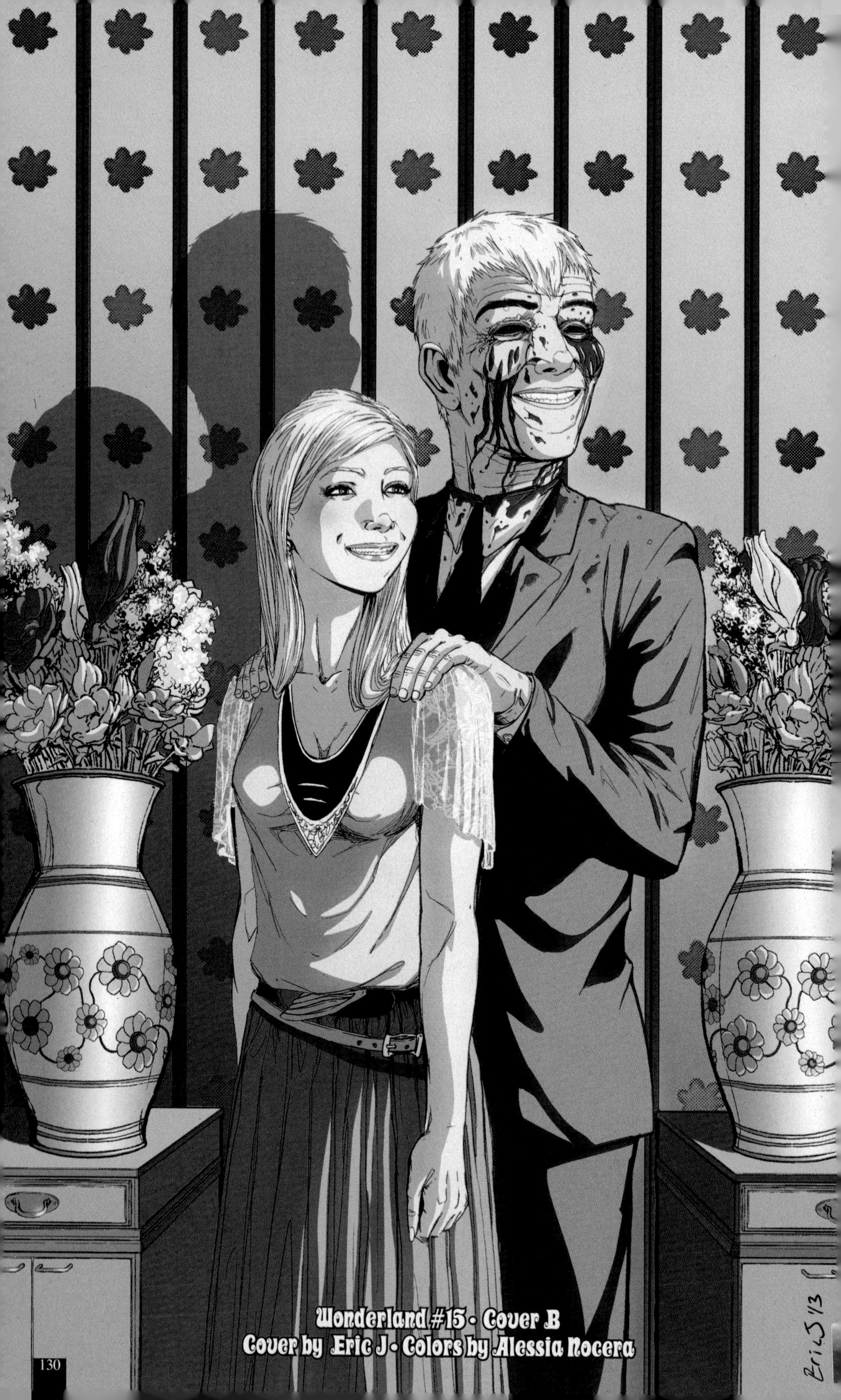
Eric J '13

Wonderland #15 • Cover B
Cover by Eric J • Colors by Alessia Nocera

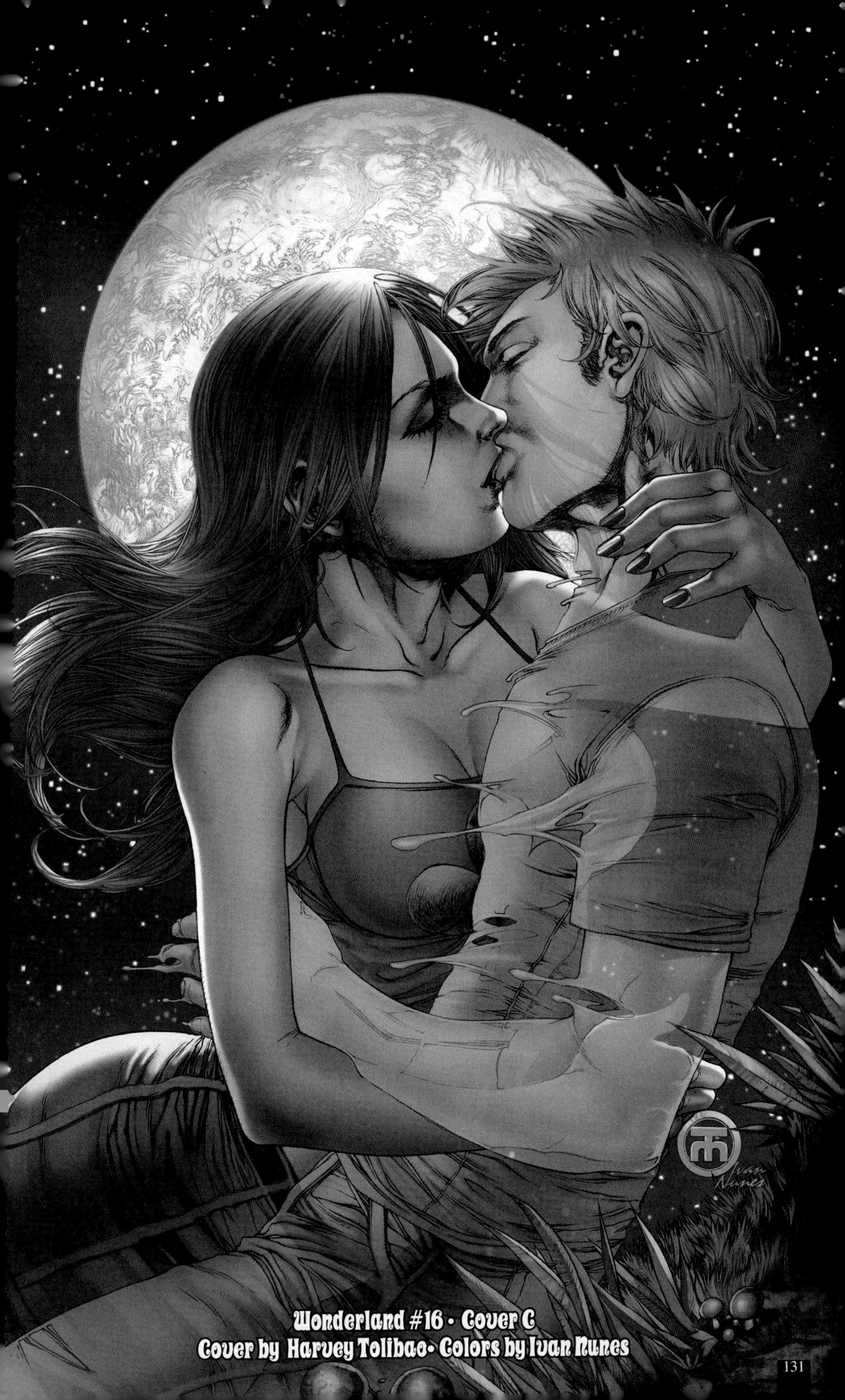

Wonderland #16 • Cover C
Cover by Harvey Tolibao• Colors by Ivan Nunes

Exclusive sneak preview...

Grimm Fairy Tales presents

Wonderland

Issue #16

Writer
Raven Gregory

Pencils
Sergio Osuna

Colors
Leonardo Paciarotti

Letters
Jim Campbell

Cover
Michael Dooney
Yelenia Di Napoli

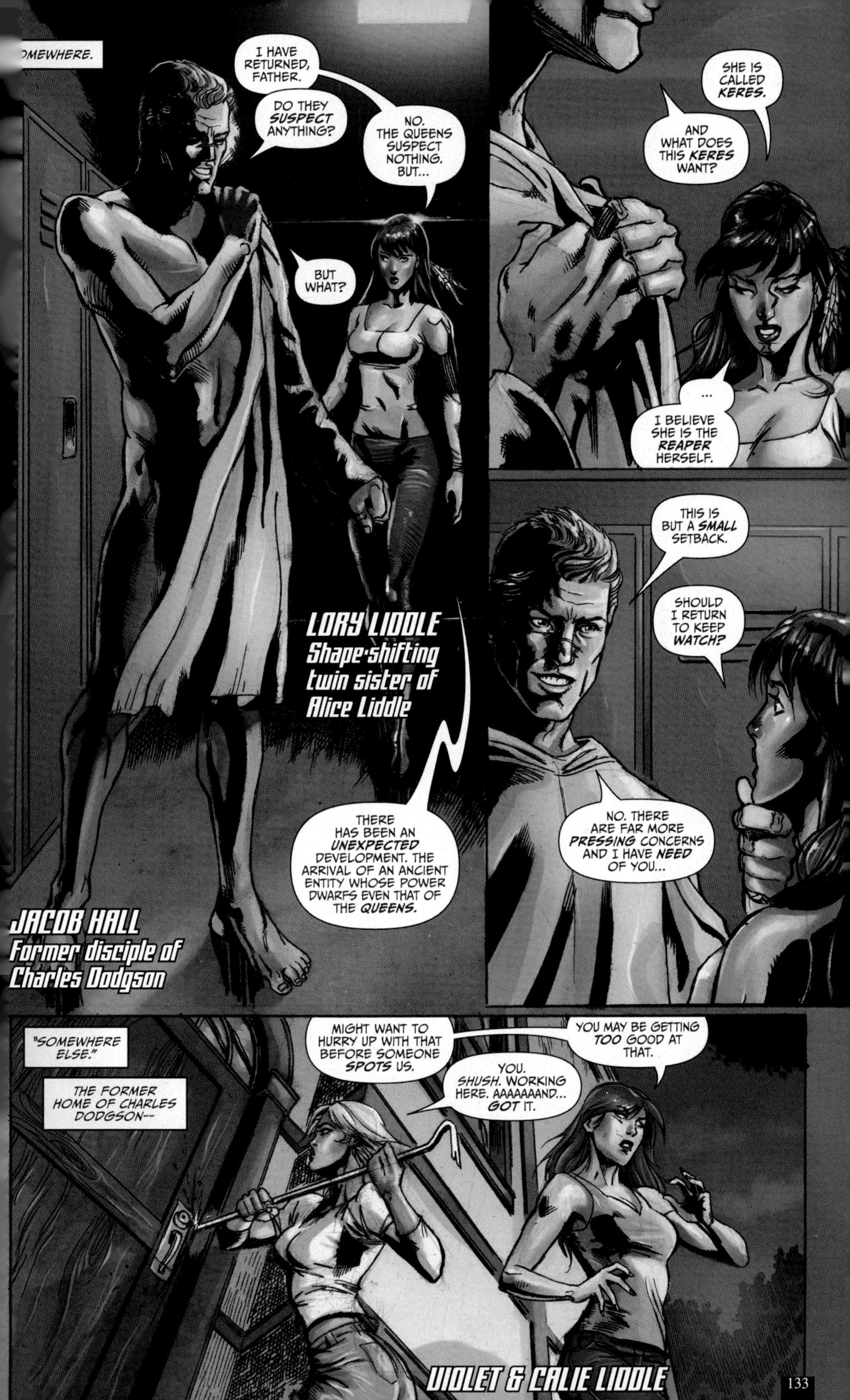

...OMEWHERE.
I HAVE RETURNED, FATHER.
DO THEY SUSPECT ANYTHING?
NO. THE QUEENS SUSPECT NOTHING. BUT...
BUT WHAT?
LORY LIDDLE
Shape-shifting twin sister of Alice Liddle
THERE HAS BEEN AN UNEXPECTED DEVELOPMENT. THE ARRIVAL OF AN ANCIENT ENTITY WHOSE POWER DWARFS EVEN THAT OF THE QUEENS.
JACOB HALL
Former disciple of Charles Dodgson
SHE IS CALLED KERES.
AND WHAT DOES THIS KERES WANT?
... I BELIEVE SHE IS THE REAPER HERSELF.
THIS IS BUT A SMALL SETBACK.
SHOULD I RETURN TO KEEP WATCH?
NO. THERE ARE FAR MORE PRESSING CONCERNS AND I HAVE NEED OF YOU...
"SOMEWHERE ELSE."
THE FORMER HOME OF CHARLES DODGSON--
MIGHT WANT TO HURRY UP WITH THAT BEFORE SOMEONE SPOTS US.
YOU MAY BE GETTING TOO GOOD AT THAT.
YOU. SHUSH. WORKING HERE. AAAAAAAND... GOT IT.
VIOLET & CALIE LIDDLE

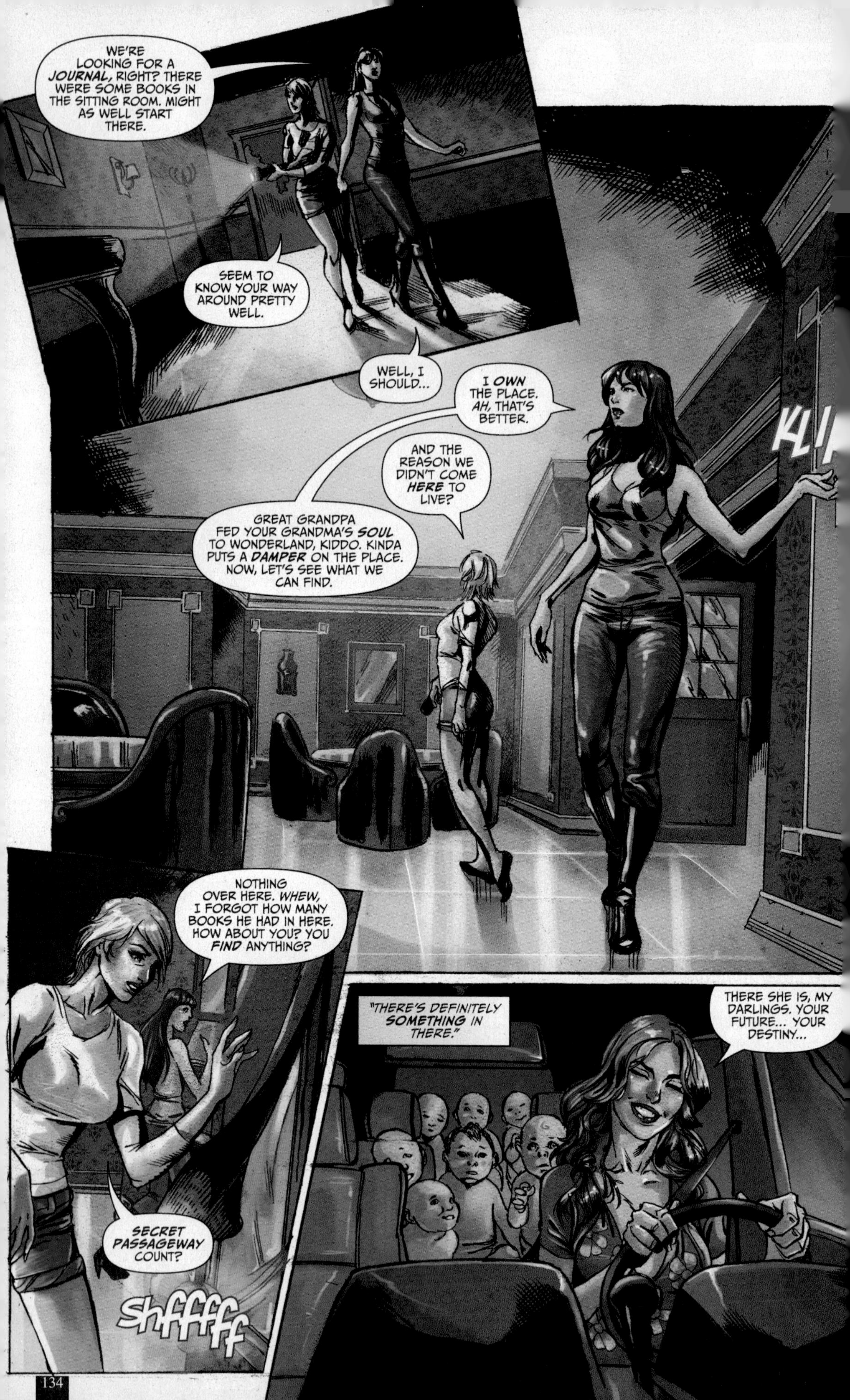
WE'RE LOOKING FOR A JOURNAL, RIGHT? THERE WERE SOME BOOKS IN THE SITTING ROOM. MIGHT AS WELL START THERE.
SEEM TO KNOW YOUR WAY AROUND PRETTY WELL.
WELL, I SHOULD...
I OWN THE PLACE. AH, THAT'S BETTER.
AND THE REASON WE DIDN'T COME HERE TO LIVE?
GREAT GRANDPA FED YOUR GRANDMA'S SOUL TO WONDERLAND, KIDDO. KINDA PUTS A DAMPER ON THE PLACE. NOW, LET'S SEE WHAT WE CAN FIND.
NOTHING OVER HERE. WHEW, I FORGOT HOW MANY BOOKS HE HAD IN HERE. HOW ABOUT YOU? YOU FIND ANYTHING?
SECRET PASSAGEWAY COUNT?
Shffffff
"THERE'S DEFINITELY SOMETHING IN THERE."
THERE SHE IS, MY DARLINGS. YOUR FUTURE... YOUR DESTINY...

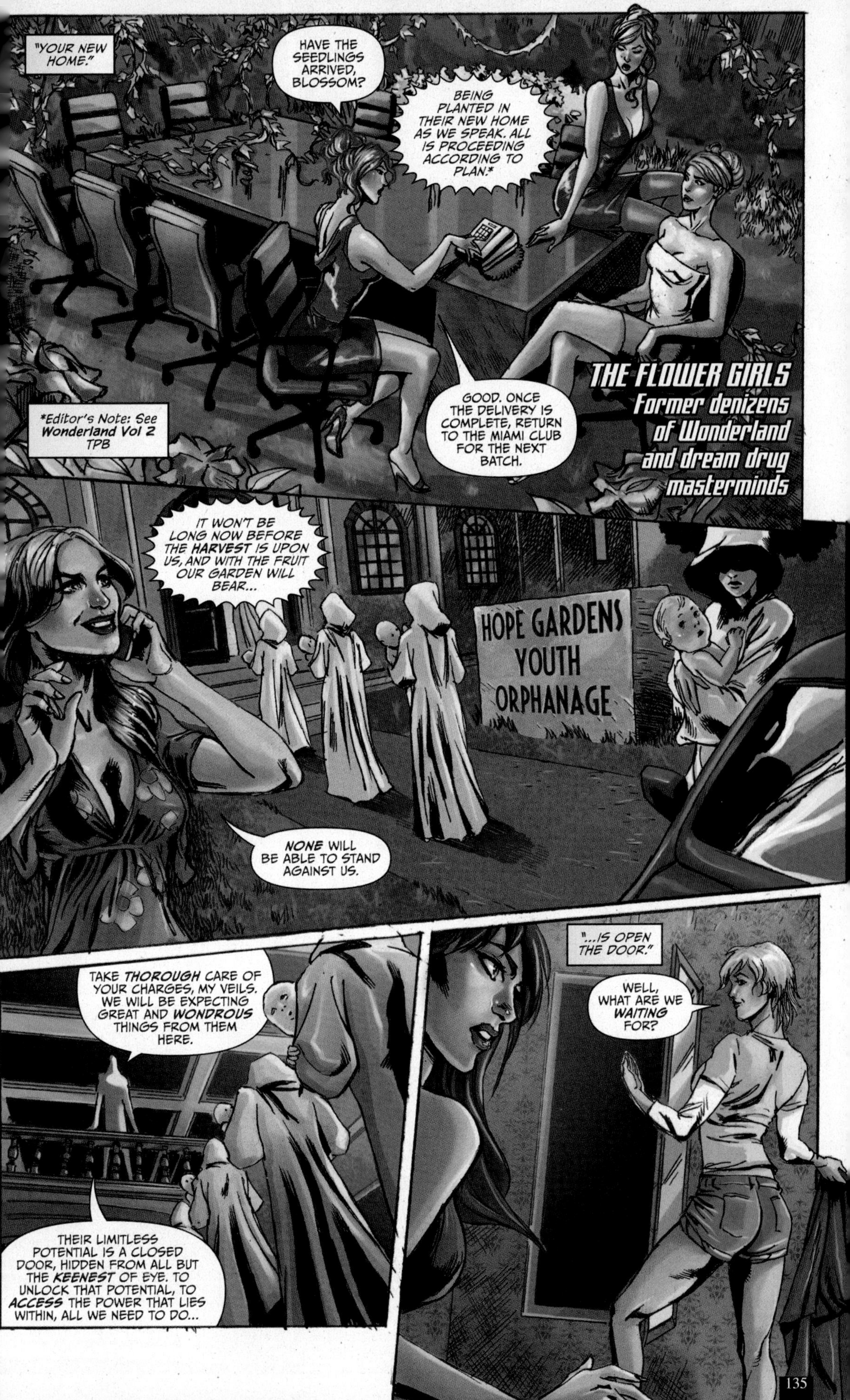

"YOUR NEW HOME."
HAVE THE SEEDLINGS ARRIVED, BLOSSOM?
BEING PLANTED IN THEIR NEW HOME AS WE SPEAK. ALL IS PROCEEDING ACCORDING TO PLAN.*
GOOD. ONCE THE DELIVERY IS COMPLETE, RETURN TO THE MIAMI CLUB FOR THE NEXT BATCH.
*Editor's Note: See Wonderland Vol 2 TPB
THE FLOWER GIRLS Former denizens of Wonderland and dream drug masterminds
IT WON'T BE LONG NOW BEFORE THE HARVEST IS UPON US, AND WITH THE FRUIT OUR GARDEN WILL BEAR...
HOPE GARDENS YOUTH ORPHANAGE
NONE WILL BE ABLE TO STAND AGAINST US.
TAKE THOROUGH CARE OF YOUR CHARGES, MY VEILS. WE WILL BE EXPECTING GREAT AND WONDROUS THINGS FROM THEM HERE.
THEIR LIMITLESS POTENTIAL IS A CLOSED DOOR, HIDDEN FROM ALL BUT THE KEENEST OF EYE. TO UNLOCK THAT POTENTIAL, TO ACCESS THE POWER THAT LIES WITHIN, ALL WE NEED TO DO...
"...IS OPEN THE DOOR."
WELL, WHAT ARE WE WAITING FOR?

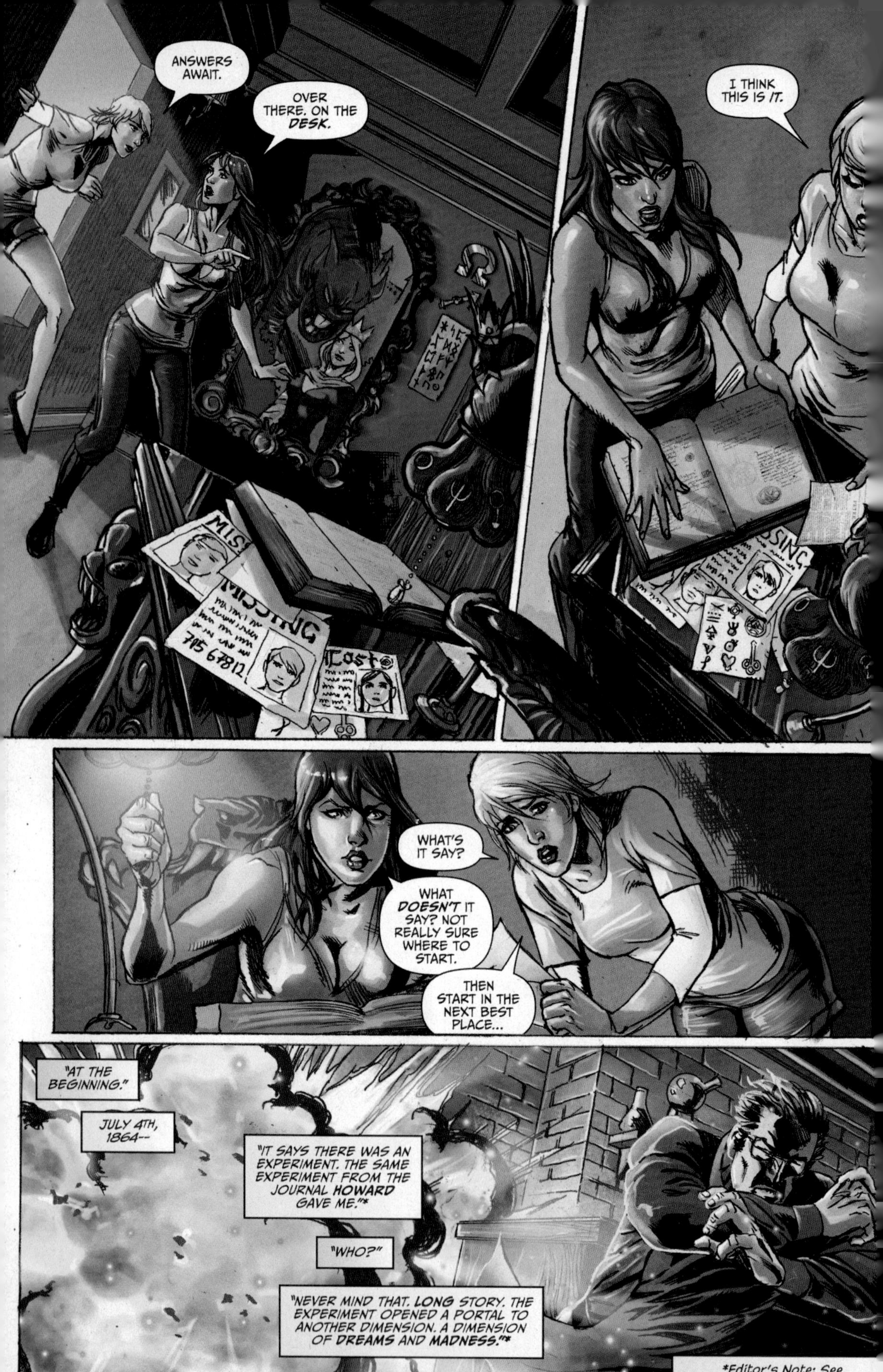
ANSWERS AWAIT.
OVER THERE. ON THE **DESK.**
MISSING
MISSING
715 67812
Lost
I THINK THIS IS *IT.*
MISSING
WHAT'S IT SAY?
WHAT **DOESN'T** IT SAY? NOT REALLY SURE WHERE TO START.
THEN START IN THE NEXT BEST PLACE...
"AT THE BEGINNING."
JULY 4TH, 1864--
"IT SAYS THERE WAS AN EXPERIMENT. THE SAME EXPERIMENT FROM THE JOURNAL **HOWARD** GAVE ME."*
"WHO?"
"NEVER MIND THAT. **LONG** STORY. THE EXPERIMENT OPENED A PORTAL TO ANOTHER DIMENSION. A DIMENSION OF **DREAMS** AND **MADNESS.**"*
*Editor's Note: See **Tales From Wonderland Vol 1** and **Escape From Wonderland**

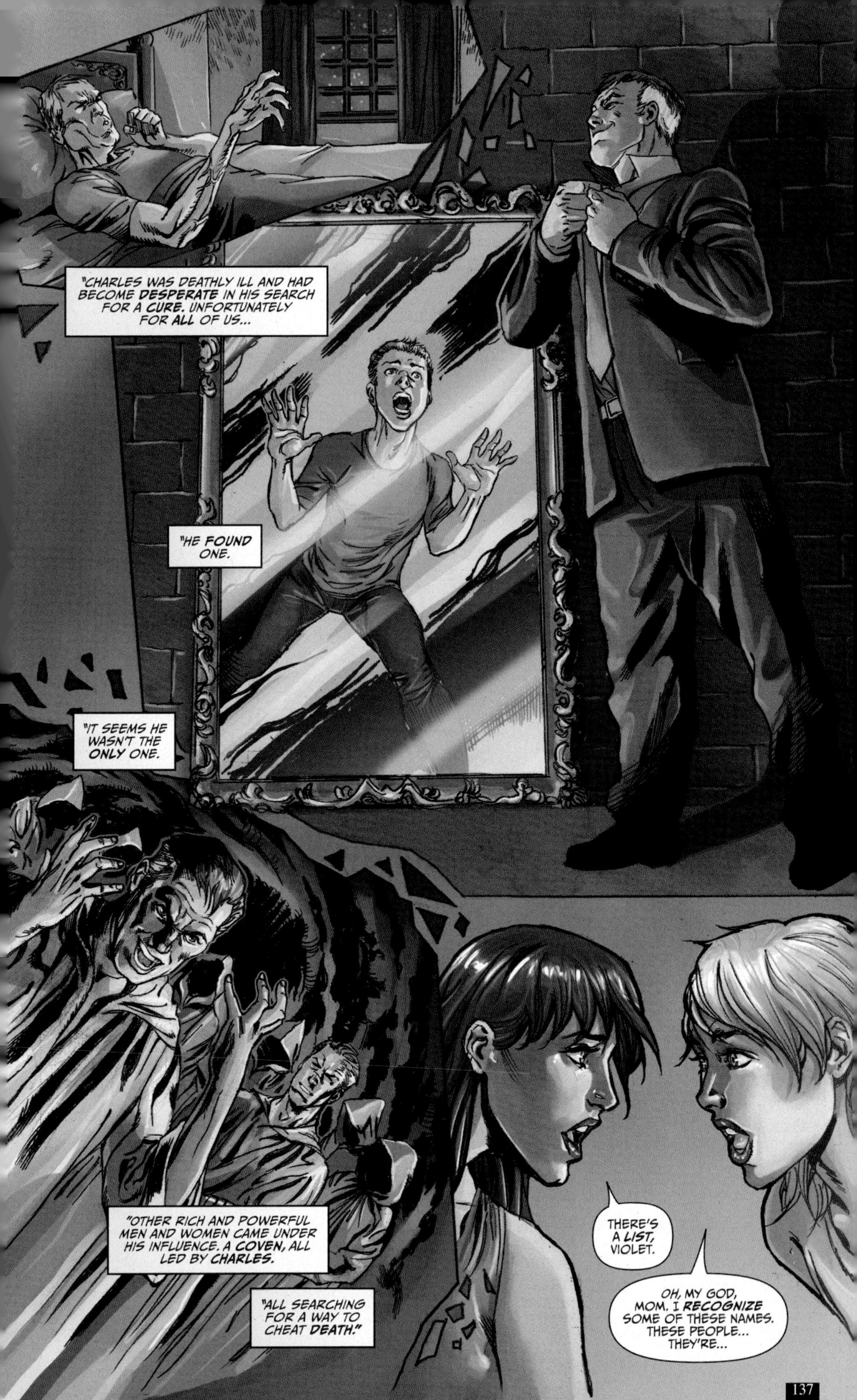
"CHARLES WAS DEATHLY ILL AND HAD BECOME DESPERATE IN HIS SEARCH FOR A CURE. UNFORTUNATELY FOR ALL OF US...
"HE FOUND ONE.
"IT SEEMS HE WASN'T THE ONLY ONE.
"OTHER RICH AND POWERFUL MEN AND WOMEN CAME UNDER HIS INFLUENCE. A COVEN, ALL LED BY CHARLES.
"ALL SEARCHING FOR A WAY TO CHEAT DEATH."
THERE'S A LIST, VIOLET.
OH, MY GOD, MOM. I RECOGNIZE SOME OF THESE NAMES. THESE PEOPLE... THEY'RE...

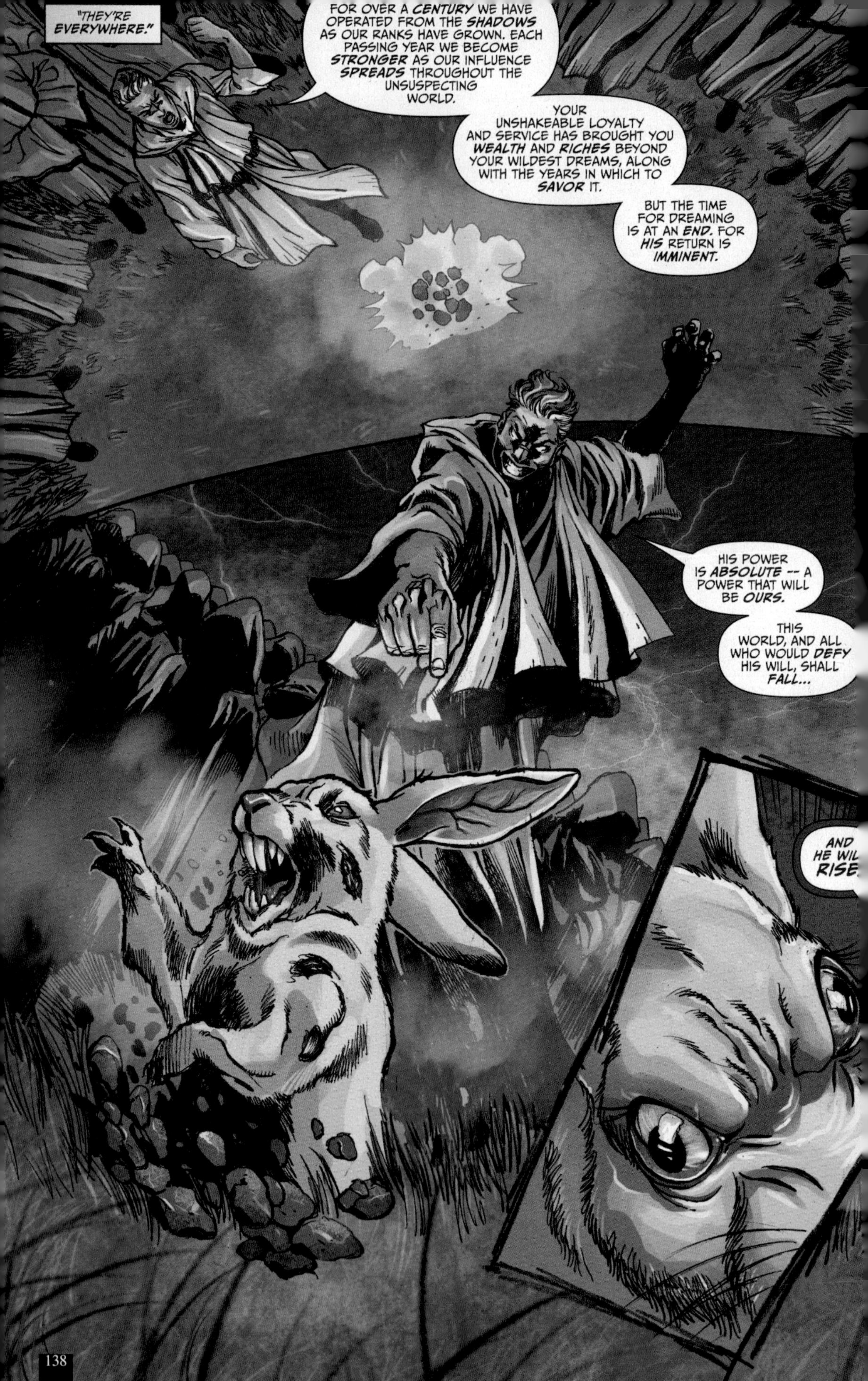
"THEY'RE EVERYWHERE."
FOR OVER A CENTURY WE HAVE OPERATED FROM THE SHADOWS AS OUR RANKS HAVE GROWN. EACH PASSING YEAR WE BECOME STRONGER AS OUR INFLUENCE SPREADS THROUGHOUT THE UNSUSPECTING WORLD.
YOUR UNSHAKEABLE LOYALTY AND SERVICE HAS BROUGHT YOU WEALTH AND RICHES BEYOND YOUR WILDEST DREAMS, ALONG WITH THE YEARS IN WHICH TO SAVOR IT.
BUT THE TIME FOR DREAMING IS AT AN END. FOR HIS RETURN IS IMMINENT.
HIS POWER IS ABSOLUTE -- A POWER THAT WILL BE OURS.
THIS WORLD, AND ALL WHO WOULD DEFY HIS WILL, SHALL FALL...
AND HE WIL RISE

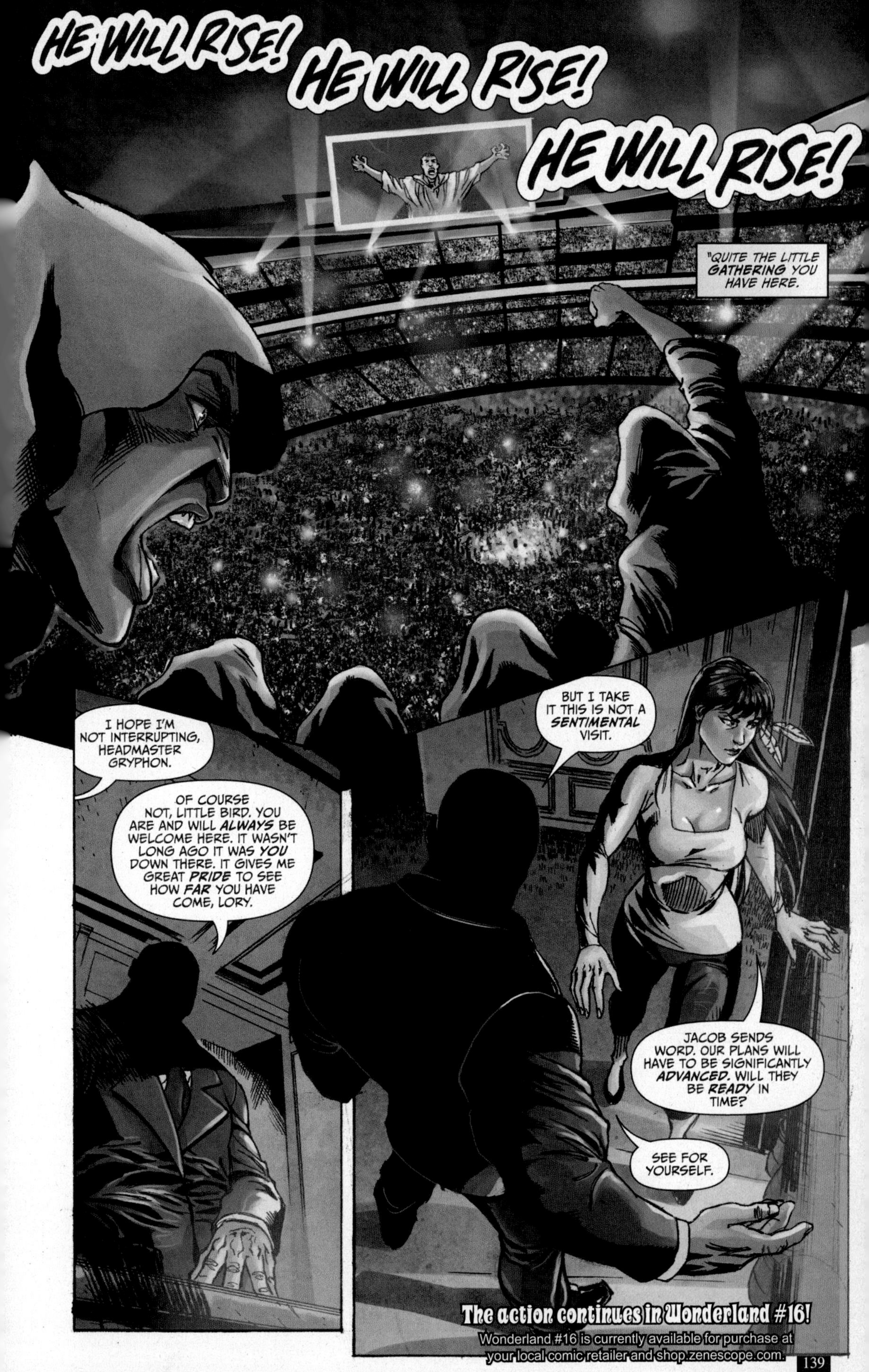
HE WILL RISE! HE WILL RISE!
HE WILL RISE!
"QUITE THE LITTLE GATHERING YOU HAVE HERE.
I HOPE I'M NOT INTERRUPTING, HEADMASTER GRYPHON.
OF COURSE NOT, LITTLE BIRD. YOU ARE AND WILL ALWAYS BE WELCOME HERE. IT WASN'T LONG AGO IT WAS YOU DOWN THERE. IT GIVES ME GREAT PRIDE TO SEE HOW FAR YOU HAVE COME, LORY.
BUT I TAKE IT THIS IS NOT A SENTIMENTAL VISIT.
JACOB SENDS WORD. OUR PLANS WILL HAVE TO BE SIGNIFICANTLY ADVANCED. WILL THEY BE READY IN TIME?
SEE FOR YOURSELF.

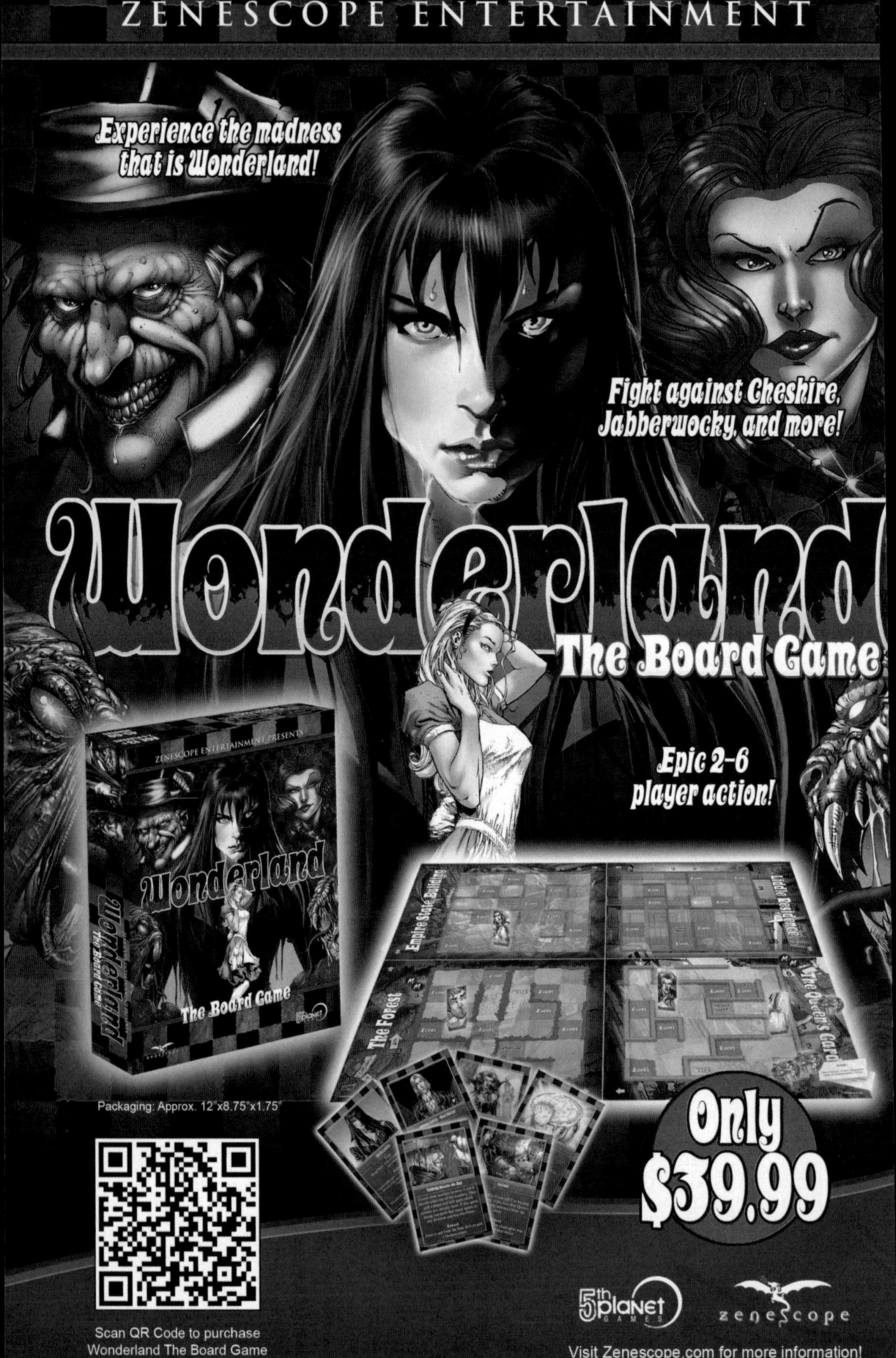
ZENESCOPE ENTERTAINMENT
Experience the madness that is Wonderland!
Fight against Cheshire, Jabberwocky, and more!
Wonderland
The Board Game
Epic 2-6 player action!
ZENESCOPE ENTERTAINMENT PRESENTS
Wonderland
The Board Game
Empire State Building
The Forest
Packaging: Approx. 12"x8.75"x1.75"
Only $39.99
Scan QR Code to purchase Wonderland The Board Game
5th planet GAMES
zenescope
Visit Zenescope.com for more information!

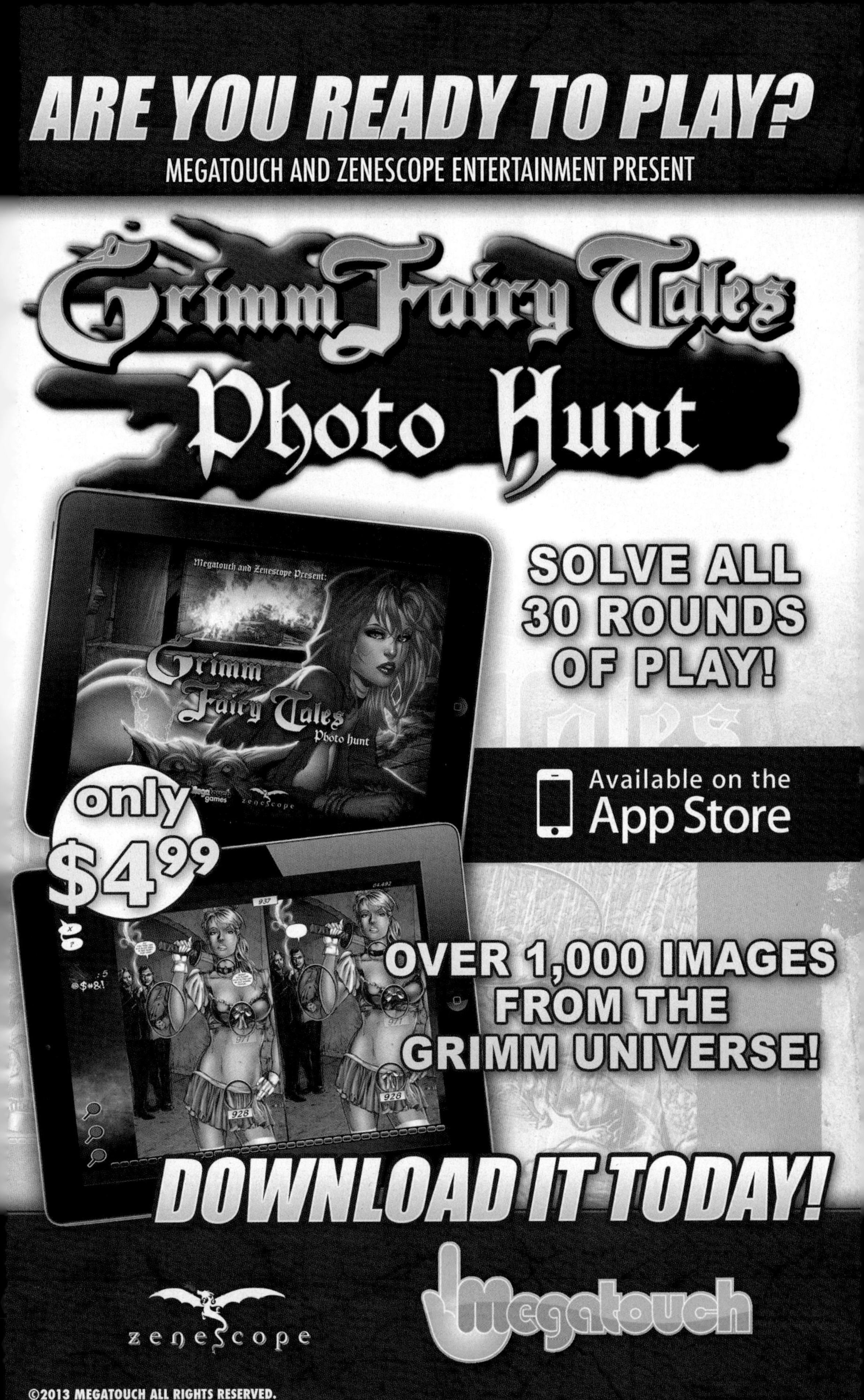
ARE YOU READY TO PLAY?
MEGATOUCH AND ZENESCOPE ENTERTAINMENT PRESENT
Grimm Fairy Tales
Photo Hunt
Megatouch and Zenescope Present:
Grimm Fairy Tales
Photo hunt
zenescope
only
$4.99
SOLVE ALL 30 ROUNDS OF PLAY!
Available on the
App Store
OVER 1,000 IMAGES FROM THE GRIMM UNIVERSE!
DOWNLOAD IT TODAY!
zenescope
Megatouch

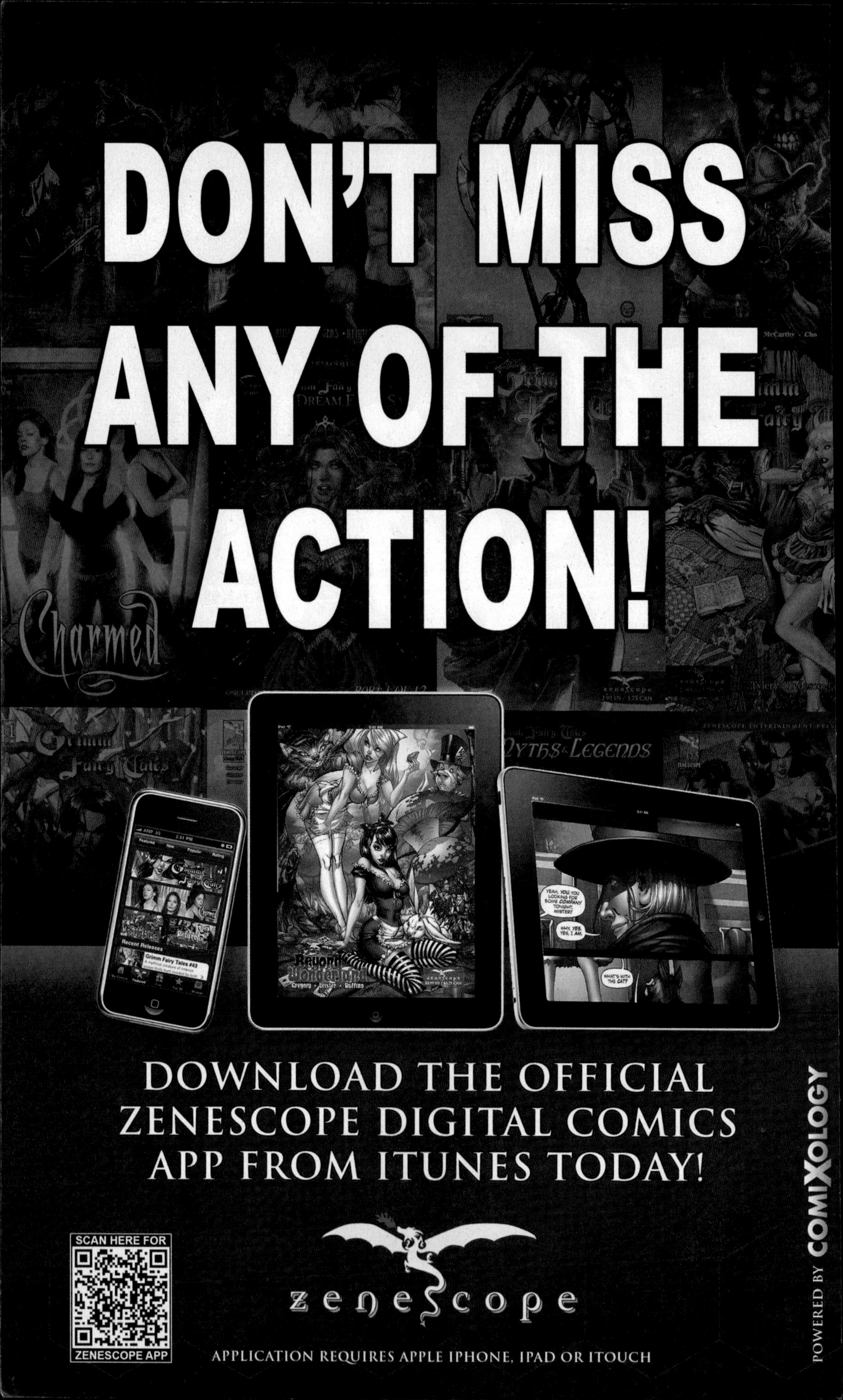

DON'T MISS
ANY OF THE
ACTION!
Charmed
Myths & Legends
Beyond Wonderland
YEAH, YOU YOU LOOKING FOR SOME COMPANY TONIGHT, MISTER?
WHY, YES. YES, I AM.
WHAT'S WITH THE CAT?
DOWNLOAD THE OFFICIAL
ZENESCOPE DIGITAL COMICS
APP FROM ITUNES TODAY!
SCAN HERE FOR
ZENESCOPE APP
zenescope
APPLICATION REQUIRES APPLE IPHONE, IPAD OR ITOUCH
POWERED BY COMIXOLOGY

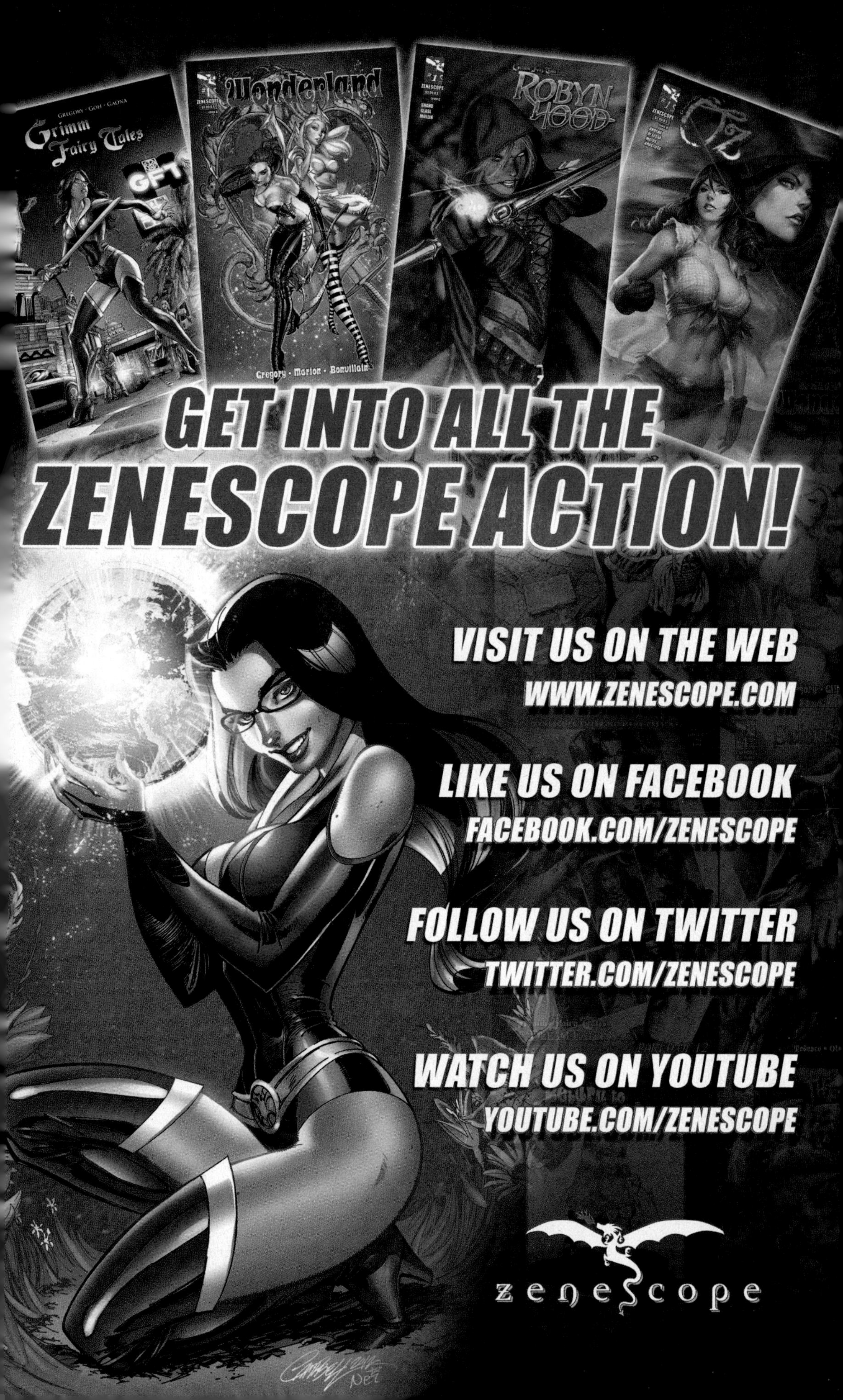
GET INTO ALL THE ZENESCOPE ACTION!
VISIT US ON THE WEB
WWW.ZENESCOPE.COM
LIKE US ON FACEBOOK
FACEBOOK.COM/ZENESCOPE
FOLLOW US ON TWITTER
TWITTER.COM/ZENESCOPE
WATCH US ON YOUTUBE
YOUTUBE.COM/ZENESCOPE
zenescope

Grimm Fairy Tales presents

Wonderland